Grades K-2

Newcomer

English Language Development

Teacher's Guide

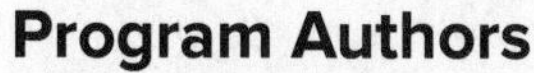

Program Authors

Dr. Diane August
Managing Director,
American Institutes for Research
Washington, D.C.

Dr. Jana Echevarria
California State University, Long Beach
Long Beach, California

Dr. Josefina V. Tinajero
University of Texas at El Paso
El Paso, Texas

Cover: Nathan Love

www.mheonline.com/readingwonders

Send all inquiries to:
McGraw-Hill Education
2 Penn Plaza
New York, New York 10121

ISBN: 978-0-02-131495-9
MHID: 0-02-131495-0

Printed in the United States of America.

5 6 7 8 LOV 23 22 21

A

TABLE OF CONTENTS

UNIT 3: Community

UNIT 4: The World

INTRODUCTION

The *Wonders for English Learners* Newcomer components are designed to help your students build their listening, speaking, reading, and writing skills in English.

These components will help newcomers develop oral language by creating frequent opportunities for students to engage in conversations with their classmates.

Teaching Strategies for Newcomers: Building Oral Language

To progress academically, newcomers must have access to basic, high-utility vocabulary from which they can build English language skills. Much of this vocabulary will become a part of their everyday speech when they are given opportunities to converse with their classmates. Here are some general strategies to keep in mind as you build a classroom environment that encourages conversation:

- Provide enough time for students to answer questions.
- Allow responses in the native language.
- Utilize nonverbal cues, such as pointing, acting out, or drawing.
- Use corrective feedback to model correct form for a response.
- Repeat correct answers to validate and motivate students.
- Elaborate on answers to model fluent speaking and grammatical patterns.
- Elicit more detailed responses by asking follow-up questions.
- Remind students that listening is as important as speaking.

USING THE *WONDERS FOR ENGLISH LEARNERS* NEWCOMER COMPONENTS

Teacher's Guide

The Teacher's Guide provides instruction with three lessons for each conversation topic.

Set Purpose
Prepare students for the lesson purpose and objective.

Teach/Model Vocabulary
Sing the song/chant before teaching new vocabulary and language structures.

Practice/Apply
Pair students to engage in collaborative conversations and apply what they've learned.

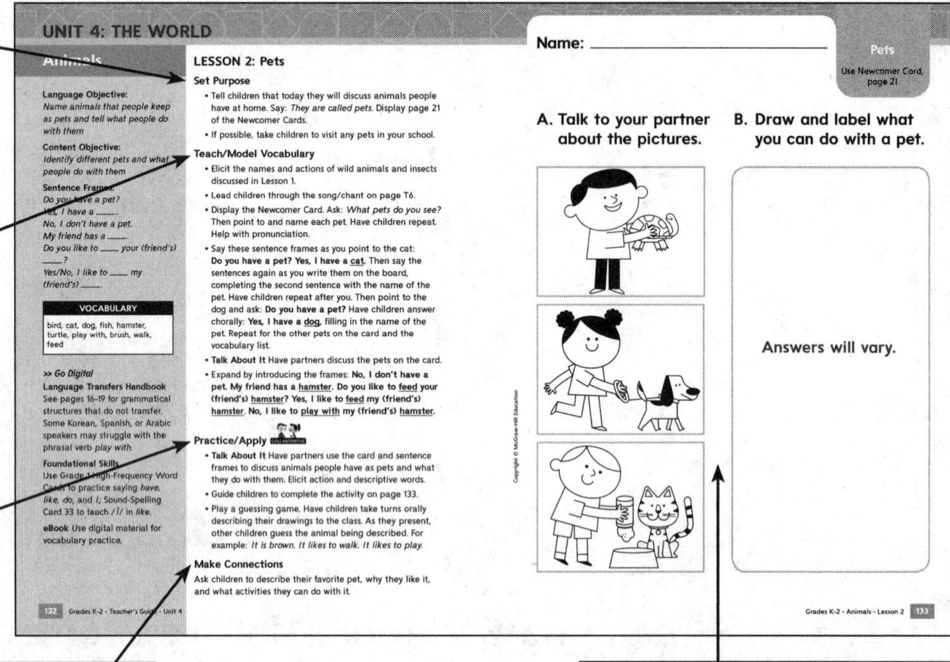

UNIT 4: THE WORLD

Animals

Language Objective:
Name animals that people keep as pets and tell what people do with them

Content Objective:
Identify different pets and what people do with them

Sentence Frames:
Do you have a pet?
Yes, I have a ____.
No, I don't have a pet.
My friend has a ____.
Do you like to ____ your (friend's) ____?
Yes/No, I like to ____ my (friend's) ____.

VOCABULARY
bird, cat, dog, fish, hamster, turtle, play with, brush, walk, feed

>> Go Digital
Language Transfers Handbook See pages 16–19 for grammatical structures that do not transfer. Some Korean, Spanish, or Arabic speakers may struggle with the phrasal verb *play with*.

Foundational Skills Use Grade 1 High-Frequency Word Cards to practice saying *have, like, do,* and *I*; Sound-Spelling Card 33 to teach /ī/ in *like*.

eBook Use digital material for vocabulary practice.

LESSON 2: Pets

Set Purpose

- Tell children that today they will discuss animals people have at home. Say: *They are called pets.* Display page 21 of the Newcomer Cards.
- If possible, take children to visit any pets in your school.

Teach/Model Vocabulary

- Elicit the names and actions of wild animals and insects discussed in Lesson 1.
- Lead children through the song/chant on page T6.
- Display the Newcomer Card. Ask: *What pets do you see?* Then point to and name each pet. Have children repeat. Help with pronunciation.
- Say these sentence frames as you point to the cat: **Do you have a pet? Yes, I have a cat.** Then say the sentences again as you write them on the board, completing the second sentence with the name of the pet. Have children repeat after you. Then point to the dog and ask: **Do you have a pet?** Have children answer chorally: **Yes, I have a dog**, filling in the name of the pet. Repeat for the other pets on the card and the vocabulary list.
- **Talk About It** Have partners discuss the pets on the card.
- Expand by introducing the frames: **No, I don't have a pet. My friend has a hamster. Do you like to feed your (friend's) hamster? Yes, I like to feed my (friend's) hamster. No, I like to play with my (friend's) hamster.**

Practice/Apply COLLABORATIVE

- **Talk About It** Have partners use the card and sentence frames to discuss animals people have as pets and what they do with them. Elicit action and descriptive words.
- Guide children to complete the activity on page 133.
- Play a guessing game. Have children take turns orally describing their drawings to the class. As they present, other children guess the animal being described. For example: *It is brown. It likes to walk. It likes to play.*

Make Connections

Ask children to describe their favorite pet, why they like it, and what activities they can do with it.

132 Grades K-2 • Teacher's Guide • Unit 4

Name: ____________________

Pets
Use Newcomer Card, page 21

A. Talk to your partner about the pictures.

B. Draw and label what you can do with a pet.

Answers will vary.

Copyright © McGraw-Hill Education

Grades K-2 • Animals • Lesson 2 133

Make Connections
Extend learning beyond the lesson and connect to students' personal lives.

Provide opportunities to practice and write about what they've learned.

Unit Overview

Each unit overview provides a snapshot of the content.

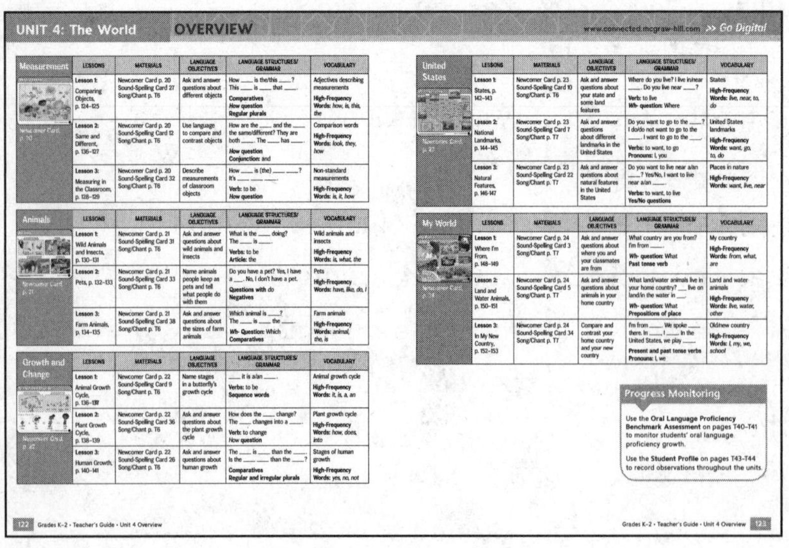

UNIT 4: The World OVERVIEW

www.connected.mcgraw-hill.com >> Go Digital

Measurement	LESSONS	MATERIALS	LANGUAGE OBJECTIVES	LANGUAGE STRUCTURES/ GRAMMAR	VOCABULARY
Newcomer Card p. 20	**Lesson 1:** Comparing Objects, p. 124–125	Newcomer Card p. 20 Sound-Spelling Card 27 Song/Chant p. T6	Ask and answer questions about different objects	How ____ is the/this ____? This ____ is ____ that ____. **Comparatives** ***How* question** **Regular plurals**	Adjectives describing measurements **High-Frequency Words:** *how, is, this, the*
	Lesson 2: Same and Different, p. 126–127	Newcomer Card p. 20 Sound-Spelling Card 12 Song/Chant p. T6	Use language to compare and contrast objects	How are the ____ and the ____ the same/different? They are both ____. The ____ has ____. ***How* question** **Conjunction:** and	Comparison words **High-Frequency Words:** *look, they, how*
	Lesson 3: Measuring in the Classroom, p. 128–129	Newcomer Card p. 20 Sound-Spelling Card 32 Song/Chant p. T6	Describe measurements of classroom objects	How ____ is (the) ____ ____? It's ____ ____ ____. **Verb:** to be ***How* question**	Non-standard measurements **High-Frequency Words:** *is, it, how*

Animals	LESSONS	MATERIALS	LANGUAGE OBJECTIVES	LANGUAGE STRUCTURES/ GRAMMAR	VOCABULARY
Newcomer Card p. 21	**Lesson 1:** Wild Animals and Insects, p. 130–131	Newcomer Card p. 21 Sound-Spelling Card 31 Song/Chant p. T6	Ask and answer questions about wild animals and insects	What is the ____ doing? The ____ is ____. **Verbs:** to be **Article:** the	Wild animals and insects **High-Frequency Words:** *is, what, the*
	Lesson 2: Pets, p. 132–133	Newcomer Card p. 21 Sound-Spelling Card 33 Song/Chant p. T6	Name animals people keep as pets and tell what people do with them	Do you have a pet? Yes, I have a ___. No, I don't have a pet. **Questions with** *do* **Negatives**	Pets **High-Frequency Words:** *have, like, do, I*
	Lesson 3: Farm Animals, p. 134–135	Newcomer Card p. 21 Sound-Spelling Card 38 Song/Chant p. T6	Ask and answer questions about the sizes of farm animals	Which animal is ____? The ____ is ____ the ____. ***Wh-* Question:** Which **Comparatives**	Farm animals **High-Frequency Words:** *animal, the, is*

Growth and Change	LESSONS	MATERIALS	LANGUAGE OBJECTIVES	LANGUAGE STRUCTURES/ GRAMMAR	VOCABULARY
Newcomer Card p. 22	**Lesson 1:** Animal Growth Cycle, p. 136–137	Newcomer Card p. 22 Sound-Spelling Card 9 Song/Chant p. T6	Name stages in a butterfly's growth cycle	____ it is a/an ____. **Verbs:** to be **Sequence words**	Animal growth cycle **High-Frequency Words:** *it, is, a, an*
	Lesson 2: Plant Growth Cycle, p. 138–139	Newcomer Card p. 22 Sound-Spelling Card 36 Song/Chant p. T6	Ask and answer questions about the plant growth cycle	How does the ____ change? The ____ changes into a ____. **Verb:** to change ***How* question**	Plant growth cycle **High-Frequency Words:** *how, does, into*
	Lesson 3: Human Growth, p. 140–141	Newcomer Card p. 22 Sound-Spelling Card 26 Song/Chant p. T6	Ask and answer questions about human growth	The ____ is ____ than the ____. Is the ____ ____ than the ____? **Comparatives** **Regular and irregular plurals**	Stages of human growth **High-Frequency Words:** *yes, no, not*

122 Grades K-2 • Teacher's Guide • Unit 4 Overview

United States	LESSONS	MATERIALS	LANGUAGE OBJECTIVES	LANGUAGE STRUCTURES/ GRAMMAR	VOCABULARY
Newcomer Card p. 23	**Lesson 1:** States, p. 142–143	Newcomer Card p. 23 Sound-Spelling Card 10 Song/Chant p. T6	Ask and answer questions about your state and some land features	Where do you live? I live in/near ____. Do you live near ____? **Verb:** to live ***Wh-* question:** Where	States **High-Frequency Words:** *live, near, to, do*
	Lesson 2: National Landmarks, p. 144–145	Newcomer Card p. 23 Sound-Spelling Card 7 Song/Chant p. T7	Ask and answer questions about different landmarks in the United States	Do you want to go to the ____? I do/do not want to go to the ____. I want to go to the ____. **Verbs:** to want, to go **Pronouns:** I, you	United States landmarks **High-Frequency Words:** *want, go, to, do*
	Lesson 3: Natural Features, p. 146-147	Newcomer Card p. 23 Sound-Spelling Card 22 Song/Chant p. T7	Ask and answer questions about natural features in the United States	Do you want to live near a/an ____? Yes/No, I want to live near a/an ____. **Verbs:** to want, to live **Yes/No questions**	Places in nature **High-Frequency Words:** *want, live, near*

My World	LESSONS	MATERIALS	LANGUAGE OBJECTIVES	LANGUAGE STRUCTURES/ GRAMMAR	VOCABULARY
Newcomer Card p. 24	**Lesson 1:** Where I'm From, p. 148–149	Newcomer Card p. 24 Sound-Spelling Card 3 Song/Chant p. T7	Ask and answer questions about where you and your classmates are from	What country are you from? I'm from ____. ***Wh-* question:** What **Past tense verb**	My country **High-Frequency Words:** *from, what, are*
	Lesson 2: Land and Water Animals, p. 150–151	Newcomer Card p. 24 Sound-Spelling Card 5 Song/Chant p. T7	Ask and answer questions about animals in your home country	What land/water animals live in your home country? ___ live on land/in the water in ___. ***Wh-* question:** What **Prepositions of place**	Land and water animals **High-Frequency Words:** *live, water, other*
	Lesson 3: In My New Country, p. 152–153	Newcomer Card p. 24 Sound-Spelling Card 34 Song/Chant p. T7	Compare and contrast your home country and your new country	I'm from ____. We spoke ____ there. In ____, I ____. In the United States, we play ____. **Present and past tense verbs** **Pronouns:** I, we	Old/new country **High-Frequency Words:** *I, my, we, school*

Progress Monitoring

Use the **Oral Language Proficiency Benchmark Assessment** on pages T40–T41 to monitor students' oral language proficiency growth.

Use the **Student Profile** on pages T43–T44 to record observations throughout the units.

Grades K-2 • Teacher's Guide • Unit 4 Overview 123

Teacher Support

Includes Games, Songs/Chants, Answer Key, and Progress Monitoring.

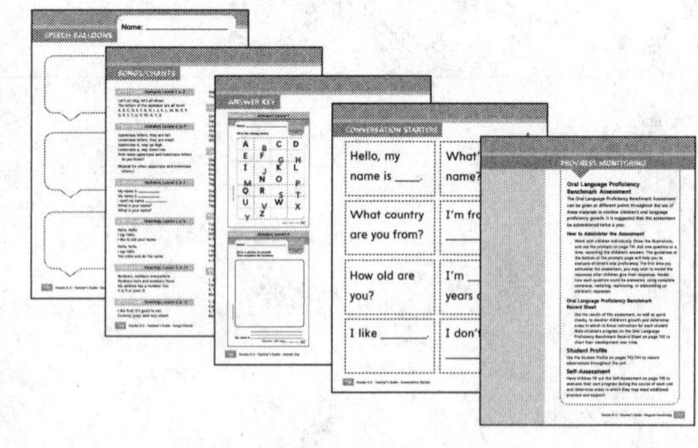

Newcomer Cards

Newcomer cards include colorful illustrations and photographs to stimulate conversations. Each card presents a topic supported in the Teacher's Guide over three lessons.

>> Go Digital
www.connected.mcgraw-hill.com

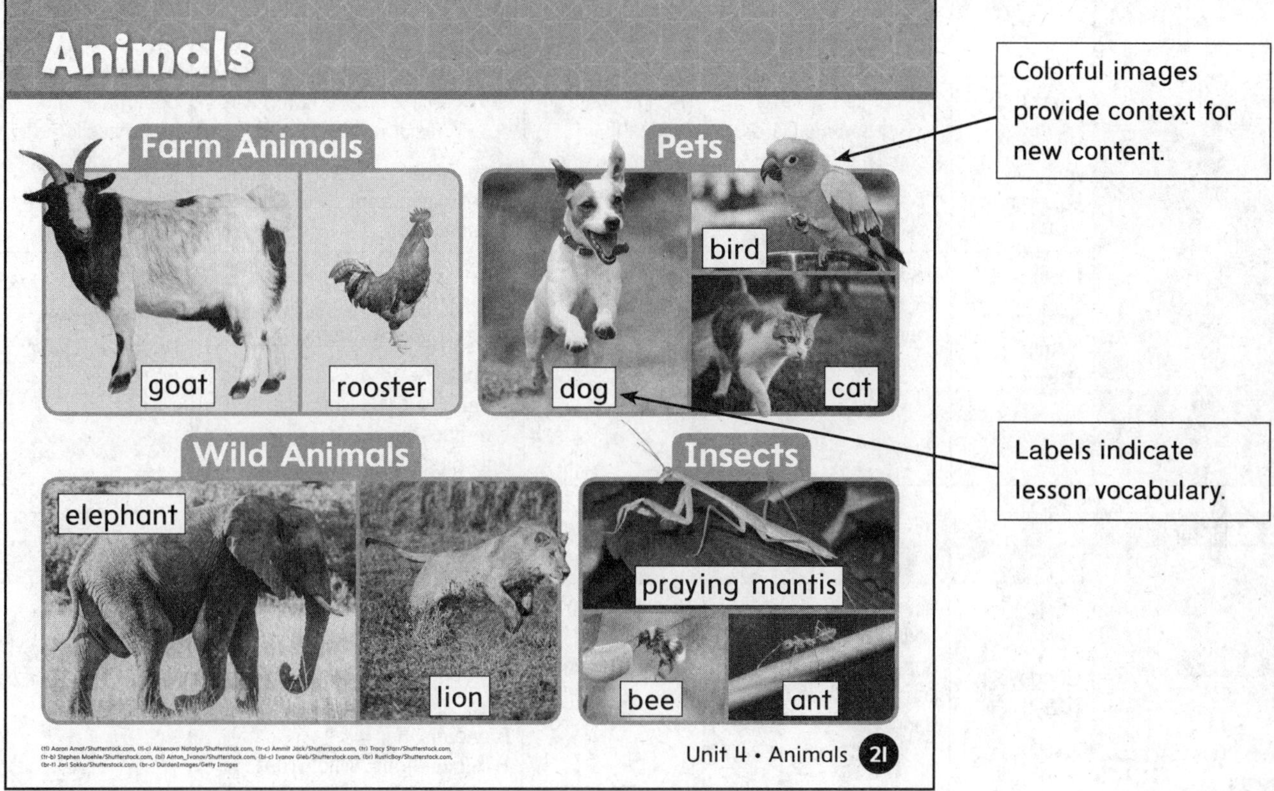

Digital

eBook

Presents Newcomer Cards in a student-friendly eBook with additional activities that include audio support and recording features.

Online Games

Offer additional interaction and practice with the vocabulary.

Online Visuals

Offer additional images for each topic to extend students' collaborative conversations.

Components (Grades K-2)

- Newcomer Teacher's Guide
- Newcomer Cards
- eBook of Newcomer Cards
- Online Games
- Online Visuals

Wonders Materials also referenced:

- Language Transfers Handbook
- Foundational Skills
  - High-Frequency Word Cards (Grades K, 1, 2)
  - Sound-Spelling Cards

Alphabet

Newcomer Card, p. 1

LESSONS	MATERIALS	LANGUAGE OBJECTIVES	LANGUAGE STRUCTURES/ GRAMMAR	VOCABULARY
Lesson 1: ABC Song, p. 2–3	Newcomer Card p. 1 Sound-Spelling Card 9 Song/Chant p. 154 Language Transfers Handbook	Name the letters of the alphabet	Is this the letter ____? Yes, it is. No, it isn't the letter __. It's the letter ____. **Verb:** to be **Yes/No questions** **Contraction:** it's **Pronouns:** this, it	Letters **High-Frequency Words:** *this, is, yes, no*
Lesson 2: Uppercase and Lowercase, p. 4–5	Newcomer Card p. 1 Sound-Spelling Card 9 Song/Chant p. 154 Language Transfers Handbook	Use language to identify uppercase and lowercase letters	Is this an uppercase/lowercase ____? Yes, it is. No, it's a(n) ___. **Verb:** to be **Yes/No questions** **Pronouns:** this, it	Uppercase and lowercase letters **High-Frequency Words:** *it, is, yes, no*
Lesson 3: Spelling My Name, p. 6–7	Newcomer Card p. 1 Sound-Spelling Card 5 Song/Chant p. 154 Language Transfers Handbook	Say and spell first name	What's your name? My name is ____. How do you spell your name? I spell my name _____. **Verb:** to be **Pronouns:** I, you, your, my ***Wh-* questions:** What **How questions**	Names **High-Frequency Words:** *my, your, what, how*

Greetings

Newcomer Card, p. 2

LESSONS	MATERIALS	LANGUAGE OBJECTIVES	LANGUAGE STRUCTURES/ GRAMMAR	VOCABULARY
Lesson 1: Hello and Goodbye, p. 8–9	Newcomer Card p. 2 Sound-Spelling Card 8 Song/Chant p. 154 Language Transfers Handbook	Use language to greet and introduce people	Who is this? I'm ____. What's your/his/her name? My/His/Her name is ____. **Verb:** to be **Pronouns:** her, his ***Wh-* questions:** Who, What **Contractions:** I'm, what's	Introductions **High-Frequency Words:** *my, your, her, this*
Lesson 2: Talking about You and Me, p. 10–11	Newcomer Card p. 2 Sound-Spelling Card 30 Song/Chant p. 154 Language Transfers Handbook	Ask and answer questions about yourself and others	Where do you live? I/We/They live in/on ____. What's your phone number? My phone number is ____. **Verb:** to be **Pronouns:** I, my, you, we, they **Prepositions of place** ***Wh-* questions:** Where, What	Personal information **High-Frequency Words:** *I, we, they, live*
Lesson 3: Likes and Dislikes, p. 12–13	Newcomer Card p. 2 Sound-Spelling Card 12 Song/Chant p. 154 Language Transfers Handbook	Express likes and dislikes	I like/don't like ____. She/He likes/doesn't like _____. Do you like ____? **Verb:** to like **Helping verb:** to do **Contractions:** don't, doesn't **Pronouns:** I, you, he, she	Things people like or dislike **High-Frequency Words:** *I, we, they, like*

Shapes and Colors

Newcomer Card, p. 3

LESSONS	MATERIALS	LANGUAGE OBJECTIVES	LANGUAGE STRUCTURES/ GRAMMAR	VOCABULARY
Lesson 1: Shapes, p. 14–15	Newcomer Card p. 3 Sound-Spelling Card 37 Song/Chant p. 154 Language Transfers Handbook	Name shapes	What is this/that? It's a ____. Point to the ____. I see a ____. **Verb:** to be ***Wh-* questions:** What **Pronouns:** this, that **Imperative**	Shapes **High-Frequency Words:** *this, what, is, see*
Lesson 2: Colors, p. 16–17	Newcomer Card p. 3 Sound-Spelling Card 3 Song/Chant p. 154 Language Transfers Handbook	Name colors	What color is it? It's ____. What color and shape is the ____? It's a ____ ____. **Verb:** to be **Nouns and adjectives** **Contraction:** it's	Colors **High-Frequency Words:** *green, blue, color*
Lesson 3: Shapes and Colors Around Us, p. 18–19	Newcomer Card p. 3 Sound-Spelling Card 11 Song/Chant p. 154 Language Transfers Handbook	Name shapes and colors around us	The ___ is a ___. The ___ is ___. The ___ ___ is a ___. **Verb:** to be **Articles:** a, the	Objects with shapes and colors around us **High-Frequency Words:** *the, is, a*

Numbers

Newcomer Card, p. 4

PROGRESS MONITORING
Use pages T40-T41 to monitor oral language proficiency.

Use pages T43-T44 to record observations throughout the units.

LESSONS	MATERIALS	LANGUAGE OBJECTIVES	LANGUAGE STRUCTURES/ GRAMMAR	VOCABULARY
Lesson 1: Numbers 1–20, p. 20–21	Newcomer Card p. 4 Sound-Spelling Card 14 Song/Chant p. 154 Language Transfers Handbook	Say and count numbers 1–20	What number is this? This is the number ____. Count from ____ to ____. **Verb:** to be ***Wh-* questions:** What **Pronoun:** this **Imperative**	Numbers and counting **High-Frequency Words:** *from, to, this*
Lesson 2: How Old Are You?, p. 22–23	Newcomer Card p. 4 Sound-Spelling Card 32 Song/Chant p. T1 Language Transfers Handbook	Talk about age using numbers	How old are you? I'm ____ years old. **Verb:** to be ***How* questions** **Contraction:** I'm	Numbers and ages **High-Frequency Words:** *how, old, are, you*
Lesson 3: How Many?, p. 24–25	Newcomer Card p. 4 Sound-Spelling Card 22 Song/Chant p. T1 Language Transfers Handbook	Name the number of objects	How many do you have? I/They/We have ____ ____. She/He has ____ ____. **Verb:** to have **Pronouns:** I, she, he, we, they	Counting objects **High-Frequency Words:** *we, she, he, they*

Alphabet

Language Objective:
Name the letters of the alphabet

Content Objective:
Identify the letters of the alphabet

Sentence Frames:
Is this the letter ____?
Yes, it is.
No, it isn't the letter ___. It's the letter ____.

VOCABULARY
A, B, C, D, E, F, G, H, I, J, K, L, M, N, O, P, Q, R, S, T, U, V, W, X, Y, Z

>> Go Digital

Language Transfers Handbook
See pages 16-19 for grammatical structures that do not transfer. Some Korean, Spanish, or Vietnamese speakers may omit subject pronouns.

Foundational Skills
Use the Grade 1 High-Frequency Word Cards to practice saying the words *this, is, yes,* and *no.* Use Sound-Spelling Card 9 to teach children how to identify and pronounce the /y/ sound in *yes.*

eBook Use digital material for vocabulary practice.

LESSON 1: ABC Song

Set Purpose

- Tell children that today they will discuss letters of the alphabet. Show page 1 of the Newcomer Cards.

Teach/Model Vocabulary

- Lead children through the song/chant on page 154.
- Display the card again. Ask: *What do you see?* Children name things they know. Then point to and name each letter. Have children repeat. Help with pronunciation.
- Say these sentence frames as you point to a letter: **Is this the letter A?** Nod your head as you say: **Yes, it is.** Then say the sentences again as you write them on the board, completing the first sentence with the name of the letter. Then point to the letter *B* and ask: **Is this the letter B?** Have children chorally answer: **Yes, it is.** Repeat for other letters. Provide support as needed.
- **Talk About It** Have partners take turns pointing to and naming different letters on the card and in the classroom.
- Extend by pointing to the letter *O* and asking: **Is this the letter B?** Shake your head as you introduce the sentence frames: **No, it isn't the letter B. It's the letter O.**

Practice/Apply COLLABORATIVE

- **Talk About It** Have partners use the Newcomer Card and sentence frames they learned to talk about letters.
- Guide children to complete the activity on page 3.
- Play a version of musical chairs with the letters of the alphabet. Write the letters on index cards and place the cards on chairs in a circle. Have children walk around the chairs while you play music. When the music stops, have children sit in the nearest chair and say the letter.

Make Connections

Have children make an alphabet book of their favorite letters. Help them fold four pieces of blank paper in half and then tie them together with string to make a booklet. Provide children with copies of the alphabet to trace and color. Then have children cut out the letters and glue them onto the pages of the booklet. Afterwards, have children read the alphabet book aloud to each other.

Name: ____________________

ABC Song

Use Newcomer Card, page 1

Fill in the missing letters.

A		C	D
E	F		
I		K	L
	N	O	
Q	R		
U		W	
	Z		

Alphabet

Language Objective:
Use language to identify uppercase and lowercase letters

Content Objective:
Identify uppercase and lowercase letters

Sentence Frames:
Is this an uppercase ____?
Is this a lowercase ____?
Yes, it is.
No, it's a(n) ____.

VOCABULARY

uppercase, lowercase,
A a, B b, C c, D d, E e, F f, G g,
H h, I i, J j, K k, L l, M m, N n,
O o, P p, Q q, R r, S s, T t, U u,
V v, W w, X x, Y y, Z z

>> Go Digital

Language Transfers Handbook
See pages 16-19 for grammatical structures that do not transfer. Hmong, Vietnamese, Korean, Arabic, Tagalog, or Cantonese speakers may mistake *one* for *a/an.*

Foundational Skills
Use the Grade 1 High-Frequency Word Cards to practice saying the words *it, is, yes,* and *no.* Use Sound-Spelling Card 9 to teach children how to identify and pronounce the /i/ sound in *it* and *is.*

eBook Use digital material for vocabulary practice.

LESSON 2: Uppercase and Lowercase

Set Purpose

- Tell children that today they will discuss uppercase and lowercase letters. Show page 1 of the Newcomer Card.

Teach/Model Vocabulary

- Elicit names of letters from Lesson 1.
- Lead children through the song/chant on page 154.
- Display the Newcomer Card again. Say: *Tell me about the letters.* Then point to and name the uppercase and lowercase letters. Have children repeat. Help with pronunciation.
- Say these sentence frames as you point to the letters: **Is this an uppercase A? Yes, it is.** Then say the sentences again as you write them on the board. Have children repeat after you. Then point to the lowercase letter *j* and ask: **Is this the lowercase letter j?** Have children chorally answer: **Yes, it is.** Repeat for other letters.
- **Talk About It** Have partners talk about uppercase and lowercase letters in the classroom.
- Expand by pointing to the uppercase letter *R* and asking: **Is this a lowercase R?** Shake your head as you introduce the sentence frame: **No, it's an uppercase R.** Repeat for other letters.

Practice/Apply COLLABORATIVE

- **Talk About It** Have partners use the Newcomer Card and sentence frames they learned to discuss what they know about uppercase and lowercase letters.
- Guide children to complete the activity on page 5.
- Partners can play concentration. Have each child write four uppercase and lowercase letters on index cards and place them face down in two rows. Children take turns choosing two cards, saying the letters, and looking for a match between uppercase and lowercase. When there's a match, the child gets a point and replaces the cards with a new pair.

Make Connections

In pairs, have one child say the name of a letter and whether it's uppercase or lowercase. The partner writes the correct letter. Then they switch roles.

Name: ______________________

Uppercase and Lowercase

Use Newcomer Card, page 1

Match the uppercase letter to the correct lowercase letter.

V	i
L	b
G	l
I	g
B	v
H	c
E	y
C	e
Y	a
A	h

Write two uppercase and two lowercase letters.

____

Alphabet

Language Objective:
Say and spell first name

Content Objective:
Learn names and how to spell them

Sentence Frames:
What's your name?
My name is ____.
How do you spell your name?
I spell my name ____.

VOCABULARY
spell, name, A, B, C, D, E, F, G, H, I, J, K, L, M, N, O, P, Q, R, S, T, U, V, W, X, Y, Z

>> Go Digital

Language Transfers Handbook
See pages 16-19 for grammatical structures that do not transfer. Cantonese, Hmong, or Vietnamese speakers may omit the linking verb *is*.

Foundational Skills
Use the Grade 1 High-Frequency Word Cards to practice saying the words *my, your, what,* and *how*. Use Sound-Spelling Card 5 to teach children how to identify and pronounce the /e/ sound in *spell*.

eBook and Games Provide audio support, interaction, and practice with the vocabulary.

LESSON 3: Spelling My Name

Set Purpose

- Tell children that today they will discuss how to say and spell names. Display page 1 of the Newcomer Card.

Teach/Model Vocabulary

- Elicit names of letters from Lessons 1 and 2.
- Lead children through the song/chant on page 154.
- Display the Newcomer Card again. Ask: *What do you think they are saying?*
- Say and write down the sentence frames: **Hello! My name is Mr./Mrs./Ms. ____. I spell my last name ____.** Introduce yourself to children and spell your last name.
- Read aloud the text in the speech balloons, modeling their conversation: **Hello! What's your name? Hi! My name is Lin. How do you spell your name? I spell my name L-i-n.** Play the role of either girl as you repeat the conversation a few times with individual children.
- **Talk About It** Have partners practice saying hello to each other and asking each other how to spell their first names.
- Remind children that our first and last name begin with an uppercase letter, followed by lowercase letters. Have children practice saying and writing their name.

Practice/Apply 

- **Talk About It** Have partners use the Newcomer Card and sentence frames they learned to discuss what they know about names and how to spell them.
- Guide children to complete the activity on page 7.
- Have children play a spelling bee game. Ask one child: *How do you spell your name?* Have the child answer. Say the name aloud and have children spell it chorally. Provide help as needed. Continue until all children have spelled their names.

Make Cultural Connections

Have children respond to the following prompt about their home country: *Tell me the names of family or friends from your home country.*

Name: ____________________

Spelling My Name

Use Newcomer Card, page I

Draw a picture of yourself. Then complete the sentence.

My name is ____________________.

Greetings

Language Objective:
Use language to greet and introduce people

Content Objective:
Demonstrate understanding of greetings and introductions

Sentence Frames:
Who is this?
I'm ____./ I'm Mr./Ms. ____.
What's your name?
My name is ____.
What's her/his name?
Her/His name is ____.

VOCABULARY
hello, goodbye, name, good morning, hi, bye

>> Go Digital

Language Transfers Handbook
See pages 16-19 for grammatical structures that do not transfer. Hmong, Spanish, Vietnamese, or Arabic speakers may use prepositions to describe possessives.

Foundational Skills
Use the Grade 1 High-Frequency Word Cards to practice saying *my, your, her,* and *this.* Use Sound-Spelling Card 8 to teach children how to identify and pronounce /h/ in *hello* and *hi.*

eBook Use digital materials for vocabulary practice.

LESSON 1: Hello and Goodbye

Set Purpose

- Tell children that today they will discuss how to say hello and goodbye. Display page 2 of the Newcomer Cards.

Teach/Model Vocabulary

- Lead children through the song/chant on page 154.
- Display the Newcomer Card and ask: *What do you see?*
- Say and write the sentence frames: **Hello. I'm Mr./Ms./Mrs. ____.** Introduce yourself, filling in your last name. Explain the different times to say *hello* and *hi.* Then say and write the other sentence frames for introducing ourselves to others: **I'm ____** and **My name is ____.** Repeat your introduction and ask a volunteer: **What's your name?** Partners can exchange greetings and names.
- Read aloud the text in the speech balloons in the first box, modeling their conversation: **Hello. I'm Lei. What's your name? My name is Ravi.** Have children repeat.
- **Talk About It** Partners can use the Conversation Starters on page T28 to introduce themselves to each other.
- Extend by introducing the sentence frames: **Who is this? I'm ____. What's her/his name? Her/His name is ____.** Have children use the Speech Balloons on page T26 to practice a conversation.
- Explain when we say "good morning." Then explain that when we leave new friends or adults, we say *goodbye* or *bye.* Have partners practice saying goodbye to each other.

Practice/Apply

- **Talk About It** Have partners use the sentence frames to ask about the names of other classmates.
- Guide children to complete the activity on page 9.
- Have children stand in a circle. Choose one child to stand in the middle and ask: **What's your name?** Have the child answer the question. Then ask the other children **What's her/his name?** Emphasize the correct pronoun. Have children answer chorally: **Her/His name is ____.** Repeat with other children.

Make Connections

Have children tell you how they greet a family member when they get home from school.

Name: ______________________

Use Newcomer Card, page 2

Draw a picture of yourself meeting new friends in class. Then write their names.

Greetings

Language Objective:
Ask and answer questions about yourself and others

Content Objective:
Determine a person's address and phone number

Sentence Frames:
Where do you live?
What's your/their address?
I/We/They live in ____.
I/We/They live on ____.
What's your phone number?
My phone number is ____.

VOCABULARY
live, address, phone number, street, avenue, lane
Cognates: número, avenida

>> Go Digital

Language Transfers Handbook
See pages 16-19 for grammatical structures that do not transfer. Korean, Spanish, or Arabic speakers may confuse the related phrasal verbs *live on* and *live in.*

Foundational Skills
Use the Grade 1 High-Frequency Word Cards to practice saying *I, we, they,* and *live.* Use Sound-Spelling Card 30 to teach how to identify and pronounce /hw/ in *what* and *where.*

eBook Use digital material for vocabulary practice.

LESSON 2: Talking about You and Me

Set Purpose

- Tell children that today they will learn more about friends. Display page 2 of the Newcomer Cards.

Teach/Model Vocabulary

- Elicit greetings from Lesson 1.
- Lead children through the song/chant on page 154.
- Display the Newcomer Card and point to the second and third illustrations. Ask: *What do you think the children are doing?* Then say and write these sentence frames, filling them in with information about yourself: **Where do you live? I live on ____.** Then have children take turns asking and answering the question: *Where do you live?*
- Read aloud the text in the speech balloons in the second box: **Where do you live? I live on Main Street.** Have children repeat after you.
- **Talk About It** Have children use the Conversation Starters on page T29 and the Speech Balloons on page T26 to practice exchanging information with a partner.
- Repeat the instruction for exchanging phone numbers. Then extend the instruction by reusing the sentence frames with the pronouns *you, your, I,* and *we.* Teach the phrasal verb *live in* to indicate the city/town, state, or country name.

Practice/Apply

- **Talk About It** Have partners use the Newcomer Card and sentence frames they learned to discuss the addresses of friends and family.
- Guide children to complete the activity on page 11.
- Have partners talk about their addresses. Then have children write their partner's name and address on an envelope and draw a picture to put inside. Collect the envelopes and have children take turns role-playing a mail carrier to deliver the envelopes.

Make Connections

Ask children to talk about where they have seen addresses or phone numbers, such as in phone books, television ads, or billboards.

Name: ____________________

Talking About You and Me

Use Newcomer Card, page 2

Circle the numbers in your phone number. Then write your phone number on the line.

1	2	3
4	5	6
7	8	9
	0	

Greetings

Language Objective:
Express likes and dislikes

Content Objective:
Identify likes and dislikes

Sentence Frames:
I like ____.
I don't like ____.
She/He likes ____.
She/He doesn't like ____.
We/They like ____.
We/They don't like ____.
Do you like ____?

VOCABULARY
like, fruit, grapes, apples, bananas, books, cats, dogs
Cognates: fruta, bananas

>> Go Digital

Language Transfers Handbook
See pages 16-19 for grammatical structures that do not transfer. Cantonese, Hmong, Korean, Vietnamese, Arabic, or Tagalog speakers may omit the present tense, third-person ending *-s.*

Foundational Skills
Use the Grade 1 High-Frequency Word Cards to practice saying *I, we, they,* and *like.* Use Sound-Spelling Card 12 to teach children how to identify and pronounce /l/ as in *like.*

eBook and Games Provide audio support, interaction, and practice with the vocabulary.

LESSON 3: Likes and Dislikes

Talk About It

- Tell children that today they will discuss likes and dislikes. Display page 2 of the Newcomer Cards.

Teach/Model Vocabulary

- Elicit sentence frames from Lessons 1 and 2.
- Lead children through the song/chant on page 154.
- Display the Newcomer Card again and point to the last illustration. Say and write these sentence frames: **I like ____. I don't like ____**, filling them in with information about yourself. Then have children take turns using the sentence frames to tell what they like and don't like.
- Read aloud the text in the speech balloons: **Do you like bananas? I don't like bananas.** Have children repeat after you. Repeat for other likes and dislikes listed in the vocabulary list and that children provide.
- **Talk About It** Have partners talk about what they like or dislike. Challenge them to say *why* they like or dislike something.
- Expand by introducing the sentence frames: **She/He likes/doesn't like ____** and **We/They like/don't like ____** to review pronouns. Gesture to indicate the pronouns you're using as you use them.

Practice/Apply INTERPRETIVE

- **Talk About It** Have partners use the Newcomer Card, the Conversation Starters on page T28, and the sentence frames they learned to discuss fruit they like and dislike.
- Guide children to complete the activity on page 13.
- Have children play a thumbs-up or thumbs-down game. Point to a game and say: **I like games. Do you like games?** Have children use their thumbs to say if they like or dislike games. Repeat with the names of items in the classroom. Then have partners take turns asking and answering questions about likes and dislikes.

Make Cultural Connections

Have children respond to the following prompt: *Tell me about a fruit from your home country that you like or dislike. Tell why you like it or don't like it.*

Name: ______________________________

Likes and Dislikes

Use Newcomer Card, page 2

Write or draw fruits you like. Then write or draw fruits you don't like. Talk to a partner about them.

☺	☹

Shapes and Colors

Language Objective:
Name shapes

Content Objective:
Identify shapes

Sentence Frames:
What's this?
It's a ____.
Point to the ____.
I see a ____.

VOCABULARY
shape, circle, square, triangle, rectangle, star, diamond
Cognates: círculo, triángulo, rectángulo, diamante

>> Go Digital

Language Transfers Handbook
See pages 16-19 for grammatical structures that do not transfer. Cantonese, Hmong, Korean, Vietnamese, Arabic, or Tagalog speakers may omit articles.

Foundational Skills
Use the Grade 1 High-Frequency Word Cards to practice saying the words *what, is, this,* and *see.* Use Sound-Spelling Card 37 to teach children how to identify and pronounce the /är/ sound in *star.*

eBook Use digital material for vocabulary practice.

LESSON 1: Shapes

Set Purpose

- Tell children that today they will discuss shapes. Display page 3 of the Newcomer Cards.

Teach/Model Vocabulary

- Lead children through the song/chant on page 154.
- Display the Newcomer Card again. Ask: *What do you see?* Children can name things they know. Then point to and name each shape. Have children repeat. Help with pronunciation. Then have children take turns naming and tracing the shapes with their finger.
- Say these sentence frames as you point to the circle: **What's this? It's a circle.** Say the sentence frames again as you write them on the board. Have children repeat after you. Then point to the square and ask: **What's this?** Have children answer chorally: **It's a square,** filling in the name of the shape. Repeat for other shapes on the card and in the vocabulary list.
- **Talk About It** Have partners use the Conversation Starters on page T30 to talk about the different shapes on the card.
- Extend by introducing the sentence frames: **Point to the ____. I see a ____.**

Practice/Apply COLLABORATIVE

- **Talk About It** Have partners use the Newcomer Card and the sentence frames they learned to talk about shapes they see in the classroom.
- Guide children to complete the activity on page 15.
- Cut shapes out of colored paper. Spread the shapes on the floor and have children talk about the shapes they see. Then have children close their eyes while you take away one shape. When children open their eyes, have them name the shapes and tell the shape that is missing.

Make Connections

Ask children to draw and name an object from their home that is in the shape of a circle, a rectangle, a square, and a triangle.

Name: ______________________

Use Newcomer Card, page 3

Write the name of each shape. Use words from the box.

circle	diamond	rectangle
square	star	triangle

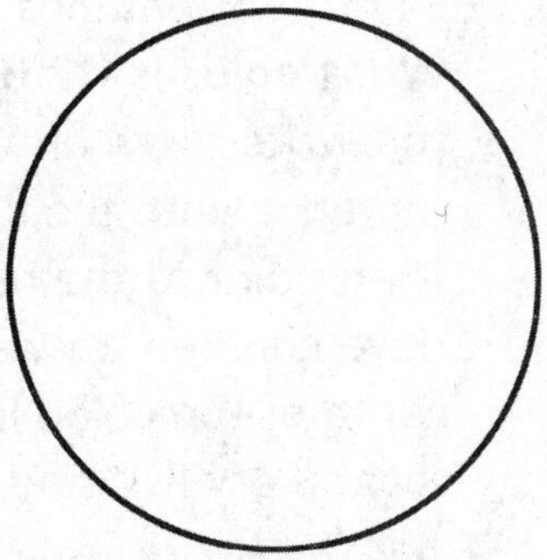

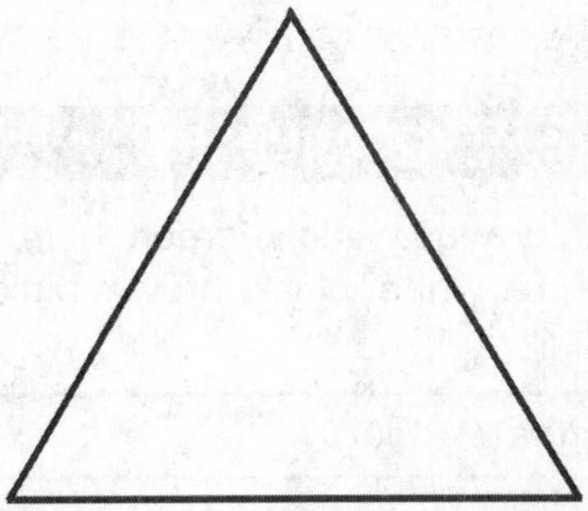

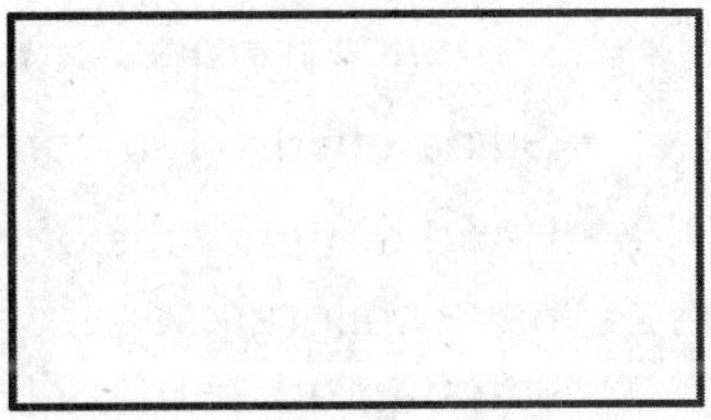

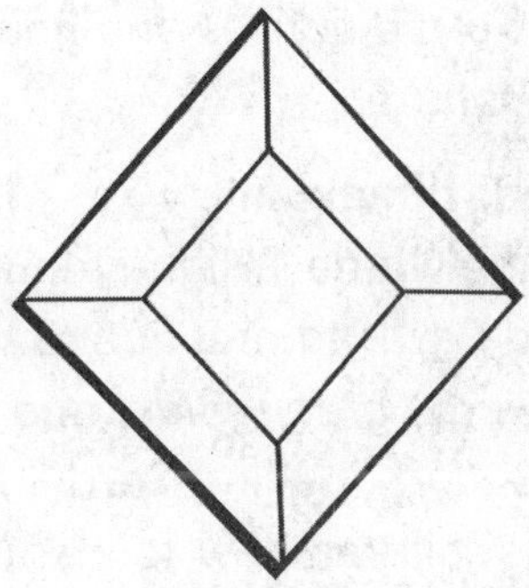

Shapes and Colors

Language Objective:
Name colors

Content Objective:
Name colors and colors of shapes and objects

Sentence Frames:
What color is it?
What color and shape is the ____?
It's ____.
It's a ____ ____.

VOCABULARY
red, orange, yellow, green, blue, purple, white, black, brown, pink, color
Cognate: color

>> Go Digital

Language Transfers Handbook
See pages 16–19 for grammatical structures that do not transfer. Cantonese, Korean, Hmong, Spanish, Vietnamese, or Arabic speakers may struggle with the order of adjectives and nouns (*red square*).

Foundational Skills
Use the Grade 1 High-Frequency Word Cards to practice saying the words *green, blue,* and *color.* Use Sound-Spelling Card 3 to teach children how to identify and pronounce the /k/ sound in *color* and *black.*

eBook Use digital materials for vocabulary practice.

LESSON 2: Colors

Set Purpose

- Tell children that today they will discuss colors and the color of shapes. Display page 3 of the Newcomer Cards.

Teach/Model Vocabulary

- Elicit names of shapes from Lesson 1.
- Lead children through the song/chant on page 154.
- Display the Newcomer Card again. Ask: *What words can we use to describe the shapes?* Children can name the colors they know. Then point to and name each color. Have children repeat. Help with pronunciation.
- Say these sentence frames as you point to the blue star: **What color is it? It's blue.** Say the sentences again as you write them on the board, completing the second sentence with the color. Have children repeat after you. Then point to the red circle and ask: **What color is it?** Have children answer chorally: **It's red**, filling in the name of the color. Repeat for other colors on the card, vocabulary list, and in the classroom.
- **Talk About It** Have children talk about the colors they see on the card and around the classroom.
- Expand by introducing the sentence frame: **What color and shape is the clock? It's a (color) circle**, filling in the name of the color and shape. Continue with other shapes and colors.

Practice/Apply INTERPRETIVE

- **Talk About It** Have partners use the Newcomer Card and sentence frames to discuss their favorite colors.
- Guide children to complete the activity on page 17.
- Hand out crayons of different colors. Name a color and have children see if their crayon's color matches the color you named. If there is a match, the child holds up his/her crayon and says the color using the sentence frame: **It's ____.**

Make Connections

Have partners talk about the different colors they see in each other's clothes. If there are shapes as well as colors, encourage children to use the sentence frame: **It's a ____ ____.**

Name: ______________________________

Colors

Use Newcomer Card, page 3

Say and trace the words. Then fill in each shape with the correct color.

1. 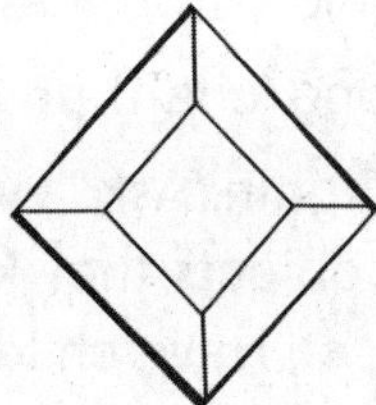 blue diamond

2. 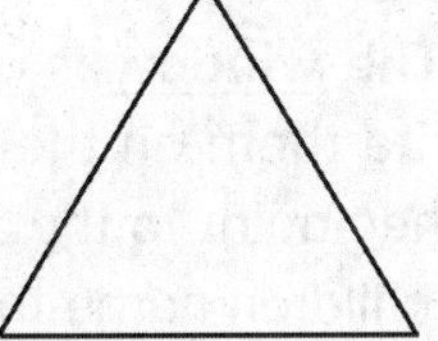 red triangle

3.  orange rectangle

4.  green star

5. 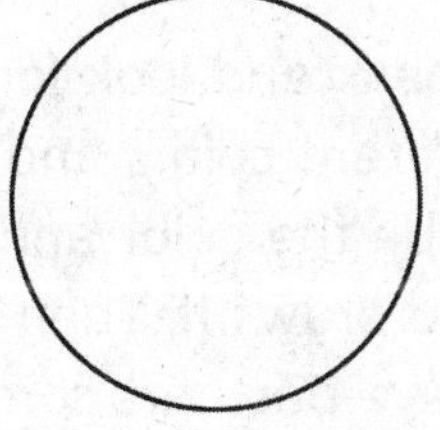 yellow circle

6. 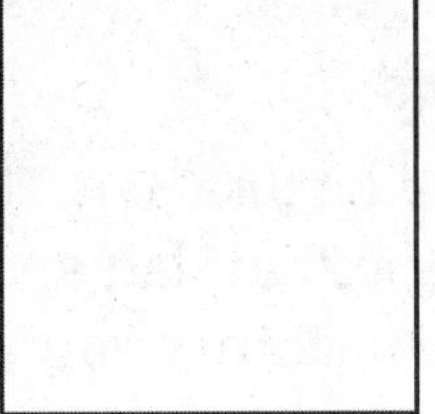 purple square

Shapes and Colors

Language Objective:
Name shapes and colors around us

Content Objective:
Identify shapes and colors around us

Sentence Frames:
The ____ is a ____.
The ____ is ____.
The ____ ____ is a ____.

VOCABULARY
clock, window, book, square

>> Go Digital

Language Transfers Handbook
See pages 16–19 for grammatical structures that do not transfer. Vietnamese speakers may overuse pronouns with nouns.

Foundational Skills
Use the Grade 1 High-Frequency Word Cards to practice saying the words *the, is,* and *a.* Use Sound-Spelling Card 11 to teach children how to identify and pronounce the /k/ sound in *clock* and *book.*

eBook and Games Provide audio support, interaction, and practice with the vocabulary.

LESSON 3: Shapes and Colors Around Us

Set Purpose

- Tell children that today they will discuss shapes and colors around us. Show page 3 of the Newcomer Cards.

Teach/Model Vocabulary

- Elicit names of shapes and colors from Lessons 1 and 2.
- Lead children through the song/chant on page 154.
- Display the Newcomer card again. Ask: *What do you see?* Children can name the objects they know. Then point to and name each object. Have children repeat. Help with pronunciation.
- Say these sentence frames as you point to the window: **The window is a square. The window is green.** Say the sentences again as you write them on the board. Have children repeat after you. Then point to the clock and say: **The clock is a circle.** Have children name the color of the clock by chorally stating: **The clock is red.** Repeat for other objects on the card and in the vocabulary list.
- **Talk About It** Have partners talk about the colors and shapes of objects in the classroom.
- Expand by introducing the frame: **The (color) (object) is a (shape).** Demonstrate the use of adjectives and nouns by filling in the blanks.

Practice/Apply COLLABORATIVE

- **Talk About It** Have partners use the Newcomer Card and sentence frames they learned to discuss what they know about shapes and colors in the world around us.
- Guide children to complete the activity on page 19.
- Have partners sit back to back and look for objects in the classroom that are different colors and shapes. Have one child name and describe the color and shape of an object while the other child draws it. Then have them switch roles. Afterwards, have partners compare their drawings to the real objects.

Make Cultural Connections

Show the United States flag or a picture of it. Then ask children to name colors and shapes in that flag and to name colors and shapes in their home country's flag.

Name: ____________________

Color each object. Write the name of the object and the color. Use words from the box.

Colors	red orange yellow green blue purple black brown pink brown
Objects	book clock window

1. 

The ________ is ________ .

2. 
The ________ is ________ .

3. 
The ________ is ________ .

Numbers

Language Objective:
Say and count numbers 1–20

Content Objective:
Identify and sequence numbers 1–20

Sentence Frames:
What number is this?
This is the number ____.
Count from ____ to ____.

VOCABULARY
1, 2, 3, 4, 5, 6, 7, 8, 9, 10, 11, 12, 13, 14, 15, 16, 17, 18, 19, 20, count
Cognate: contar

>> Go Digital

Language Transfers Handbook
See pages 16–19 for grammatical structures that do not transfer. Korean or Vietnamese speakers may omit object pronouns (*this*).

Foundational Skills
Use the Grade 1 High-Frequency Word Cards to practice saying *from, to,* and *this*; Sound-Spelling Card 14 to teach how to identify and pronounce /n/ in *number.*

eBook Use digital material for vocabulary practice.

LESSON 1: Numbers 1-20

Set Purpose

- Tell children that today they will discuss numbers. Display page 4 of the Newcomer Cards.

Teach/Model Vocabulary

- Lead children through the song/chant on page 154.
- Display the Newcomer Card again. Ask: *What do you see?* Then point to and name each number. Have children repeat. Then hold up your fingers and have children practice counting to twenty with you. Partners can practice by holding up their fingers and counting together.
- Say these sentence frames as you point to a number. **What number is this? This is the number 4.** Say the sentences again as you write them on the board, completing the second sentence with the number. Then point to the number *12* and ask: **What number is this?** Have children answer chorally: **This is the number 12.** Repeat for other numbers on the Newcomer Card and around your classroom.
- **Talk About It** Have partners name the numbers they know and point to them on the card.
- Extend by introducing the sentence frame: **Count from ____ to ____.** Have children practice counting from one number to another.

Practice/Apply COLLABORATIVE

- **Talk About It** Have partners use the card and sentence frames to discuss the numbers they know. Elicit how they know these numbers.
- Guide children to complete the activity on page 21.
- In pairs, have one child use a finger to draw a number on the back of his or her partner's back and ask: **What number is this?** Have the partner guess the number and the child answers: **Yes/No.** Then have them switch roles.

Make Connections

Have children talk to a partner about numbers they see at home or at school, such as numbers in their address, phone number, sports jersey, above a classroom, etc.

Name: ______________________

Numbers 1-20

Use Newcomer Card, page 4

Fill in the missing numbers. Then write the missing numbers on the line.

1	2	__
4	5	6
__	8	__
10	__	12
13	14	15
__	17	__
19	20	

Numbers

Language Objective:
Talk about age using numbers

Content Objective:
Understand which numbers are in a person's age

Sentence Frames:
How old are you?
I'm ____ years old.

VOCABULARY
one, two, three, four, five, six, seven, eight, nine, ten, years old

>> Go Digital

Language Transfers Handbook
See pages 16-19 for grammatical structures that do not transfer. Spanish or Arabic speakers may use *have* instead of *be*.

Foundational Skills
Use the Grade 1 High-Frequency Word Cards to practice saying *how, old, are,* and *you.* Sound-Spelling Card 32 to teach how to identify and pronounce the long *a* sound in *eight.*

eBook Use digital material for vocabulary practice.

LESSON 2: How Old Are You?

Set Purpose

- Tell children that today they will use numbers to discuss age. Display page 4 of the Newcomer Cards.

Teach/Model Vocabulary

- Elicit numbers discussed in Lesson 1.
- Lead children through the song/chant on page T1.
- Display the Newcomer Card again. Ask: *What numbers do you see?* Have children turn to a partner and say which numbers they see. Point to and read the birthday card. Have children repeat. Help with pronunciation.
- Say these sentence frames as you point to the boy with the hat on: **How old are you? I'm <u>six</u> years old.** Then say the sentences again as you write them on the board, completing the second sentence with the number. Have children repeat after you. Then have all children who are six years old stand up and ask: **How old are you?** Have children who are standing answer chorally: **I'm <u>six</u> years old.** Repeat for other ages in the class.
- **Talk About It** Have partners take turns asking each other their age, using the sentence frames.

Practice/Apply COLLABORATIVE

- **Talk About It** Have partners use the Newcomers Card, the Conversation Starters on page T28, and the sentence frames they learned to ask and answer questions about their ages.
- Guide the children to complete the activity on page 23.
- Have children stand in a circle. Pass a ball to the child next to you and ask him or her the question: **How old are you?** Have the child answer the question with: **I'm ____ years old.** Then have children pass the ball around the circle as they count to the number that the child answered. For example, if the child says: *I'm 7 years old,* then children will pass the ball seven times, then repeat the question for the child holding the ball.

Make Connections

Have children draw themselves on a recent, fun day. Have children ask each other: **How old are you?** Have children respond by saying their age using numbers.

Name: ______________________________

How Old Are You?

Use Newcomer Card, page 4

Draw a picture of yourself celebrating at your last birthday. Write how old you are at the bottom.

Numbers

Language Objective:
Name the number of objects

Content Objective:
Count the number of objects

Sentence Frames:
How many do you have?
I have ____ ____.
We have ____ ____.
They have ____ ____.
She/He has ____ ____.

VOCABULARY
apples, gifts, balls, muffins, bananas, strawberries, balloons, flags, shoes
Cognate: bolas

>> Go Digital

Language Transfers Handbook
See pages 16-19 for grammatical structures that do not transfer. Korean, Spanish, or Vietnamese speakers may omit subject pronouns.

Foundational Skills
Use the Grade 1 High-Frequency Word Cards to practice saying *we, she, he,* and *they*. Sound-Spelling Card 22 to teach how to identify and pronounce the /v/ sound in *have*.

eBook and Games Provide audio support, interaction, and practice with the vocabulary.

LESSON 3: How Many?

Set Purpose

- Tell children that today they will discuss the number of objects. Display page 4 of the Newcomer Cards.
- If possible, take the children to the playground and talk about the the things you see and how many there are.

Teach/Model Vocabulary

- Elicit numbers and ages discussed in Lessons 1 and 2.
- Lead the children through the song/chant on page T1.
- Display the Newcomer card again. Ask: *What things do you see*? Children can name things they know. Then point to and name the objects. Have children repeat. Help with pronunciation.
- Say this sentence frame as you point to the objects: **They have <u>four</u> <u>apples</u>.** Then count the objects and say the sentences again as your write them on the board, completing the sentence with number and name of the objects. Have children repeat after you. Then count the balloons and prompt children to say chorally: **They have <u>seven</u> <u>balloons</u>.** Repeat for other objects on the card.
- **Talk About It** Have partners talk about the different objects they see on the card and in the classroom. Elicit the number of objects from the children.
- Extend by introducing the frames: **How many do you have? I/We have ____ ____. She/He has ____ ____.**

Practice/Apply

- **Talk About It** Have children use the card and sentence frames to discuss the number of different objects they both know about in the school.
- Guide children to complete the activity on page 25.
- In pairs, have one child use the sentence frame: **I have <u>ten</u> <u>crayons</u>.** The partner draws a picture of the objects. Then have them switch roles. Be sure they use different numbers and objects. Afterwards, have partners share and talk about their drawings with their classmates.

Make Cultural Connections

Have partners talk about number games they played in their home countries. Have children teach the class their game and then play the number game with the class.

Name: ____________________

How Many?

Use Newcomer Card, page 4

A. Read the number. Count the items in the pictures. Circle the picture that matches the number.

7

3

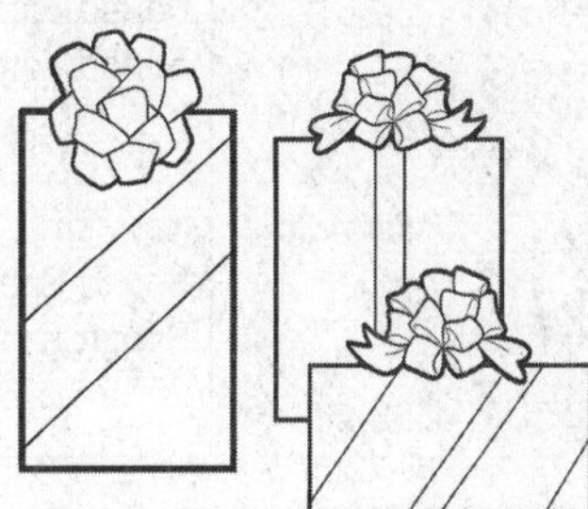

B. Write a sentence about the number of gifts.

UNIT 1: Life at School OVERVIEW

In the Classroom

Newcomer Card, p. 5

LESSONS	MATERIALS	LANGUAGE OBJECTIVES	LANGUAGE STRUCTURES/ GRAMMAR	VOCABULARY
Lesson 1: Classroom Objects, p. 28–29	Newcomer Card p. 5 Sound-Spelling Card 1 Song/Chant p. T1	Say the names, amounts, and colors of classroom objects	What color is his/her/your/their ____? He/She/I/We/They has/have ____ ____. **Verb:** to be, to have **Regular plurals**	Classroom objects **High-Frequency Words:** *what, color, have, has*
Lesson 2: Classroom Activities, p. 30–31	Newcomer Card p. 5 Sound-Spelling Card 31 Song/Chant p. T1	Talk about what we do in the classroom	What is he/she doing? He's/She's ____. What are you doing? I'm ____. **Verb:** present continuous of *do* **Contractions:** I'm, she's, he's	Classroom activities **High-Frequency Words:** *you, he, she, we*
Lesson 3: Classroom Commands, p. 32–33	Newcomer Card p. 5 Sound-Spelling Card 19 Song/Chant p. T1	Understand classroom directions, commands, and requests	Please sit down. Please listen to ____. Please look at ____. **Imperatives** **Pronouns:** me, your	Classroom commands **High-Frequency Words:** *come, listen, look*

Computers

Newcomer Card, p. 6

LESSONS	MATERIALS	LANGUAGE OBJECTIVES	LANGUAGE STRUCTURES/ GRAMMAR	VOCABULARY
Lesson 1: Location of Objects, p. 34–35	Newcomer Card p. 6 Sound-Spelling Card 14 Song/Chant p. T1	Express where objects are in the classroom	Where is the ____? The ____ is ____ the ____. **Prepositions of place** **Wh- questions:** Where	Locations **High-Frequency Words:** *where, by, near*
Lesson 2: Asking for Help, p. 36–37	Newcomer Card p. 6 Sound-Spelling Card 17 Song/Chant p. T1	Express the need for help	Can you help me? I need ____. I don't understand. **Verb:** to need **Modal verb:** can	Help and clarifications **High-Frequency Words:** *help, say, know, question*
Lesson 3: Using Computers, p. 38–39	Newcomer Card p. 6 Sound-Spelling Card 13 Song/Chant p. T1	Name and describe computer equipment	What can you do with a ____? I/We/They/She/He can ____. **Pronouns:** I, we, they, she, he, you **Modal verb:** can	Computer equipment **High-Frequency Words:** *use, how, then*

A Day at School

Newcomer Card, p. 7

LESSONS	MATERIALS	LANGUAGE OBJECTIVES	LANGUAGE STRUCTURES/ GRAMMAR	VOCABULARY
Lesson 1: Places at School, p. 40–41	Newcomer Card p. 7 Sound-Spelling Card 9 Song/Chant p. T1	Name places in school	What is this? This is a ____. **Verb:** to be ***Wh-* questions:** What **Pronoun:** this	Places in school **High-Frequency Words:** *this, is, a*
Lesson 2: What We Do in School, p. 42–43	Newcomer Card p. 7 Sound-Spelling Card 23 Song/Chant p. T2	Name school activities	Where do we ____? We ____ in the ____. **Pronoun:** we ***Wh-* questions:** Where	School activities **High-Frequency Words:** eat, *play, write, work*
Lesson 3: People in School, p. 44–45	Newcomer Card p. 7 Sound-Spelling Card 20 Song/Chant p. T2	Name people we see in school	Who's in the ____? The ____ is in the ____. **Verb:** to be ***Wh-* questions:** Who	People in school **High-Frequency Words:** *who, the, is*

Calendar	LESSONS	MATERIALS	LANGUAGE OBJECTIVES	LANGUAGE STRUCTURES/ GRAMMAR	VOCABULARY
Newcomer Card, p. 8	**Lesson 1:** Days and Months, p. 46–47	Newcomer Card p. 8 Sound-Spelling Card 4 Song/Chant p. T2	Name days of the week and months of the year	What day is/was ____? What month is it? It is ____. **Simple past tense** ***Wh-* questions:** What	Days and months **High-Frequency Words:** *day, today, month, year*
	Lesson 2: School-Day Routine, p. 48–49	Newcomer Card p. 8 Sound-Spelling Card 7 Song/Chant p. T2	Retell the order of events during a school day	First I ____. Then I ____. Next I ____. Finally I ____. **Pronouns:** she, he, I, my **Sequence words**	School-day events **High-Frequency Words:** *get, have, go, my*
	Lesson 3: Times of the Day, p. 50–51	Newcomer Card p. 8 Sound-Spelling Card 12 Song/Chant p. T2	Ask and answer questions about different times of day	When do we ____? We ____ in the/at ____. ***Wh-* questions:** When **Pronoun:** we	Times of the day **High-Frequency Words:** *when, early, we*

Weather	LESSONS	MATERIALS	LANGUAGE OBJECTIVES	LANGUAGE STRUCTURES/ GRAMMAR	VOCABULARY
Newcomer Card, p. 9	**Lesson 1:** Weather Conditions, p. 52–53	Newcomer Card p. 9 Sound-Spelling Card 40 Song/Chant p. T2	Ask and answer questions about types of weather	What is the weather outside? It's ____. It's ____ and ____. **Verb:** to be **Conjunction:** and	Weather conditions **High-Frequency Words:** *warm, what, and*
	Lesson 2: Seasons, p. 54–55	Newcomer Card p. 9 Sound-Spelling Card 21 Song/Chant p. T2	Ask and answer questions about the seasons	What season is it? It is ____. There is/are ____. ***Wh-* questions:** What **Present continuous verb**	Seasons **High-Frequency Words:** *it, is, fall, are*
	Lesson 3: Up in the Sky, p. 56–57	Newcomer Card p. 9 Sound-Spelling Card 33 Song/Chant p. T2	Talk about what we see in the sky	We can see the ____ in the sky. We see the ____ during the day/at night. **Modal verb:** can **Prepositions of time**	Objects in the sky **High-Frequency Words:** *can, day, see*

Progress Monitoring

Use the **Oral Language Proficiency Benchmark Assessment** on pages T40–T41 to monitor students' oral language proficiency growth.

Use the **Student Profile** on pages T43–T44 to record observations throughout the units.

In the Classroom

Language Objective:
Say the names, amounts, and colors of classroom objects

Content Objective:
Identify classroom objects and their colors

Sentence Frames:
What color is his/her ____?
She/He has ____.
What color is your/their ____?
I/You/We/They have ____.

VOCABULARY
book, pencil, ruler, pen, crayons, marker, desk, glue, flag, thing, have, we, they, two

>> Go Digital

Language Transfers Handbook
See pages 16-19 for grammatical structures that do not transfer. Hmong, Vietnamese, Korean, Arabic, Tagalog, or Cantonese speakers may mistake the article *one* for *a/an.*

Foundational Skills
Use the Grade 1 High-Frequency Word Cards to practice saying the words *what, color, have,* and *has.* Use Sound-Spelling Card 1 to teach children how to identify and pronounce the /a/ sound in *has* and *have.*

eBook Use digital material for vocabulary practice.

LESSON 1: Classroom Objects

Set Purpose

- Tell children that today they will discuss classroom objects. Show page 5 of the Newcomer Cards.

Teach/Model Vocabulary

- Lead children through the song/chant on page T1.
- Display the Newcomer Card again. Ask: *What do you see?* Then point to and name each classroom object. Have children repeat. Help with pronunciation.
- Say these sentence frames as you point to an object: **What color is her pencil? She has a yellow pencil.** Say the sentences again as you write them on the board. Have children repeat after you. Then point to the book and ask: **What color is his book?** Have children answer chorally: **He has a blue book.** Repeat for other classroom objects on the Newcomer Card.
- **Talk About It** Have partners discuss different objects on the card, in the vocabulary list, and around the room.
- Extend by introducing the sentence frames: **What color is your/their ____? I/You/We/They have ____.** Then expand by reusing the sentence frames with numbers of objects and the plural ending *-s.*

Practice/Apply

- **Talk About It** Have partners use the Newcomer Card and sentence frames they learned to discuss the classroom objects they're using today.
- Guide children to complete activity on page 29.
- Have children play a game in pairs. Name a color and ask children to look for objects in the classroom that have that color. Then ask the pairs to tell how many objects of that color they found using the sentence frame: **We have (number)(color) thing(s).**

Make Connections

Have children respond to this prompt: *Tell me more about classroom objects you use every day.* Have children tell you the names of the objects, as well as the colors and shapes.

Classroom Objects

Use Newcomer Card, page 5

Name: ____________________

Read and trace each word. Then draw a line to the picture that matches the word.

1. 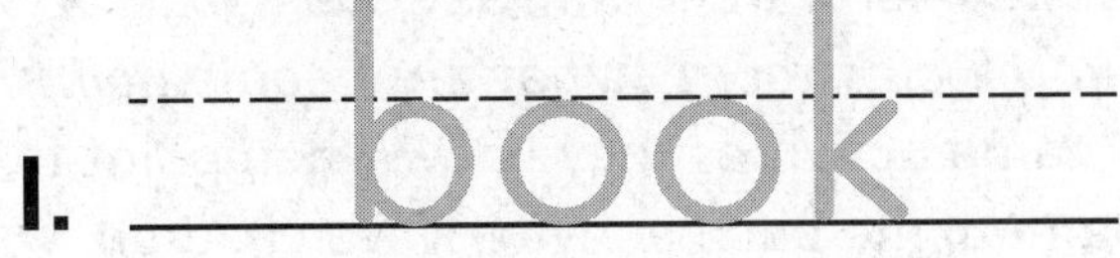

2. 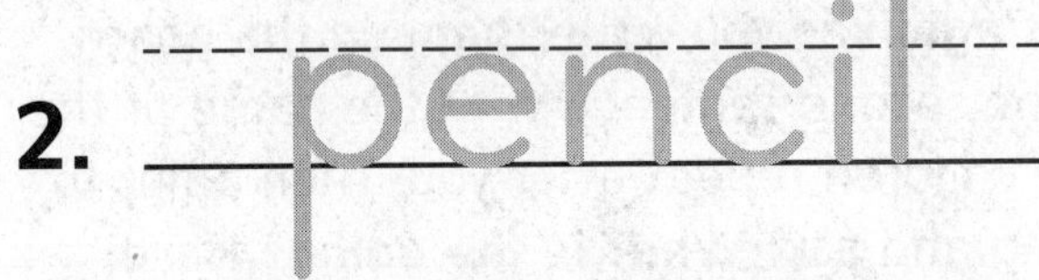

3. 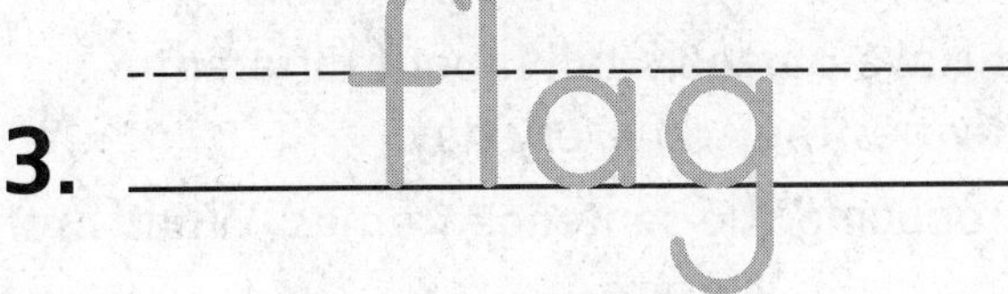

4. 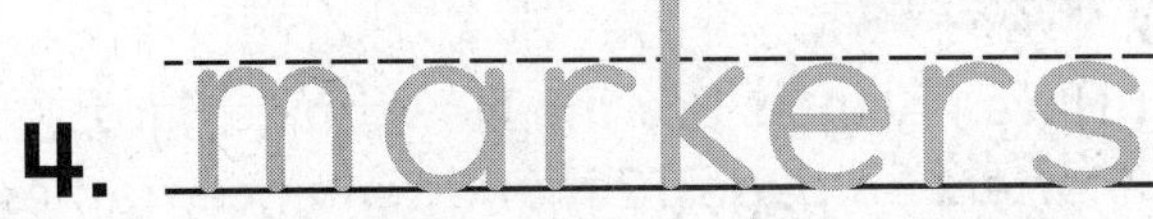

5. desk

6. ruler

a. 

b. 

c. 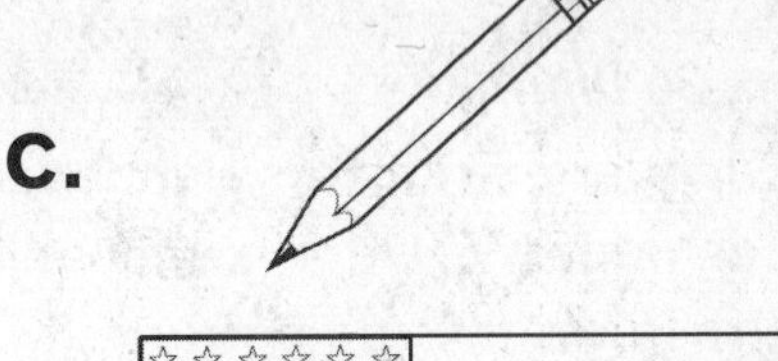

d. 

e. 

f. 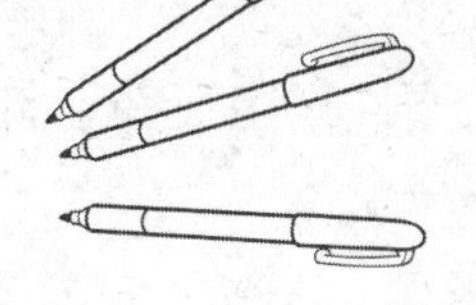

In the Classroom

Language Objective:
Talk about what we do in the classroom

Content Objective:
Demonstrate knowledge of classroom activities

Sentence Frames:
What are you doing?
I'm ____.
We are ____.
What is she/he doing?
She's/He's ____.

VOCABULARY
doing, coloring, writing, reading, listening, talking, singing, teaching, playing, counting, matching
Cognate: contar

>> Go Digital

Language Transfers Handbook
See pages 16-19 for grammatical structures that do not transfer. Cantonese, Hmong, or Vietnamese speakers may omit linking verbs.

Foundational Skills
Use the Grade 1 High-Frequency Word Cards to practice saying the words *you, he, she,* and *we*. Use Sound-Spelling Card 31 to teach how to identify and pronounce the /ng/ sound in *-ing* verbs.

eBook Use digital material for vocabulary practice.

LESSON 2: Classroom Activities

Set Purpose

- Tell children that today they will discuss classroom activities. Show page 5 of the Newcomer Cards.

Teach/Model Vocabulary

- Elicit names of objects discussed in Lesson 1.
- Lead children through the song/chant on page T1.
- Display the Newcomer Card again. Say: *Let's look at what we do in the classroom. What are people doing?* Children can name activities they know. Then point to, name, and pantomime each activity. Have children repeat your words and actions. Help with pronunciation.
- Say these sentence frames as you point to an activity in the picture: **What is he doing? He's reading.** Then say the sentences again as you write them on the board, completing the second sentence with the name of the activity. Have children repeat after you. Then point to the girl writing and ask: **What is she doing?** Have children answer chorally: **She's writing.** Repeat for other activities on the card and in the vocabulary list.
- **Talk About It** Have partners talk about different classroom activities they do every day.
- Extend by introducing the sentence frames: **What are you doing? I'm ____. We are ____.**

Practice/Apply

- **Talk About It** Have partners use the Newcomer Card, Conversation Starters on page T29, and sentence frames they learned to ask and answer questions about activities they do in the classroom.
- Guide children to complete the activity on page 31.
- Play charades. Children can take turns acting out classroom activities while others name the activity using the sentence frame: **She's/He's ____.** For an extra challenge, ask children to say what they are reading, writing with, counting, and so on.

Make Connections

Have partners talk about their favorite classroom activities, and tell why they like them. Then have individual children present to the class.

Name: ______________________

Use Newcomer Card, page 5

A. Read each word. Circle the picture that matches the classroom activity.

1. reading

2. writing

3. counting

B. What classroom activity do you see?

____

In the Classroom

Language Objective:
Understand classroom directions, commands, and requests

Content Objective:
Demonstrate understanding by appropriately responding to directions, commands, and requests

Sentence Frames:
Please sit down/come here.
Please listen to ____.
Please check your work.
Please stop/work together.
Please look at ____.
Please raise your hand.
Please write your name.

VOCABULARY
come here, sit down, listen, raise your hand, stop, look at
False cognates: come

>> *Go Digital*

Language Transfers Handbook
See pages 16–19 for grammatical structures that do not transfer. Cantonese or Hmong speakers may omit prepositions.

Foundational Skills
Use the Grade 1 High-Frequency Word Cards to practice saying the words *come, listen,* and *look.* Use Sound-Spelling Card 19 to teach children how to identify and pronounce the /s/ sound in *listen.*

eBook Provide audio support, interaction, and practice with the vocabulary.

LESSON 3: Classroom Commands

Set Purpose

- Tell children that today they will discuss classroom commands. Show page 5 of the Newcomer Cards.

Teach/Model Vocabulary

- Elicit objects and activities from Lessons 1 and 2.
- Lead children through the song/chant on page T1.
- Display the Newcomer Card again. Ask: *What is the teacher saying?* Point to and read the classroom commands as you use gestures to show what they mean. Have children repeat. Help with pronunciation. Repeat with other commands listed in the sidebar.
- **Talk About It** Have volunteers take turns giving commands as the class responds.
- **Talk About It** Pretend you are a student and one of the children is the teacher. Have the "teacher" give a command, which you respond to incorrectly (looking at a book instead of raising your hand). Have children say what your action was and show what your response should have been. As children learn the game, partners or small groups can play by themselves

Practice/Apply 

- **Talk About It** Have partners use the Newcomer Card and sentence frames they learned to discuss classroom commands they've heard today.
- Guide children to complete the activity on page 33.
- Have children work in small groups to play a game of Simon Says using commands they learned. Have one child play the leader and say a command while the rest of the group acts it out. Model the activity before beginning. Encourage children to include previously learned vocabulary, and to take turns being the leader.

Make Cultural Connections

Ask children to think of different games they played in their home countries. Have children teach each other these games using commands they've learned.

Name: ____________________

Use Newcomer Card, page 5

A. Talk with a partner about the pictures.

B. Draw something your teacher tells you to do. Write the command.

Computers

Language Objective:
Express where objects are in the classroom

Content Objective:
Identify the locations of objects in the classroom

Sentence Frames:
Where is the ____?
The ____ is ____ the ____.

VOCABULARY
in, on, by, near, next to
Cognate: en

>> Go Digital

Language Transfers Handbook
See pages 16–19 for grammatical structures that do not transfer. Cantonese, Hmong, Korean, Vietnamese, Arabic, or Tagalog speakers may omit articles.

Foundational Skills
Use the Grade 1 High-Frequency Word Cards to practice saying *where, by,* and *near;* Sound-Spelling Card 14 to teach children how to identify and pronounce /n/ in *on, in,* and *near.*

eBook Use digital material for vocabulary practice.

LESSON 1: Location of Objects

Set Purpose

- Tell children that today they will discuss the location of objects. Display page 6 of the Newcomer Cards.

Teach/Model Vocabulary

- Lead children through the song/chant on page T1.
- Display the Newcomer Card again. Ask: *What do you see?* Children can name things they know. Then point to and name the location of objects with prepositions. Have children repeat. Help with pronunciation. Have children turn to a partner and say where there backpack is.
- Say these sentence frames as you point to an object: **Where is the crayon? The crayon is on the desk.** Say the sentences again as you write them on the board. Cover all objects on the card and prepositions in the vocabulary box. Have children repeat after you. Then point to the backpack and ask: **Where is the backpack?** Have children answer chorally: **The backpack is on the floor.** Repeat for the other objects on the card and in your classroom.
- **Talk About It** Have partners talk about the location of different objects on the card and in their classroom using the Conversation Starters on page T30.

Practice/Apply

- **Talk About It** Have partners use the Newcomer Card and sentence frames to discuss the location of other children in the classroom. Extend by having children use the sentence frames to talk about how the differences between the classroom on the card and their classroom.
- Have children play a game of "basketball" with a basket and a soft ball or a garbage can and crumpled balls of paper. Have children take turns trying to toss the ball into the basket. Children can answer the question: **Where is the ball?** by seeing where the ball landed and using the sentence frame: **The ___ is ___ the ___.** Provide support making complete sentences.
- Guide children to complete the activity on page 35.

Make Connections

Ask children to talk with a partner about the location of various objects on or in her/his desk, cubby, locker, etc.

Name: ______________________________

Use Newcomer Card, page 6

A. Read the word. Circle the picture that the word describes.

1. in

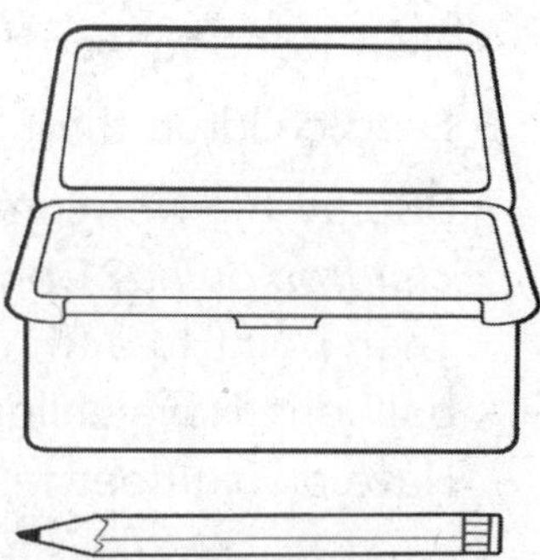

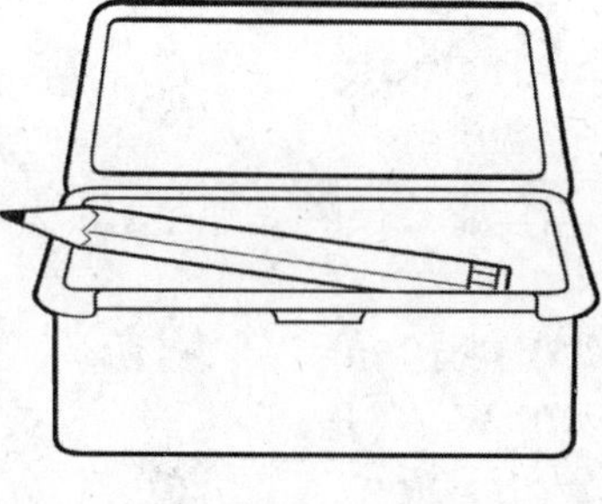

2. on

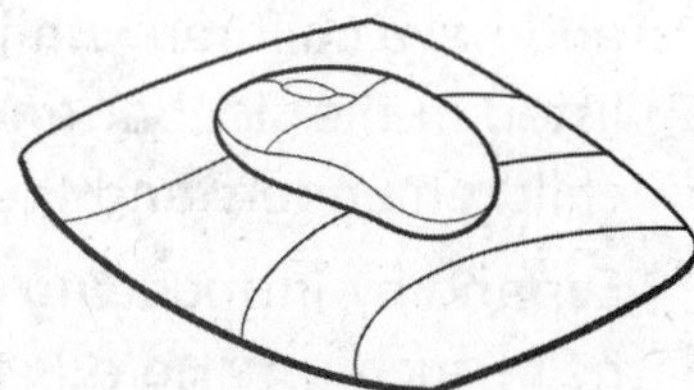

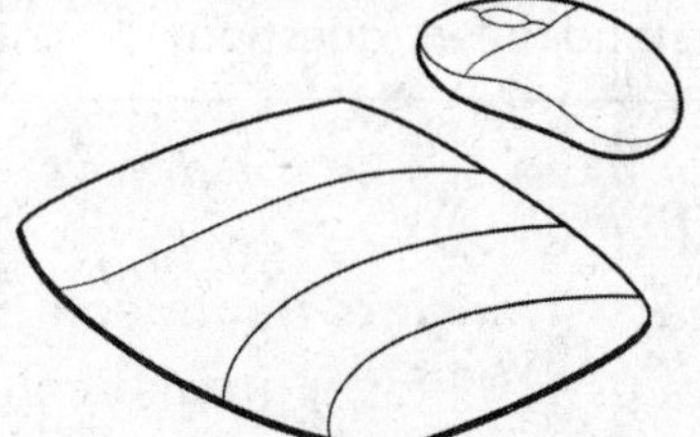

3. by

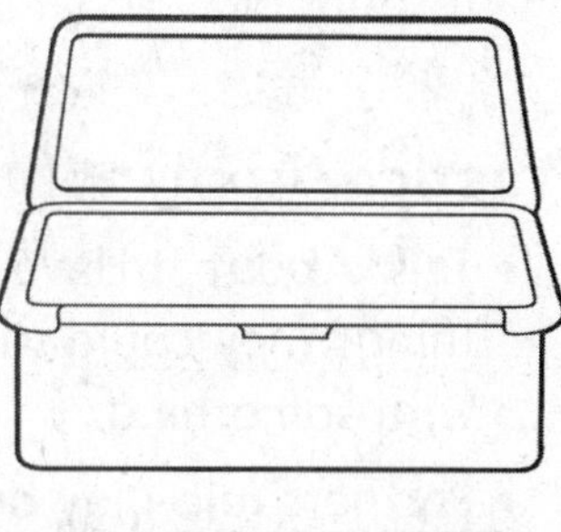

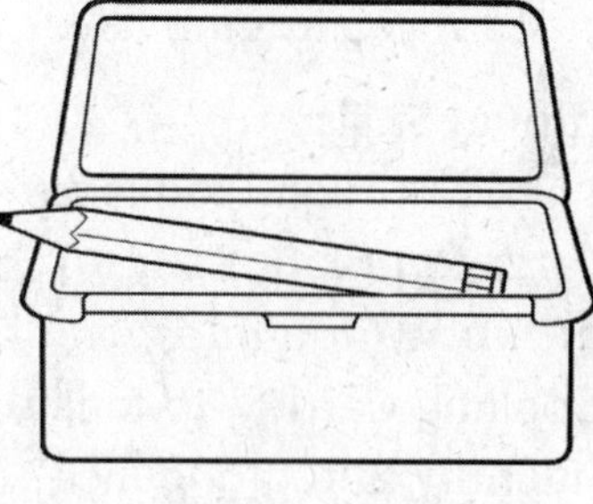

B. Where is the girl?

She is ______________ the chair.

Computers

Language Objective:
Express the need for help

Content Objective:
Understand how to ask for help

Sentence Frames:
Can you help me?
I need ____.
I don't understand.
Please say it again.
I don't know.
I have a question.

VOCABULARY
please, help, know, say, understand, need, question

>> Go Digital

Language Transfers Handbook
See pages 16-19 for grammatical structures that do not transfer. Cantonese, Korean, Spanish, or Arabic speakers may omit helping verbs in negative statements.

Foundational Skills
Use the Grade 1 High-Frequency Word Cards to practice saying *help, say, know,* and *question*; Sound-Spelling Card 17 to teach how to identify and pronounce /kw/ in *question.*

eBook Use digital material for vocabulary practice.

LESSON 2: Asking for Help

Set Purpose

- Tell children that today they will discuss how to ask for help in class. Display page 6 of the Newcomer Cards.

Teach/Model Vocabulary

- Elicit location words from Lesson 1.
- Lead children through the song/chant on page T1.
- Display the Newcomer Card again. Ask: *What are the children doing?* Children can name things they know. Then point to and read aloud the text in the speech balloons. Have children repeat. Help with pronunciation. Have a volunteer tell what these sentences mean.
- Say the sentences in the speech balloons again as you write them on the board, miming actions as necessary (looking confused while pointing to your computer; indicating a crayon on the table). Repeat a few times and have children join in. Introduce the other requests listed in the sidebar and use the same instruction to help children understand them.
- Expand by introducing simple responses to requests for help, such as: "Here is the ___." and "Of course!"
- **Talk About It** Have partners take turns asking each other for an item, such as a crayon or book, and responding.

Practice/Apply

- **Talk About It** Have partners talk about the different things they could say to the teacher if they needed help with something.
- Partners role-play being a student and a teacher. The "student" raises her/his hand. The "teacher" comes to help. The student says: **Can you help me? I have a question.** Or **I need a ____.** Have them fill in an object the student needs. Then switch roles. Model as necessary.
- Guide children to complete the activity on page 37.

Make Connections

Ask children: *Think about a time when you needed help. What did you say? Why? What will you say now?* Have children talk to a partner and draw a picture illustrating the moment. Have children present to the class.

Name: ______________________________

Use Newcomer Card, page 6

A. Talk with a partner about the pictures.

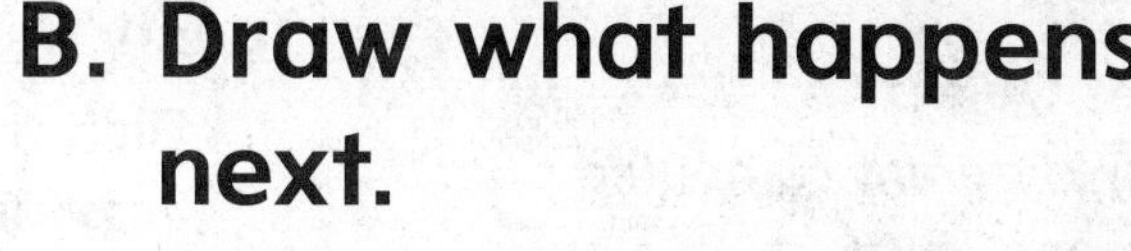

B. Draw what happens next.

Computers

Language Objective:
Name and describe computer equipment

Content Objective:
Identify different computer equipment

Sentence Frames:
What can you do with a ____?
I/We/They/She/He can ____.
I/We/They/She/He can ____ and ____.

VOCABULARY
computer, keyboard, mouse, internet, screen, use, click, turn on, use, play, games, type
Cognates: computadora, internet, usar

>> Go Digital

Language Transfers Handbook
See pages 16-19 for grammatical structures that do not transfer. Korean, Spanish, or Arabic speakers may struggle with the phrasal verb *turn on.*

Foundational Skills
Use the Grade 1 High-Frequency Word Cards to practice saying *use, how,* and *then*; Sound-Spelling Card 13 to teach children how to identify and pronounce /m/ in *mouse.*

eBook and Games Provide audio support, interaction, and practice with the vocabulary.

LESSON 3: Using Computers

Set Purpose

- Tell children that today they will discuss using the computer. Display page 6 of the Newcomer Cards.

Teach/Model Vocabulary

- Elicit the locations and ways to ask for help from Lessons 1 and 2.
- Lead children through the song/chant on page T1.
- Display the Newcomer Card again. Say: *What is the student doing with the computer?* Then point to, name, and pantomime using the various computer parts shown on the card and in the vocabulary list. Have children repeat. Help with pronunciation. Have partners talk about other computer related equipment they know of.
- Say these sentence frames as you point to the computer: **What can you do with a computer? I can play games.** Then say the sentences again as you write them on the board. Have children repeat after you. Then point to the keyboard and ask: **What can you do with a keyboard?** Have children answer chorally: **I can type on a keyboard.** Repeat for other computer parts and tasks on the card and vocabulary list.
- **Talk About It** Have partners talk about different things they do on a computer.
- Extend by introducing the sentence frame: **I can point and click on a mouse.** Have children name multiple things we can do with computer parts.

Practice/Apply

- **Talk About It** Have partners to use the card and sentence frames to discuss the different parts of a computer and how we use them. Elicit action words.
- Guide children to complete the activity on page 39.
- Have small groups play charades. One child acts out an action we do with computer equipment and the others use the sentence frame: **She/He can ____ with a ____.**

Make Cultural Connections

Have children talk with a partner about computers and technology in their home country. Have them talk about what the technology was used for and why.

Use Newcomer Card, page 6

Name: ______________________

Look at the computer. Use a word from the box to name each part.

screen	computer	mouse	keyboard

1. ______________________

2. ______________________

3. ______________________

4. ______________________

A Day at School

Language Objective:
Name places in school

Content Objective:
Identify places in school

Sentence Frames:
What is this?
This is a ____.

VOCABULARY
library, cafeteria, gym, nurse's office, main office, restroom, classroom, hallway
Cognates: cafetería, oficina **False Cognate:** librería

>> Go Digital

Language Transfers Handbook
See pages 16-19 for grammatical structures that do not transfer. Vietnamese speakers may avoid using the *'s* in *nurse's office.*

Foundational Skills
Use the Grade 1 High-Frequency Word Cards to practice saying *this, is,* and *a.* Use Sound-Spelling Card 9 to teach children how to identify and pronounce /o/ in *office.*

eBook Use digital material to practice vocabulary.

LESSON 1: Places at School

Set Purpose

- Tell children that today they will discuss places at school. Display page 7 of the Newcomer Cards.
- If possible, take children on a quick tour of your school, naming the different places.

Teach/Model Vocabulary

- Lead children through the song/chant on page T1.
- Display the Newcomer Card again. Say: *This is the inside of a school. What do you see?* Children can name things they know. Then point to and name each place. Have children repeat. Help with pronunciation.
- Say these sentence frames as you point to a place: **What is this? This is a <u>library</u>.** Then say the sentences again as you write them on the board, completing the second sentence with the name of the place. Have children repeat after you. Then point to the gym and ask: **What is this?** Have children answer chorally: **This is a <u>gym</u>,** filling in the name of the place. Repeat for other places on the Newcomer Card and in your school.
- **Talk About It** Have partners talk about and compare different places on the card and at their school.

Practice/Apply

- **Talk About It** Have partners use the Newcomer Card and sentence frames to ask and answer questions about places in school.
- Guide children to complete the activity on page 41. Ask them to tell you why those places are their favorites.
- Have children play "Sneak a Peek." Cover each place on the Newcomer Card with a sticky note. Then give children a quick peek of a place and ask: **What is this?** Children then say the name of the place, based on the quick peek. Provide extra peeks, if necessary.

Make Connections

Ask the following question: *What else can you tell me about ____?* Fill in with one of the places at school they learned about and have children tell a partner more about that place. Then have partners share with you.

Name: ______________________________

Use Newcomer Card, page 7

Draw your two favorite places at school. Write the names.

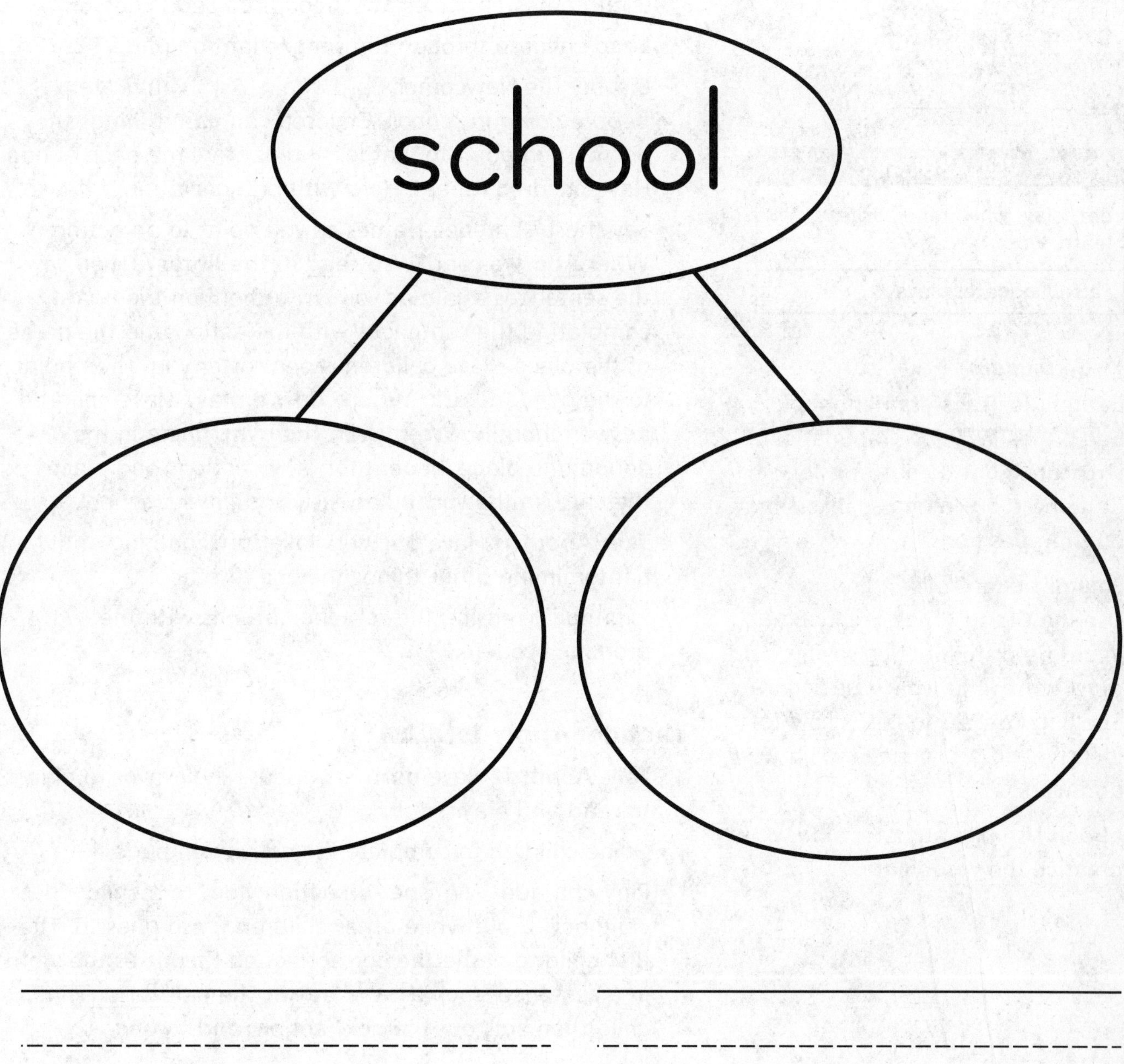

A Day at School

Language Objective:
Name school activities

Content Objective:
Identify school activities

Sentence Frames:
Where do we ____?
We ____ in the ____.

VOCABULARY
eat, play, walk, read, write, learn, work
False Cognate: playa

>> Go Digital

Language Transfers Handbook
See pages 16-19 for grammatical structures that do not transfer. Cantonese or Hmong speakers may omit prepositions.

Foundational Skills
Use the Grade 1 High-Frequency Word Cards to practice saying *eat, play, write,* and *work*. Use Sound-Spelling Card 23 to teach how to identify and pronounce /w/ in *walk* and *work*.

eBook Use digital material to practice the vocabulary.

LESSON 2: What We Do in School

Set Purpose

- Tell children that today they will discuss different school activities. Show page 7 of the Newcomer Cards.

Teach/Model Vocabulary

- Elicit names of places at school discussed in Lesson 1.
- Lead children through the song/chant on page T2.
- Display the Newcomer Card again. Ask: *What are people doing in school?* Children can name things they know. Then point to, name, and pantomime each action. Have children repeat. Help with pronunciation.
- Say these sentence frames as you point to an action: **Where do we read? We read in the library.** Then say the sentences again as you write them on the board, completing the sentences with the action and the name of the place. Have children repeat after you. Then point to the gym and ask: **Where do we play?** Have children answer chorally: **We play in the gym,** filling in the action and place. Repeat for other actions and places on the card, in the vocabulary list, and in your school.
- **Talk About It** Have partners take turns naming and pantomiming other things they do at school.
- Expand by reusing the sentence frames with the pronouns *you* and *I*.

Practice/Apply

- **Talk About It** Have partners discuss their favorite places to read and play.
- Guide children to complete the activity on page 43.
- Play charades. Whisper an action word to a child. That child acts it out while other children try to guess it. The first child to name the correct action then uses the word in a sentence, such as: **We eat in the cafeteria.** That child then acts out the next action, and so on.

Make Connections

Have children stand up. Say sentences using vocabulary from this lesson, mixing in vocabulary from previous lessons. When children hear an action word from this lesson, they must act it out and then sit down. Then have children tell a partner their favorite thing to do in school.

Name: ____________________

Match each activity with a place.

1. 

2. 

3. 

4. 

5. 

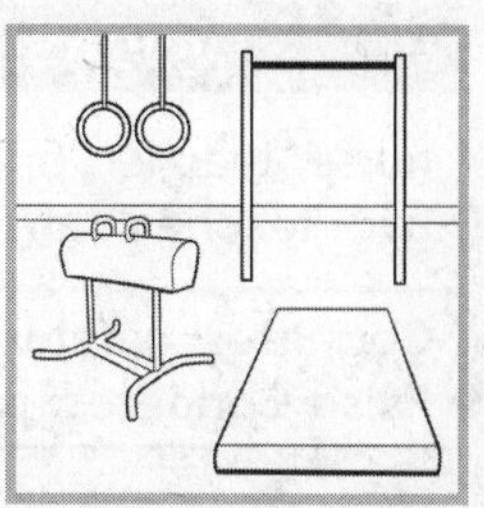

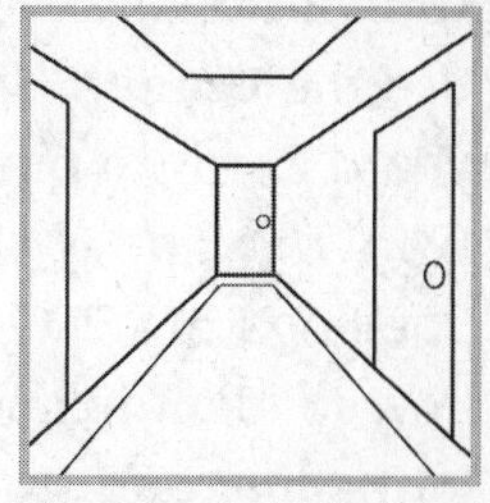

Where do we play? We __________ in the __________.

A Day at School

Language Objective:
Name people we see in school

Content Objective:
Identify people we see in school

Sentence Frames:
Who's in the ____?
The ____ is in the ____.

VOCABULARY
nurse, teacher, principal, student, gym teacher, cafeteria worker
Cognates: cafeteria, estudiante **False Cognates:** principal

>> Go Digital

Language Transfers Handbook
See pages 16-19 for grammatical structures that do not transfer. Vietnamese speakers may overuse pronouns with nouns.

Foundational Skills Kit
Use the Grade 1 High-Frequency Word Cards to practice saying *who, the,* and *is.* Use Sound-Spelling Card 20 to teach children how to identify and pronounce /t/ in *teacher* and *student.*

eBook and Games Provide audio support, interaction, and practice with the vocabulary.

LESSON 3: People in School

Set Purpose

- Tell children that today they will discuss people we see in school. Show page 7 of the Newcomer Cards.

Teach/Model Vocabulary

- Review places and activities from Lessons 1 and 2.
- Lead children through the song/chant on page T2.
- Display the Newcomer Card again. Say: *Look at all the people in school. Who do you see?* Point to and name each person. Children repeat. Help with pronunciation.
- Say these sentence frames as you point to a person: **Who's in the nurse's office? The nurse is in the nurse's office.** Say the sentences again as you write them on the board. Have children repeat after you. Then point to the office and ask: **Who's in the main office?** Have children answer chorally: **The principal is in the main office,** filling in the name of the person and place. Repeat for other people and places on the card and in your school.
- **Talk About It** Have partners talk about different people they know in their school.
- Extend by reusing the sentence frames with the activities from Lesson 2. For example, **The principal works in the main office** and **The student reads in the library**. Teach the inflectional ending *-s,* as necessary.

Practice/Apply

- **Talk About It** Have partners use the Newcomer Card and sentence frames they learned to talk about what they know about people in school.
- Guide children to complete the activity on page 45.
- Make up silly questions about people at school. For example, ask: **Is the cafeteria worker in the gym?** Have children say *yes* or *no.* If the answer is no, ask where they see that person. Encourage children to make up silly questions to ask their classmates about people at school.

Make Cultural Connections

Ask children to think of different games or activities they did in their home country. Have them share with a partner by pantomiming or drawing a picture and describing it.

Name: ______________________________

People in School

Use Newcomer Card, page 7

Draw a person in school and where you see that person. Then complete the sentence.

The ____________________ is in the ____________________.

Calendar

Language Objective:
Name days of the week and months of the year

Content Objective:
Identify and sequence days of the week and months of the year

Sentence Frames:
What day is today/tomorrow?
What day was yesterday?
Today /Tomorrow is ____.
Yesterday was ____.
What month is it? It is ____.
Last month was ____.
Next month is ____.

VOCABULARY

Sunday, Monday, Tuesday, Wednesday, Thursday, Friday, Saturday, day, week, yesterday, today, tomorrow, month, January, February, March, April, May, June, July, August, September, October, November, December

>> Go Digital

Language Transfers Handbook
See pages 16–19 for grammatical structures that do not transfer. Hmong, Spanish, Arabic, Tagalog, Cantonese, or Korean speakers may overuse articles.

Foundational Skills
Use the Grade 1 High-Frequency Word Cards to practice saying *day, today, month,* and *year*; Sound-Spelling Card 4 to teach children how to identify and pronounce /d/ in *day.*

eBook Use digital materials to practice vocabulary.

LESSON 1: Days and Months

Set Purpose

- Tell children that today they will discuss days and months. Display page 8 of the Newcomer Cards.

Teach/Model Vocabulary

- Lead children through the song/chant on page T2.
- Display the Newcomer Card again. Ask: *What do you see?* Children can name things they know. Then point to and name each day of the week. Repeat for months of the year on your own yearly calendar. Have children repeat. Help with pronunciation.
- Say these sentence frames as you point to today: **What day is today? Today is (day of the week).** Say the sentences again as you write them on the board. Then point to the next day and ask: **What day is tomorrow?** Have children answer chorally: **Tomorrow is (day).**
- Repeat the instruction with the other sentence frames in the sidebar.
- Explain that the word *was* is in the sentence frame: **Yesterday was (day).** Explain that *was* is the past tense of *is.* Explain how to create the simple paste tense of verbs they have already learned (adding -ed), and have children practice with *talk, listen, play,* etc.

Practice/Apply COLLABORATIVE

- **Talk About It** Have partners use the Newcomer Card and sentence frames to ask and answer questions about days and months. Elicit descriptive words.
- Have children write the days of the week and months on two different sets of index cards. Have partners work together to put the cards in order. Then have them use the sentence frames to tell each other what day and month it is, was, and is going to be.
- Guide children to complete the activity on page 47.

Make Connections

Have children talk to a partner answering the following prompt: *What is your favorite day? Why? What do you like to do on that day?* Encourage children to use the past tense and talk about their favorite day last week.

Name: ______________________________

Days and Months

Use Newcomer Card, page 8

A. Read the days of the week.

Put a ◯ around today.

Put a □ around yesterday.

Put a △ around tomorrow.

Sunday	Monday	Tuesday	Wednesday	Thursday	Friday	Saturday

B. Write the name of one day you don't go to school.

____

C. Write the month of your birthday.

____

Calendar

Language Objective:
Retell the order of events during a school day

Content Objective:
Understand sequencing and routines

Sentence Frames:
First I/she/he/they ____.
Then I/she/he/they ____.
Next I/she/he/they ____.
Finally I/she/he/they ____.

VOCABULARY
get up, brush teeth, brush hair, get dressed, eat breakfast, go to school, go home, play, have dinner, take a bath, take a shower, go to sleep
Cognate: escuela

>> Go Digital

Language Transfers Handbook
See pages 16–19 for grammatical structures that do not transfer. Cantonese, Korean, Spanish, Arabic, or Hmong speakers may confuse transitive and intransitive verbs .

Foundational Skills
Use the Grade 1 High-Frequency Word Cards to practice saying *get, have, go* and *my*; Sound-Spelling Card 7 to teach how to identify and pronounce /g/ in *go* and *get.*

eBook Use digital material to practice vocabulary.

LESSON 2: School-Day Routine

Set Purpose

- Tell children that today they will discuss their school-day routine. Show page 8 of the Newcomer Cards.

Teach/Model Vocabulary

- Elicit the days and months discussed in Lesson 1.
- Lead children through the song/chant on page T2.
- Display the Newcomer Card again. Ask: *What do you see the children doing?* Point to, name, and act out each action. Have children repeat. Help with pronunciation.
- Say the sentence frames as you point to the activities on the card: **First she brushes her teeth. Then she goes to bed.** Then say the sentences again as you write them on the board, completing them with the activities. Have children repeat after you. Then point to the other activities on the card and say: **First they go to school. Then...** Point to the next picture and have children chorally fill in what happens next: **...they play.** Repeat for other activities on the card and in the vocabulary list.
- **Talk About It** Have partners talk about what they do when they wake up in the morning.
- Expand by having children talk about, compare, and contrast their own school-day routines.

Practice/Apply COLLABORATIVE

- **Talk About It** Have partners use the card and sentence frames to discuss the order of different activities they do during the day and why.
- Make up silly questions about school-day routines. For example, ask: *What is the last thing you do? Do you have breakfast?* Have children say *yes* or *no.* If the answer is no, ask them to name the last thing they do during a school day. Repeat for other routine activities.
- Guide children to complete the activity on page 49.

Make Connections

Say: *Tell your partner more about your school-day routine. How is your routine different from your partner's routine?* Encourage children to use the sentence frames they learned and to use descriptive words.

Use Newcomer Card, page 8

Name: ______________________________

Draw a picture in each box to show what you do *First, Then, Next,* and *Finally* in the morning.

First

↓

Then

↓

Next

↓

Finally

Calendar

Language Objective:
Ask and answer questions about different times of day

Content Objective:
Identify times of day

Sentence Frames:
When do we ____?
We ____ in the ____.
We ____ at night.
When do we ____?
We ____ early/late.

VOCABULARY
morning, afternoon, evening, night, early, late

>> Go Digital

Language Transfers Handbook
See pages 16–19 for grammatical structures that do not transfer. Cantonese, Korean, or Hmong speakers may struggle with placement of adverbs (*early, late*).

Foundational Skills
Use the Grade 1 High-Frequency Word Cards to practice saying *when, early,* and *we*; Sound-Spelling Card 12 to teach children how to identify and pronounce /l/ in *late* and *school*.

eBook and Games Provide audio support, interaction, and practice with the vocabulary.

LESSON 3: Times of the Day

Set Purpose

- Tell children that today they will learn about times of the day. Display page 8 of the Newcomer Cards.

Teach/Model Vocabulary

- To review, elicit days, months, and school-day routines.
- Lead children through the song/chant on page T2.
- Display the Newcomer Card again. Ask: *What do you see?* Then point to and name each time of the day. Have children repeat. Help with pronunciation.
- Say these sentence frames as you point to the pictures and then the time of day tab: **When do we eat breakfast? We eat breakfast in the morning.** Then say the sentences again as you write them on the board. Have children repeat after you. Then point to the kids playing and ask: **When do we play?** Have children answer chorally: **We play in the afternoon**. Repeat for other activities on the card and ones children know.
- **Talk About It** Have partners talk about activities they do in the morning, afternoon, and evening.
- Expand by introducing the sentence frames: **We go to school early/late.** Explain that *early* means "before you need to" and *late* means "past the time you need to do something."

Practice/Apply 

- **Talk About It** Have partners use the card and the sentence frames to discuss when they do certain activities and why.
- Provide magazines with pictures showing people doing daily routines. Have children cut out pictures of things people do in the morning, afternoon, and night. Glue the pictures on paper to make a morning/afternoon/evening collage, putting the pictures in the correct order. Have children point to and talk about the activities.
- Guide children to complete the activity on page 51.

Make Cultural Connections

Ask partners to discuss activities they did in the morning in their home country. Have partners compare routines and present to the class.

Name: ____________________

Times of the Day

Use Newcomer Card, page 8

Use the words from the box to tell when each activity takes place.

morning	afternoon	night

1. It's ____________.

2. It's ____________.

3. It's ____________.

4. It's ____________.

5. It's ____________.

Weather

Language Objective:
Ask and answer questions about types of weather

Content Objective:
Identify types of weather

Sentence Frames:
What is the weather outside?
It's ____.
It's ____ and ____.

VOCABULARY
sunny, rainy, snowy, cloudy, foggy, cold, warm, hot

>> Go Digital

Language Transfers Handbook
See pages 16-19 for grammatical structures that do not transfer. Korean, Vietnamese, or Arabic speakers may avoid pronouns and repeat nouns.

Foundational Skills
Use Grade 1 High-Frequency Word Cards to practice saying *warm, what,* and *and*; Sound-Spelling Card 40 to teach children how to identify and pronounce /ou/ in *cloudy* and *outside*.

eBook Use digital material to practice vocabulary.

LESSON 1: Weather Conditions

Set Purpose

- Tell children that today they will discuss weather conditions. Display page 9 of the Newcomer Cards.

Teach/Model Vocabulary

- Lead children through the song/chant on page T2.
- Display the Newcomer Card again. Ask: *What do you see?* Children can name things they know. Then point to and name the weather conditions. Have children repeat. Help with pronunciation.
- Say these sentence frames as you point to the weather shown on the card: **What is the weather outside? It's rainy.** Then say the sentences again as you write them on the board, completing the second sentence with the weather condition. Have children repeat after you. Then point to the pictures and ask: **What is the weather outside?** Have children answer chorally: **It's rainy**. Have them fill in the weather condition. Repeat for other weather conditions on the card, in the vocabulary list, and with your current and recent weather conditions.
- **Talk About It** Have partners talk about and compare different weather conditions.
- Extend by introducing: **It's hot and sunny.** Children use this sentence frame to describe two weather conditions.

Practice/Apply COLLABORATIVE

- **Talk About It** Have partners use the Newcomer Card and sentence frames to discuss what they know about different types of weather. Elicit descriptive words.
- Have partners take turns pretending to be a weather forecaster. The "forecaster" talks about the weather during that day, while the other child asks follow-up questions. Encourage the "forecaster" to describe the weather conditions in the morning, afternoon, evening, and at night. Then children switch roles.
- Guide children to complete the activity on page 53.

Make Connections

Have partners talk about their favorite weather conditions. Afterwards, partners can present what they discussed to the class. Provide support with complete sentences, as needed.

Name: ______________________________

Weather Conditions

Use Newcomer Card, page 9

A. Talk about the pictures with a partner.

B. Draw a picture of the weather. Label it.

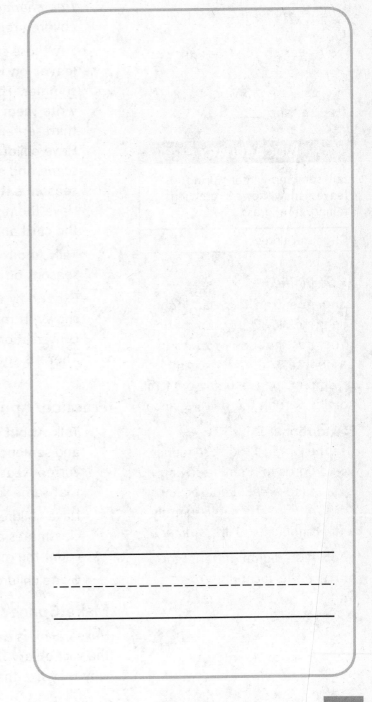

Weather

Language Objective:
Ask and answer questions about the seasons

Content Objective:
Identify and talk about the four seasons

Sentence Frames:
What season is it?
It is ____.
The leaves on the trees are ____.
There is/are ____.
The ____ are growing.
It's ____ and ____.

VOCABULARY
fall, summer, winter, spring, leaves, snow, flowers, growing, falling, tree, grass
Cognate: flores

>> Go Digital

Language Transfers Handbook
See pages 16-19 for grammatical structures that do not transfer. Cantonese, Vietnamese, Arabic, or Hmong speakers may omit the helping verb in the passive voice.

Foundational Skills Kit
Use the Grade 1 High-Frequency Word Cards to practice saying *it, is, fall,* and *are*; Sound-Spelling Card 21 to teach how to identify and pronounce /u/ in *summer.*

eBook Use digital material to practice the vocabulary.

LESSON 2: Seasons

Set Purpose

- Tell children that today they will discuss the four seasons. Display page 9 of the Newcomer Cards.

Teach/Model Vocabulary

- Review types of weather discussed in Lesson 1.
- Then lead children through the song/chant on page T2.
- Display the Newcomer Card again. Ask: *How does the tree change?* Then point to and name each season. Have children repeat. Help with pronunciation.
- Say these sentence frames as you point to the tree: **The leaves on the trees are green. What season is it? It is summer.** Then say the sentence frames again as you write them on the board, completing the second and third sentences with the color of the leaves and season. Have children repeat after you. Then point to the fall scene and ask: **The leaves on the trees are red. What season is it?** Have children answer chorally: **It is fall.** Have them fill in the season. Repeat for other seasons on the card and talk about the leaves and flowers.
- **Talk About It** Have partners talk about the different seasons on the card.
- Expand by using the sentence frames: **It's cold and snowy. It must be winter.** Then extend the children's conversations further by introducing the sentence frames: **There is snow. The flowers are growing.**

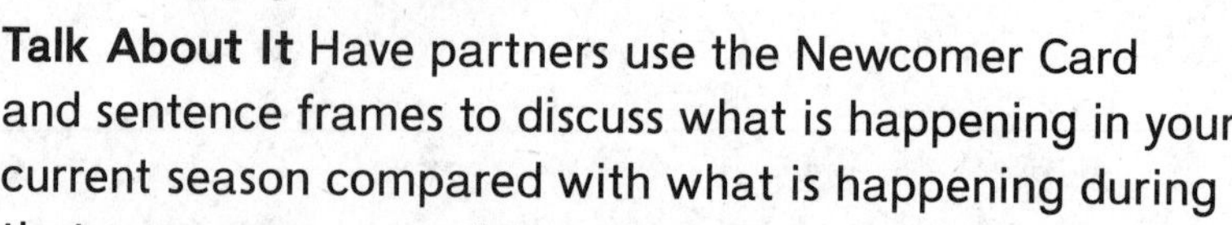

Practice/Apply

- **Talk About It** Have partners use the Newcomer Card and sentence frames to discuss what is happening in your current season compared with what is happening during that same season on the card.
- Have children make tally charts and ask each of their classmates about their favorite season. Have children count the marks and share their results with the class.
- Guide children to complete the activity on page 55.

Make Connections

Have partners describe their favorite season using some of the vocabulary they learned. Have partners tell each other why they like that season.

Name: ______________________________

Seasons

Use Newcomer Card, page 9

Draw a picture of yourself during your favorite season. Write the name of the season on the line.

Weather

Language Objective:
Talk about what we see in the sky

Content Objective:
Identify objects we see in the sky during the day and at night

Sentence Frames:
What can we see in the sky?
We can see the ____ in the sky during the day.
We can see the ____ in the sky at night.
We can see the ____ ____ in the sky.

VOCABULARY
sky, sun, stars, moon, planets, Earth, day, night
Cognates: día, planetas

>> Go Digital

Language Transfers Handbook
See pages 16-19 for grammatical structures that do not transfer. Cantonese or Hmong speakers may omit prepositions.

Foundational Skills
Use the Grade 1 High-Frequency Word Cards to practice saying *can, day,* and *see;* Sound-Spelling Card 33 to teach children how to identify and pronounce /i/ in *night* and *sky.*

eBook and Games Provide audio support, interaction, and practice with the vocabulary.

LESSON 3: Up in the Sky

Set Purpose

- Tell children that today they will discuss objects in the sky. Display page 9 of the Newcomer Cards.

Teach/Model Vocabulary

- Review weather and seasons from Lessons 1 and 2.
- Lead children through the song/chant on page T2.
- Display the Newcomer Card again. Ask: *What things do you see?* Children can name things they know. Name each object in the sky as you point to the picture. Have children repeat. Help with pronunciation.
- Say these sentence frames as you point to the sky: **What can we see in the sky? We can see the <u>sun</u> in the sky during the day.** Then say the sentences again as you write them on the board, completing the second sentence with the name of the object in the sky. Have children repeat after you. Then point to the moon and ask: **What can we see in the sky?** Have children answer chorally: **We can see the <u>moon</u> in the sky at night.** Have children fill in the name of the object. Repeat for other objects children provide and in the vocabulary list.
- **Talk About It** Have partners talk about and compare the sky in the pictures to the sky where they live. Encourage them to use descriptive words to describe the objects and the sky.
- Extend by introducing this sentence frame to encourage children to use color words to describe objects in the sky: **We can see the <u>yellow</u> <u>sun</u> in the sky.**

Practice/Apply 

- **Talk About It** Have partners use the Newcomer Card and sentence frames they learned to discuss what they can see in the sky.
- Ask the children to draw a picture of the sky at their favorite time of day or night. Have children talk with a partner about their drawing.
- Guide children to complete the activity on page 57.

Make Cultural Connections

Have partners describe what they saw in the sky in their home country and then have them share with the class.

Name: ______________________

Up in the Sky

Use Newcomer Card, page 9

A. Read and trace each word. Match the word to the correct picture.

1. sun

2. moon

3. stars

4. day

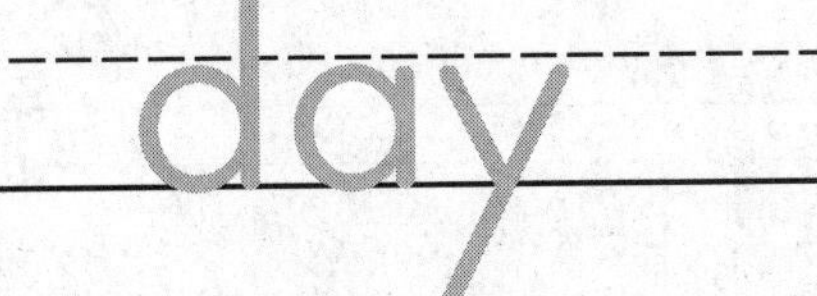

5. night

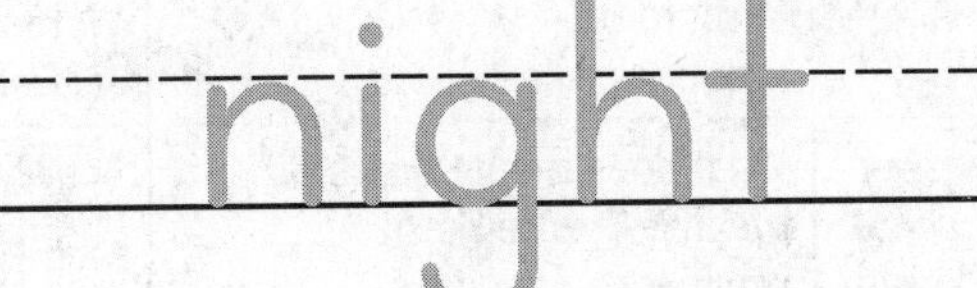

a.

b.

c.

d.

e.

B. Write what you see in the sky.

____

____

My Body	LESSONS	MATERIALS	LANGUAGE OBJECTIVES	LANGUAGE STRUCTURES/ GRAMMAR	VOCABULARY
Newcomer Card, p. 10	**Lesson 1:** Parts of My Body, p. 60–61	Newcomer Card p. 10 Sound-Spelling Card 8 Song/Chant p. T2	Ask and answer questions about different parts of the body and describe what people look like	What does she/he look like? She/He has __ __. What do you look like? I/You have __ __. ***Wh-* questions:** What **Helping verbs:** do/does	Body parts and adjectives **High-Frequency Words:** *he, she, you, I*
	Lesson 2: Healthy Routines, p. 62–63	Newcomer Card p. 10 Sound-Spelling Card 28 Song/Chant p. T2	Describe the different ways we take care of our bodies	How does she/he stay healthy? She/He ____. **Pronouns:** she, he, you *How* **questions**	Healthy activities **High-Frequency Words:** *do, does, I, my*
	Lesson 3: Five Senses, p. 64–65	Newcomer Card p. 10 Sound-Spelling Card 36 Song/Chant p. T3	Ask and answer questions about the five senses	I/We ___ with my/our ___. What do you ___? I ___ a/an/the ___. ***Wh-* questions:** What **Articles:** a, an, the	Senses **High-Frequency Words:** *the, a, an, see, eyes*

Clothing	LESSONS	MATERIALS	LANGUAGE OBJECTIVES	LANGUAGE STRUCTURES/ GRAMMAR	VOCABULARY
Newcomer Card, p. 11	**Lesson 1:** What I Wear, p. 66–67	Newcomer Card p. 11 Sound-Spelling Card 27 Song/Chant p. T3	Name and describe clothing	This is/that's a ____ ____. Those/These are ____ ____. **Regular plurals** **Pronouns:** this, that, these, those	Items of clothing **High-Frequency Words:** *this, is, what, like*
	Lesson 2: Clothing and Seasons, p. 68–69	Newcomer Card p. 11 Sound-Spelling Card 10 Song/Chant p. T3	Name items of clothing needed for different seasons	What do you wear in the ____? I wear (a) ____. **Helping verb:** to do **Pronouns:** you, I	Clothes and seasons **High-Frequency Words:** *I, you, a, do*
	Lesson 3: Activities and Clothing, p. 70–71	Newcomer Card p. 11 Sound-Spelling Card 3 Song/Chant p. T3	Name items of clothing needed for different activities	When do you need (a) ____? I need (a) ____. **Verb:** to need ***Wh-* questions:** When	Clothes and activities **High-Frequency Words:** *run, you, go*

Feelings	LESSONS	MATERIALS	LANGUAGE OBJECTIVES	LANGUAGE STRUCTURES/ GRAMMAR	VOCABULARY
Newcomer Card, p. 12	**Lesson 1:** How I Feel, p. 72–73	Newcomer Card p. 12 Sound-Spelling Card 6 Song/Chant p. T3	Name different feelings	How does she/he feel? She/He is ____. When are you ____? **Verb:** to be **Pronouns:** she, he, you, I	Feelings **High-Frequency Words:** *happy, he, she, is*
	Lesson 2: Friendship, p. 74–75	Newcomer Card p. 12 Sound-Spelling Card 16 Song/Chant p. T3	Ask and answer questions about what we do with friends	What does she/he like to do with friends? She/He likes to ____ with her/his friends. **Verb:** to like ***Wh-* questions:** What	Activities with friends **High-Frequency Words:** *play, laugh, work, eat, friend*
	Lesson 3: Helping Others, p. 76–77	Newcomer Card p. 12 Sound-Spelling Card 4 Song/Chant p. T3	Ask and answer questions about helping friends	How do you help a friend? I ____ my friend. **Helping verbs:** do/does *How* **questions**	Ways of helping **High-Frequency Words:** *friend, help, listen*

My Family	LESSONS	MATERIALS	LANGUAGE OBJECTIVES	LANGUAGE STRUCTURES/ GRAMMAR	VOCABULARY
Newcomer Card, p. 13	**Lesson 1:** Family Members, p. 78–79	Newcomer Card p. 13 Sound-Spelling Card 27 Song/Chant p. T3	Name people in a family	This is ____. Who is she/he? That is her/his/my ____. ***Wh-* questions:** Who **Pronouns:** she, he, his, her	Family members **High-Frequency Words:** *mother, father, brother*
	Lesson 2: Physical Characteristics, p. 80–81	Newcomer Card p. 13 Sound-Spelling Card 20 Song/Chant p. T3	Describe and compare family members	What does the ____ look like? She/He has ____ ____. **Verb:** to have **Comparatives and Superlatives**	Physical Characteristics **High-Frequency Words:** *eyes, look, like*
	Lesson 3: Family Activities, p. 82–83	Newcomer Card p. 13 Sound-Spelling Card 18 Song/Chant p. T3	Describe things families do together	What do families do together? They ____ together. **Helping verb:** to do **Pronoun:** they	Family activities **High-Frequency Words:** *go, to, eat, together*

My Home	LESSONS	MATERIALS	LANGUAGE OBJECTIVES	LANGUAGE STRUCTURES/ GRAMMAR	VOCABULARY
Newcomer Card, p. 14	**Lesson 1:** Where We Live, p. 84–85	Newcomer Card p. 14 Sound-Spelling Card 2 Song/Chant p. T4	Name different kinds of homes	What kind of home do you live in? I live in a/an ____. **Verb:** to live **Articles:** a, an	Types of homes **High-Frequency Words:** *do, live, in*
	Lesson 2: Rooms in Our Home, p. 86–87	Newcomer Card p. 14 Sound-Spelling Card 29 Song/Chant p. T4	Describe the location of objects in a home	Where is/are the ____? The ____ is/are in/on the ____. **Prepositions of place** ***Wh-* questions:** Where	Home objects **High-Frequency Words:** *where, is, the, in*
	Lesson 3: Helping Around the House, p. 88–89	Newcomer Card p. 14 Sound-Spelling Card 31 Song/Chant p. T4	Name things people do to help around the house	What is ____ doing? She/He is ____ in the ____. **Present continuous verbs** **Prepositions of place**	Chores **High-Frequency Words:** *what, is, he, she*

Progress Monitoring

Use the **Oral Language Proficiency Benchmark Assessment** on pages T40–T41 to monitor students' oral language proficiency growth.

Use the **Student Profile** on pages T43–T44 to record observations throughout the units.

My Body

Language Objective:
Ask and answer questions about different parts of the body and describe what people look like

Content Objective:
Identify the different parts of the body and physical characteristics

Sentence Frames:
What does she/he look like?
She/He has ____ ____.
She/He is ____.
What do you look like?
I/You have ____ ____. I am ____.

VOCABULARY
head, hair, ears, face, eyes, nose, mouth, arm, leg, foot, long, short, tall, big, small
False Cognates: ir, fase, armar

>> Go Digital

Language Transfers Handbook
See pages 16–19 for grammatical structures that do not transfer. Some Spanish or Arabic speakers may struggle with the difference between the verbs *have* and *be*.

Foundational Skills
Use Grade 1 High-Frequency Word Cards to practice saying *he, she, you,* and *I;* Sound-Spelling Card 8 to teach children how to identify and pronounce /h/ in *have* and *has.*

eBook Use digital material for vocabulary practice.

LESSON 1: Parts of My Body

Set Purpose

- Tell children that today they will talk about parts of the body and what people look like. Display page 10 of the Newcomer Cards.

Teach/Model Vocabulary

- Lead the children through the song/chant on page T2.
- Display the Newcomer Card. Ask: *What do you see?* Then point to and name each part of the body. Have children repeat and point to the parts of their own bodies. Help with pronunciation.
- Say these sentence frames as you point to the parts of the body: **What does she look like? She has long hair.** Then say the sentences again as you write them on the board. Have children repeat after you. Repeat for different body parts shown on the card and in the vocabulary list. Then point to the boy and ask: **What does he look like?** Have children answer chorally: **He has blonde hair.**
- **Talk About It** Have partners discuss how the two boys on the card are the same and different.
- Extend the conversation by introducing the sentence frames: **She/He is short. What do you look like? I have short hair. I am tall.**

Practice/Apply

- **Talk About It** Have partners use the card and sentence frames to describe each other. Elicit descriptive words.
- Have children play Simon Says using parts of the body. Children can take turns being the leader and saying to the group, for example: Simon Says, "Touch your hair." Extend the game by having children add adjectives, such as long (hair), blue (eyes), etc.
- Guide children to complete the activity on page 61.

Make Connections

Have partners work together. One child describes a person and the other child draws that person based on the description. The child describing should tell the parts of the body using descriptive words. Have children describe and share their drawings with the class.

Name: ______________________________

Parts of My Body

Use Newcomer Card, page 10

Read and trace each word. Then match the word to the correct part of the body.

1. 

2. 

3. 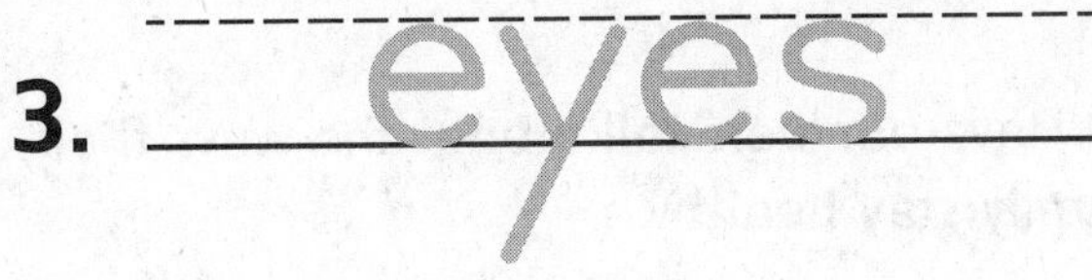

4. 

5. 

6. 

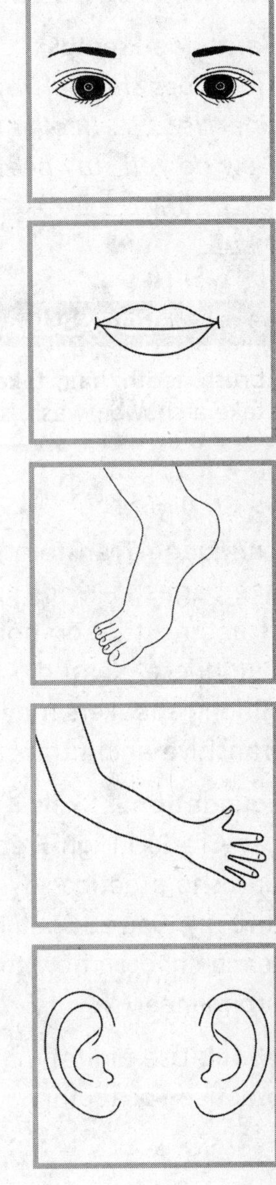

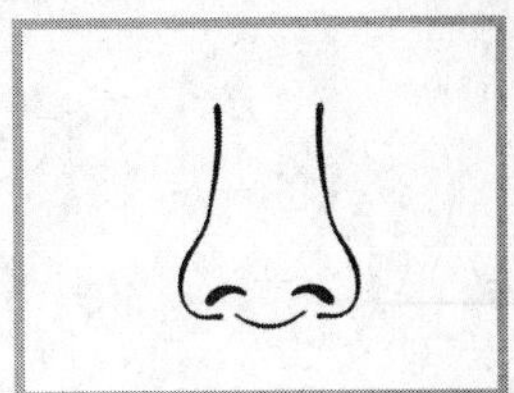

My Body

Language Objective:
Describe the different ways we take care of our bodies

Content Objective:
Understand that taking care of our bodies keeps us healthy

Sentence Frames:
How does she/he stay healthy?
She/He ____ her/his ____.
How do you stay healthy?
I ____ my ____.
I ____.

VOCABULARY
brush, teeth, hair, take a bath, take a shower, wash, stay, healthy

>> Go Digital

Language Transfers Handbook
See pages 16–19 for grammatical structures that do not transfer. Cantonese, Korean, Arabic, or Hmong speakers may struggle with transitive and intransitive verbs.

Foundational Skills Kit
Use Grade 1 High-Frequency Word Cards to practice saying *do, does, I,* and *my;* Sound-Spelling Card 28 to teach children how to identify and pronounce /sh/ in *brush* and *wash.*

eBook Use digital material to practice vocabulary.

LESSON 2: Healthy Routines

Set Purpose

- Tell children that today they will discuss what we do to stay healthy. Display page 10 of the Newcomer Cards.

Teach/Model Vocabulary

- To review, elicit vocabulary from Lesson 1.
- Lead children through the song/chant on page T2.
- Display the Newcomer Card again and point to the image on the right side. Ask: *What are the children doing?* Children can name things they know. Then point to, name, and pantomime the actions. Have children repeat. Help with pronunciation. Have children turn to a partner and say when they do these activities.
- Say these sentence frames as you point to an action: **How does she stay healthy? She brushes her teeth.** Then say the sentences again as you write them on the board, completing the second sentence with the action and part of the body. Have children repeat after you. Then point to the boy washing his hands and ask: **How does he stay healthy?** Have children answer chorally: **He washes his hands**. Repeat for other actions listed in the vocabulary list.
- **Talk About It** Have partners talk about the ways their friends and family stay healthy.
- Extend by introducing the sentence frames: **How do you stay healthy? I brush my teeth. I take a bath/shower.**

Practice/Apply

- **Talk About It** Have partners use the Newcomer Card and sentence frames to discuss what they know about taking care of their bodies.
- Have partners work together. One child in the pair pantomimes a newly learned activity, such as brushing his or her teeth. The other child says what the activity is.
- Guide children to complete the activity on page 63.

Make Connections

Have children turn to a partner and respond to this prompt: *Tell more about what you do to stay healthy.* Children can discuss their response with a partner and then share with the class.

Name: ______________________________

Use Newcomer Card, page 10

Draw two ways to stay healthy. Write the actions on the lines.

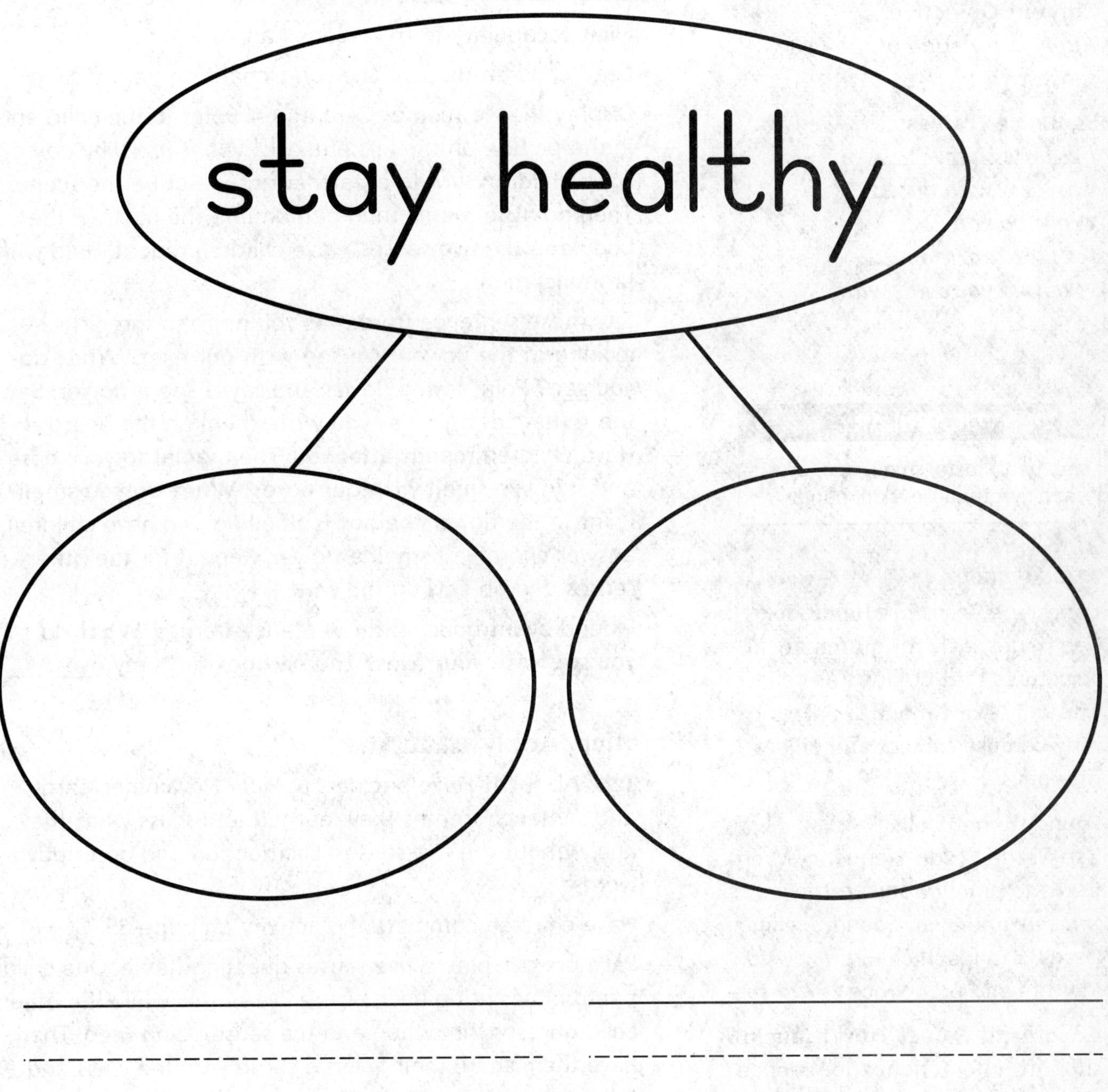

______________________________ ______________________________

______________________________ ______________________________

My Body

Language Objective:
Ask and answer questions about the five senses

Content Objective:
Apply knowledge of the five senses

Sentence Frames:
I ____ with my ____.
We ____ with our ____.
What do you ____?
I ____ a/an/the ____.
What do you ____ with your ____?
I ____ ____ with my ____.

VOCABULARY
see, hear, taste, smell, feel, eyes, ears, mouth, nose, skin, hands

>> Go Digital

Language Transfers Handbook
See pages 16–19 for grammatical structures that do not transfer. Cantonese or Hmong speakers may confuse subject and object pronouns.

Foundational Skills
Use Grade 1 High-Frequency Word Cards to practice saying *the, a, an, see,* and *eyes;* Sound-Spelling Card 36 to teach children how to identify and pronounce /ē/ in *see.*

eBook and Games Provide audio support, interaction, and practice with the vocabulary.

LESSON 3: Five Senses

Set Purpose

- Tell children that today they will discuss the five senses. Display page 10 of the Newcomer Cards.

Teach/Model Vocabulary

- Elicit vocabulary from Lessons 1 and 2.
- Lead children through the song/chant on page T3.
- Display the Newcomer Card again. Point to the children in the picture on the left and ask: *What are they doing?* Have children turn to a partner and describe the scene. Then point to, name, and pantomime the parts of the body and the five senses. Have children repeat. Help with pronunciation.
- Say these sentence frames as you point to the girl looking at the flower: **We see with our eyes. What do you see?** Point to the flower and say: **I see a flower.** Say the sentences again as you write them on the board. Have children repeat after you. Then, point to your nose and say: **We smell with our noses. What do you smell?** Point to the flower the boy is smelling and have children answer chorally: **I smell a flower.** Repeat for the other senses and objects on the card.
- Extend by introducing the sentence frames: **What do you see with your eyes? I see a book with my eyes.**

Practice/Apply

- **Talk About It** Have partners use the Newcomer Card and sentence frames they learned to discuss what they know about the five senses. Elicit action and descriptive words.
- Have children complete the activity on page 65.
- Partners can play a five senses guessing game. One child pantomimes using each of the five senses while the other child guesses the action and the sense being used. Then have them share their favorite sense with the class and tell why it's their favorite.

Make Cultural Connections

Have children draw pictures of their favorite things to hear, see, taste, smell, and feel in their home country. Then have them talk about their drawings with a partner.

Name: ______________________________

Use Newcomer Card, page 10

Write a word from the box to name each picture.

see	hear	smell	taste	feel

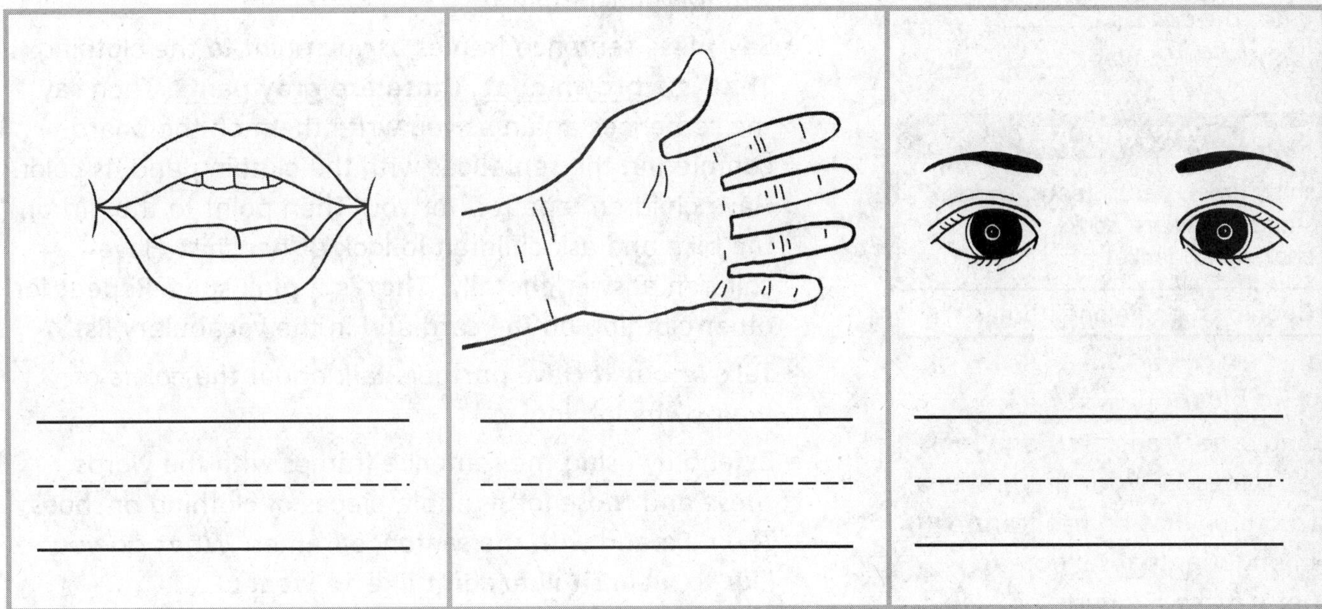

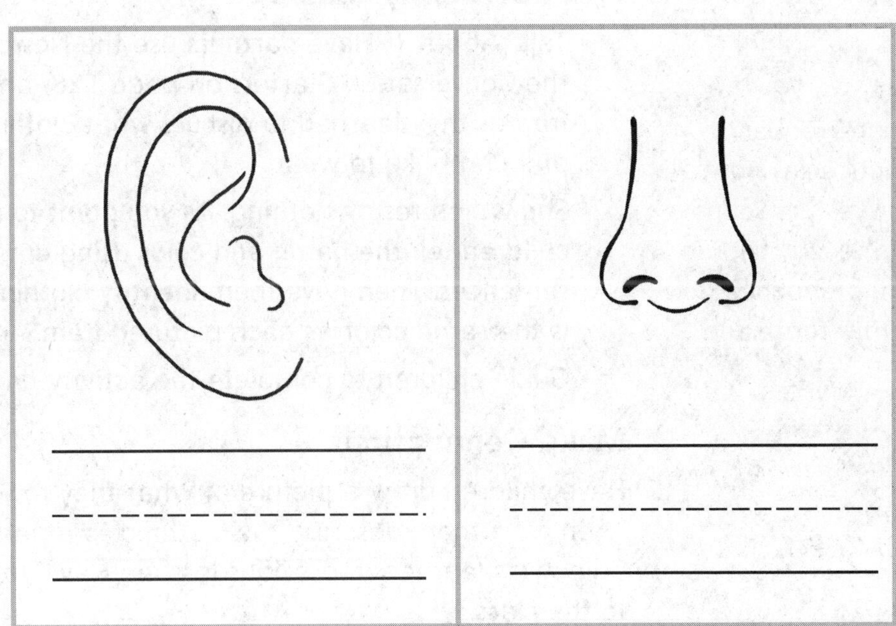

Clothing

Language Objective:
Name and describe clothing

Content Objective:
Identify different types of clothing

Sentence Frames:
This is/That's a ____ ____.
These/Those are ____ ____.
What do you like to wear?
I like to wear ____ ____.
I don't like to wear ____ ____.

VOCABULARY
shirt, dress, pants, jeans, shorts, shoes, sneakers, socks, boots, coat, wear, jacket
Cognates: pantalones, botas

>> Go Digital

Language Transfers Handbook
See pages 16–19 for grammatical structures that do not transfer. Hmong, Cantonese, Korean, Vietnamese, Spanish, or Arabic speakers may struggle with the word order of adjectives and nouns.

Foundational Skills
Use the Grade 1 High-Frequency Word Cards to practice saying *this, is, what,* and *like.* Use Sound-Spelling Card 27 to teach children how to identify and pronounce the /th/ sound in *this, those* and *these.*

eBook Use digital material for vocabulary practice.

LESSON 1: What I Wear

Set Purpose

- Tell children that today they will discuss clothing. Display page 11 of the Newcomer Cards.

Teach/Model Vocabulary

- Lead children through the song/chant on page T3.
- Display the Newcomer Card again. Ask: *What do you see?* Children can name things they know. Then point to and name items of clothing. Have children repeat. Help with pronunciation.
- Say these sentence frames as you point to the clothing: **That is a brown coat. Those are gray pants.** Then say the sentences again as you write them on the board, completing the sentences with the clothing and its color. Have children repeat after you. Then point to the girl on the bike and ask children to look at her shirt. Have children answer chorally: **That is a pink shirt**. Repeat for other clothing on the card and in the vocabulary list.
- **Talk About It** Have partners talk about the colors of their own clothing.
- Extend by using the sentence frames with the words *these* and *those* for multiple pieces of clothing or shoes. Then expand with the sentence frames: **What do you like to wear? I like/don't like to wear ____.**

Practice/Apply COLLABORATIVE

- **Talk About It** Have partners use the Newcomer Card, the Conversation Starters on page T28, and the sentence frames they learned to discuss what clothing they like and don't like to wear.
- Show pictures of clothing. As you point to an item, have children tell the name and color using complete sentences. Then have them identify clothing in class that is the same color as each pictured item.
- Guide children to complete the activity on page 67.

Make Connections

Have children draw a picture of what they're wearing. Then have them describe the clothing to a partner using adjectives learned in previous lessons. Have partners present to the class.

Name: ______________________________

Read and trace each word. Match each word to a picture.

1. 
pants

2. 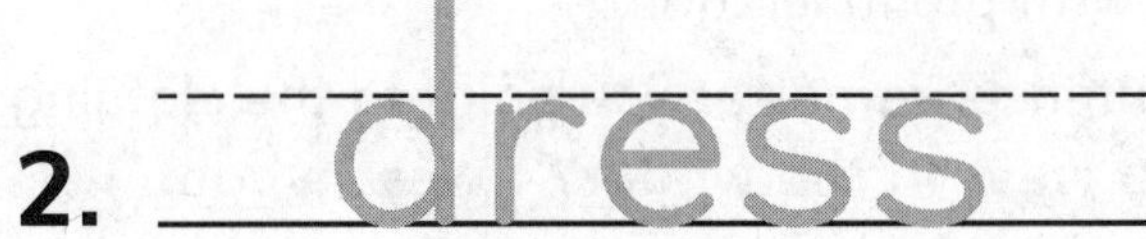
dress

3. 
shirt

4. 
socks

5. 
shorts

6. 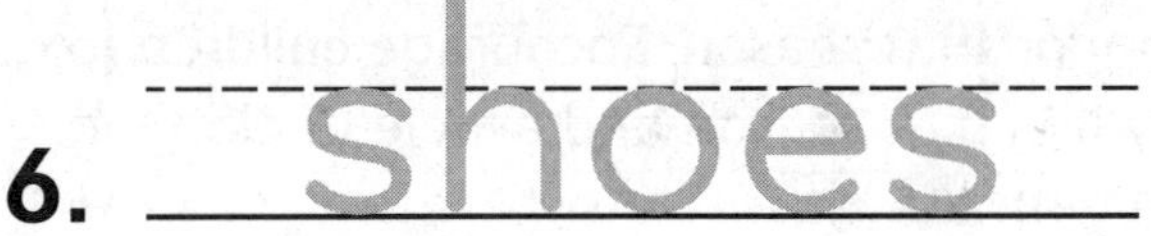
shoes

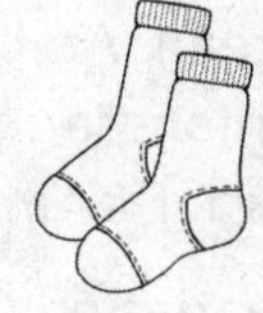

Clothing

Language Objective:
Name items of clothing needed for different seasons

Content Objective:
Identify what to wear, depending on the season

Sentence Frames:
What do you wear in the ____?
I wear a ____.
I wear ____.

VOCABULARY
coat, hat, mittens, jacket, boots, bathing suit, t-shirt, shorts
Cognates: mitones, botas

>> Go Digital

Language Transfers Handbook
See pages 16-19 for grammatical structures that do not transfer. Some Hmong, Vietnamese, Korean, Arabic, Tagalog, or Cantonese speakers may mistake *one* for *a/an.*

Foundational Skills
Use Grade 1 High-Frequency Word Cards to practice saying *I, you, a,* and *do.* Use Sound-Spelling Card 10 to teach children how to identify and pronounce the /j/ sound in *jacket.*

eBook Use digital material for vocabulary practice.

LESSON 2: Clothing and Seasons

Set Purpose

- Tell children that today they will discuss clothing we wear in different seasons. Show page 11 of the Newcomer Cards.

Teach/Model Vocabulary

- Elicit vocabulary from Lesson 1.
- Lead children through the song/chant on page T3.
- Display the Newcomer Card again. Ask: *What clothes are they wearing in the different seasons?* Children can name the seasons and clothing they know. Then point to and name the seasons and clothing. Have children repeat. Help with pronunciation.
- Say these sentence frames as you point to the clothing: **What do you wear in the winter? I wear a coat. I wear mittens.** Then say the sentences again as you write them on the board. Have children repeat after you. Then point to the summer scene and ask: **What do you wear in the summer?** Have children answer chorally: **I wear** a **bathing suit**. Repeat for the other seasons.
- **Talk About It** Have children take turns pantomiming and saying what they wear during different seasons.
- Extend by talking about the weather on the card, using previously learned vocabulary and sentence frames.

Practice/Apply INTERPRETIVE

- **Talk About It** Have partners use the Newcomer Card and sentence frames they learned to discuss what they know about clothing needed for different seasons.
- Guide children to complete the activity on page 69.
- Have children play charades. Provide index cards with the names of the seasons. Children take turns picking a card and pantomiming the season. Other children guess the season and say what they need to wear in that season.

Make Connections

Ask children to discuss their favorite season and their favorite article of clothing for that season. Encourage children to explain why they like that season and article of clothing. Have them share with the class.

Use Newcomer Card, page II

Name: ______________________

A. Talk about the clothing with a partner. Circle the correct season.

I. winter summer

2. winter spring

3. summer spring

4. spring fall

B. Write what you wear during your favorite season.

____

____

Clothing

Language Objective:
Name items of clothing needed for different activities

Content Objective:
Determine what item of clothing to wear, depending on an activity

Sentence Frames:
When do you need ____?
I need ____ to ____.
When do you need a ____?
I need a ____ to ____.

VOCABULARY
run, swim, hike, bike, go camping
Cognates: acampar

>> Go Digital

Language Transfers Handbook
See pages 16-19 for grammatical structures that do not transfer. Some Cantonese or Hmong speakers may confuse infinitives with the main verb.

Foundational Skills
Use Grade 1 High-Frequency Word Cards to practice saying *run, go,* and *you.* Use Sound-Spelling Card 3 to teach children how to identify and pronounce the /b/ sound in *bike.*

eBook and Games Provide audio support, interaction, and practice with the vocabulary.

LESSON 3: Activities and Clothing

Set Purpose

- Tell children that today they will discuss activities and clothing. Display page 11 of the Newcomer Cards.

Teach/Model Vocabulary

- Elicit vocabulary from Lessons 1 and 2.
- Lead children through the song/chant on page T3.
- Display the Newcomer Card again. Ask: *What are the children doing?* Point to, name, and pantomime the activities. Have children repeat. Help with pronunciation.
- Say these sentence frames as you point to the clothing: **When do you need sneakers? I need sneakers to bike.** Then say the sentences again as you write them on the board, completing the sentences with the name of the clothing and activity. Have children repeat after you. Then point to the girl in the bathing suit and ask: **When do you need a bathing suit?** Have children answer chorally: **I need a bathing suit to swim.** Repeat for other activities on the card and in the vocabulary list.
- **Talk About It** Have partners talk about and compare clothing needed for different activities. Encourage children to talk about other activities that require special clothing.

Practice/Apply PRODUCTIVE

- **Talk About It** Have partners use the Newcomer Card and sentence frames they learned to discuss what they know about the clothing needed for different activities.
- Guide children to complete the activity on page 71.
- Provide magazines with pictures of people doing different outdoor activities. Have partners make a collage showing what people wear for different activities. Have partners describe their collage to the class.

Make Cultural Connections

Have children name an outdoor activity people do in their home country. Have them name and describe clothing worn during this activity. Encourage them to use previously learned vocabulary to add to their descriptions.

Name: ___________________________

Use Newcomer Card, page II

Fill in the name of the correct activity. Use words from the box.

bike	run	swim

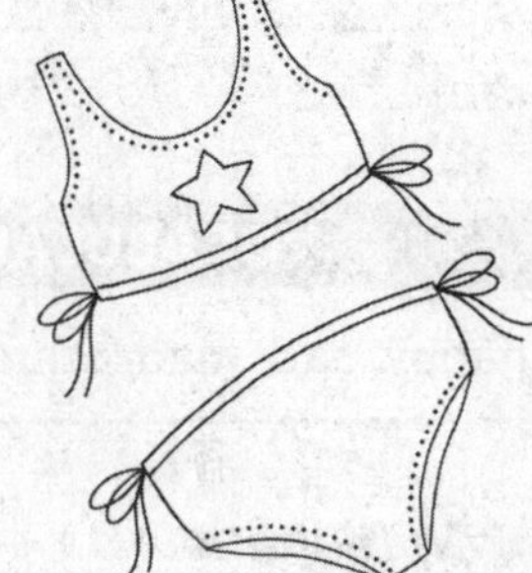

1. I need a bathing suit to ______________.

2. I need shorts to ______________.

3. I need sneakers to ______________.

Feelings

Language Objective:
Name different feelings

Content Objective:
Demonstrate understanding of different feelings

Sentence Frames:
How does she/he feel?
She/He is ____.
When are you ____?
I'm ____ when ________.
I am ____.

VOCABULARY
happy, sad, mad, scared, sleepy

>> Go Digital

Language Transfers Handbook
See pages 16–19 for grammatical structures that do not transfer. Cantonese, Hmong, Korean, Spanish, Tagalog, or Vietnamese speakers may struggle with the gender-specific pronouns *she* and *he*.

Foundational Skills
Use Grade 1 High-Frequency Word Cards to practice saying *happy, he, she,* and *is*; Sound-Spelling Card 6 to teach children how to identify and pronounce /f/ in *feel*.

eBook Use digital material to practice vocabulary.

LESSON 1: How I Feel

Set Purpose

- Tell children that today they will discuss feelings. Display page 12 of the Newcomer Cards.

Teach/Model Vocabulary

- Lead children through the song/chant on page T3.
- Display the Newcomer Card again. Say: *What do you see?* Children can name things they know. Point to, name, and pantomime each feeling on the card. Have children repeat. Help with pronunciation. Have children turn to a partner and say other feelings they know of.
- Say these sentence frames as you point to the feelings: **How does she feel? She is happy.** Then say the sentences again as you write them on the board, completing the second sentence with the name of the feeling. Have children repeat after you. Then point to the boy who is mad and ask: **How does he feel?** Have children answer chorally: **He is mad.** Repeat for other feelings on the card and in the vocabulary list.
- **Talk About It** Have partners discuss the different feelings shown on the card.
- Extend by introducing the sentence frames: **When are you happy? I'm happy when I swim.** Expand by having children talk about why they have different feelings using *because*.

Practice/Apply

- **Talk About It** Have partners use the Conversation Starters on page T29 to discuss how they feel when they see the broken scooter.
- Write the feelings from this lesson on 9x9 bingo sheets. As you name and pantomime each feeling, have children cover the words with pre-cut circles and call "Bingo!" when they have three in a row. Have the winner name the feelings in the winning row.
- Guide children to complete the activity on page 73.

Make Connections

In pairs, have children talk about their drawings in the graphic organizer. Have pairs choose their favorite drawing and describe it to the class.

Name: ______________________________

Use Newcomer Card, page 12

Draw pictures showing what makes you happy. Then complete the sentence.

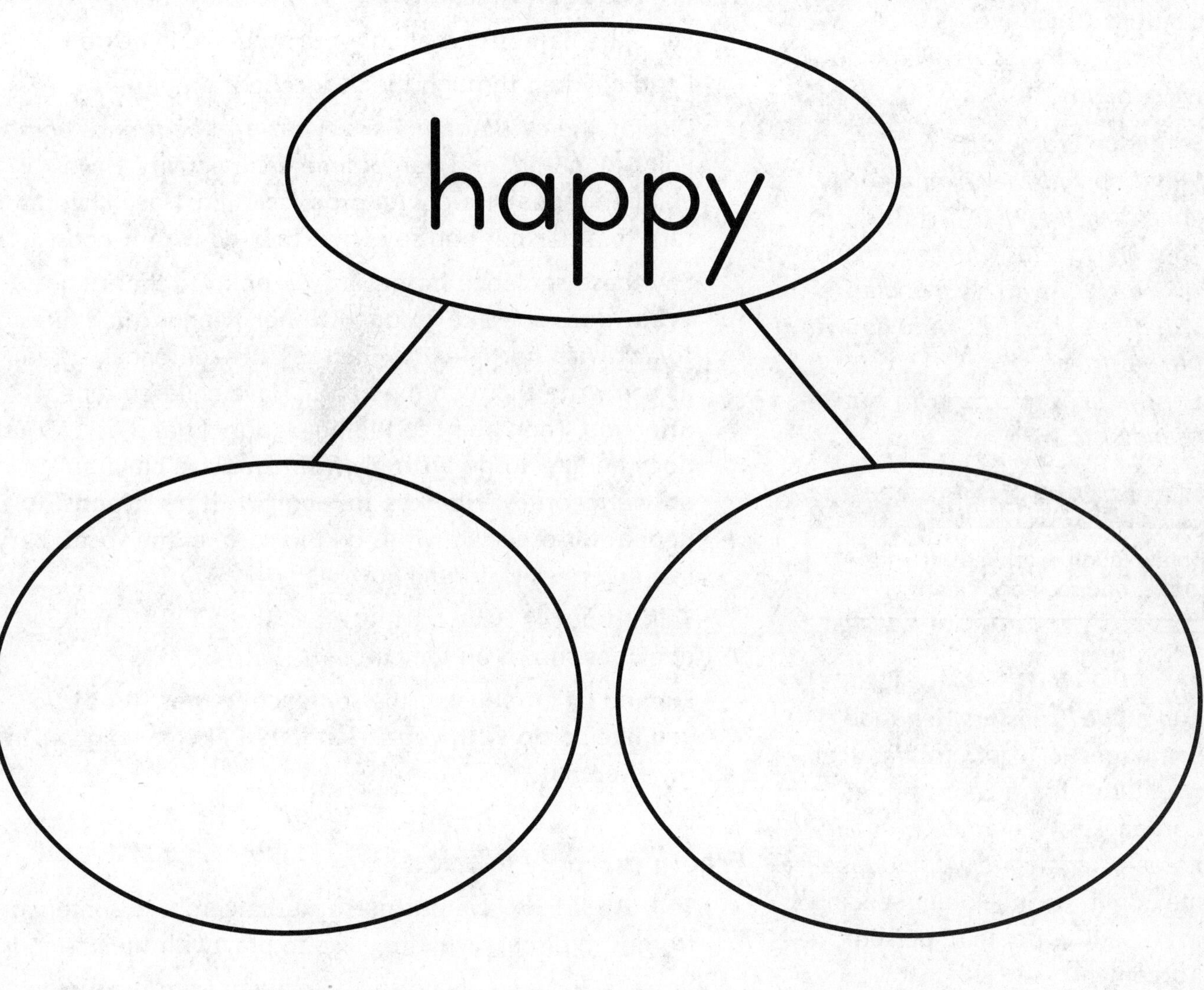

I'm happy when ______________________________.

Feelings

Language Objective:
Ask and answer questions about what we do with friends

Content Objective:
Identifying things we like to do with friends

Sentence Frames:
What do you/they like to do with your/their friend(s)?
They like to ____ with their friends.
I like to ____ with my friend(s).
What does he/she like to do with his/her friend(s)?
She/He likes to ____ with her/his friend(s).

VOCABULARY
play, laugh, work, eat, friend, rake, ride scooters, clean

>> Go Digital

Language Transfers Handbook
See pages 16–19 for grammatical structures that do not transfer. Cantonese, Vietnamese, Hmong, Korean, Tagalog, or Arabic speakers may omit the inflectional ending *-s* in present tense, third person agreement.

Foundational Skills
Use Grade 1 High-Frequency Word Cards to practice saying *play, laugh, work, eat,* and *friend*; Sound-Spelling Card 16 to teach children how to identify and pronounce /p/ in *play*.

eBook Use digital material to practice vocabulary.

LESSON 2: Friendship

Set Purpose

- Tell children that today they will discuss friendship. Display page 12 of the Newcomer Cards.

Teach/Model Vocabulary

- Elicit the names of feelings you discussed in Lesson 1.
- Lead children through the song/chant on page T3.
- Display the card again. Ask: *What are the friends doing?* Point to, name, and pantomime each activity. Have children repeat. Help with pronunciation. Have children turn to a partner and say what they do with friends.
- Say these sentence frames as you point to the friends: **What does she like to do with her friends? She likes to eat with her friends.** Then say the sentences again as you write them on the board. Have children repeat after you. Then point to the boy laughing and ask: **What does he like to do with his friends?** Have children answer chorally: **He likes to laugh with his friends.** Repeat for other activities on the card, in the vocabulary list, and ones children know.
- **Talk About It** Have partners talk about different activities shown on the card.
- Expand by introducing the sentence frames: **What do you like to do with your friend(s)? I like to laugh with my friend(s).**

Practice/Apply 

- **Talk About It** Have partners use the card and sentence frames to discuss why they like to play with their friends.
- In pairs, have one child say an activity from the lesson and the other child use the word in a sentence, telling what people like to do with friends. Model before beginning. For example, *Play*: **They like to play with their friends.** Then have partners switch roles. Encourage children to use descriptive words in their sentences to describe the activities they like to do with friends.
- Guide children to complete the activity on page 75.

Make Connections

Have partners rank their three favorite activities to do with friends. Children can describe the activities to each other.

Name: ______________________

Friendship

Use Newcomer Card, page 12

A. Talk about the pictures with a partner.

B. Draw and label what you like to do with friends.

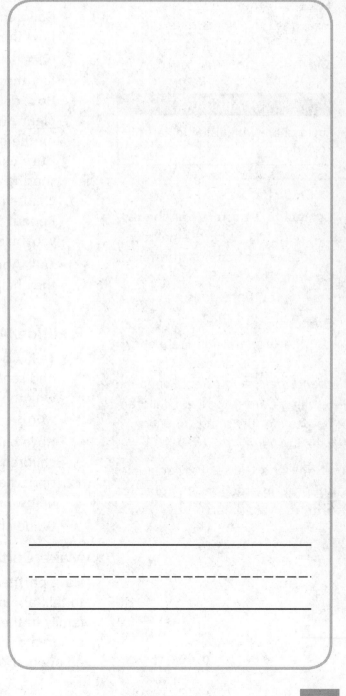

Feelings

Language Objective:
Ask and answer questions about helping friends

Content Objective:
Identify ways to help friends

Sentence Frames:
How do you help a friend?
I ____ my friend ____.
How does she/he help her/his friend(s)?
She/He ____ her/his friend ____.

VOCABULARY
help, share with, listen to, talk to, care for

>> Go Digital

Language Transfers Handbook
See pages 16–19 for grammatical structures that do not transfer. Cantonese or Hmong speakers may omit prepositions.

Foundational Skills
Use the Grade 1 High-Frequency Word Cards to practice saying *friend, help,* and *listen*; Sound-Spelling Card 4 to teach children how to identify and pronounce /sh/ in *share*.

eBook and Games Provide audio support, interaction, and practice with the vocabulary.

LESSON 3: Helping Others

Set Purpose

- Tell children that today they will discuss different ways we help others. Display page 12 of the Newcomer Cards.

Teach/Model Vocabulary

- Elicit the feelings and activities from Lessons 1 and 2.
- Lead children through the song/chant on page T3.
- Display the Newcomer Card again and point to the last box. Ask: *What do you think is happening in this picture?* Children can share their ideas. Then point to and name how the children are helping each other. Have children repeat. Help with pronunciation.
- Say these sentence frames as you point to the card: **How does she help her friend? She helps her friend clean.** Then say the sentences again as you write them on the board, completing the sentences with the action. Have children repeat after you. Then point to the girl sharing and ask: **How does she help her friend?** Have children answer chorally: **She shares with her friend.** Repeat for other activities on the card and in the vocabulary list.
- **Talk About It** Have partners talk about different ways they help their friends.

Practice/Apply COLLABORATIVE

- **Talk About It** Have partners use the Newcomer Card and sentence frames they learned to discuss how and why they help their friends. Elicit action and descriptive words.
- Have children sit in a circle. Start a timer and have the children pass the ball around the circle. When the timer rings, have the child holding the ball say how she or he helps a friend.
- Guide children to complete the activity on page 77.

Make Cultural Connections

Have partners use the vocabulary from Lessons 1, 2, and 3 to talk about different things they did with their friends and family in their home country. After the conversations, have children draw a picture to show one thing their partner talked about. Have individual students present to the class.

Name: ______________________________

Helping Others

Use Newcomer Card, page 12

A. Label the pictures with words from the box.

share	listen

B. Complete the sentences.

I ______________________ to my friend.

I ______________________ with my friend.

My Family

Language Objective:
Name people in a family

Content Objective:
Identify people in a family

Sentence Frames:
This is ____.
Who is she/he?
That's her/his/my ____.
How many ____ does he/she have?
She/He/I has/have ____ ____.

VOCABULARY
father, mother, brother, sister, grandfather, grandmother, son, daughter
False Cognates: son

>> Go Digital

Language Transfers Handbook
See pages 16-19 for grammatical structures that do not transfer. Some Cantonese, Hmong, Korean, Vietnamese, Arabic, or Spanish speakers may struggle with the plural marker *-s.*

Foundational Skills
Use Grade 1 High-Frequency Word Cards to practice saying the words *mother, father,* and *brother.* Use Sound-Spelling Card 27 to teach children how to identify and pronounce the */th/* sound in *brother* and *that.*

eBook Use digital material for vocabulary practice.

LESSON 1: Family Members

Set Purpose

- Tell children that today they will discuss people in a family. Display page 13 of the Newcomer Cards
- Have children bring in photos of their families to share.

Teach/Model Vocabulary

- Lead children through the song/chant on page T3.
- Display page 13 of the Newcomer Cards. Say: *Look at the family. Who do you see?* Children can name the family members the know. Then point to and name each family member. Have children repeat. Help with pronunciation.
- Say these sentence frames as you point to the girl with the pink shirt: **This is Luna.** Then point to the older boy and say: **Who is he? That is her brother.** Say the sentences again as you write them on the board. Have children repeat after you. Then point to the father and ask: **Who is he?** Have children answer chorally: **That is her father.** Repeat for other family members on the card and in the vocabulary list.
- **Talk About It** Have partners talk more about the family members they see on the card. Elicit descriptive words.
- Expand by pointing to Luna and asking: **How many brothers does she have? She has two brothers.** Use this exercise as a review of numbers.

Practice/Apply 

- **Talk About It** Have partners use the Newcomer Card and sentence frames they learned to discuss the relationships of people in a family.
- Guide children to complete the activity on page 79.
- Have partners ask and answer questions about people in their drawings using the sentence frame: **I have ____.** Have children name and count the number of family members. Teach the words for aunts, uncles, and cousins, as necessary.

Make Connections

Have children respond to this prompt: *Tell me more about your ____.* Fill in with a family member the child included in his or her drawing. The child can share with a partner and then with you.

Name: ______________________________

Family Members

Use Newcomer Card, page 13

Draw your family. Write a sentence about one family member.

____

My Family

Language Objective:
Describe and compare family members

Content Objective:
Understand differences between family members

Sentence Frames:
What does the ____ look like?
She/He has ____ ____.
She/He is ____.
She/He is ____ than his/her ____.
____ is the ____.

VOCABULARY

tall, long, short, dark, light, taller than, tallest, shorter than, shortest, eyes, hair, brown, black

>> Go Digital

Language Transfers Handbook
See pages 16–19 for grammatical structures that do not transfer. Cantonese, Hmong, Vietnamese, Korean, Spanish, or Arabic speakers may struggle with the word order of nouns and adjectives.

Foundational Skills
Use Grade 1 High-Frequency Word Cards to practice saying *eyes, look,* and *like.* Use Sound-Spelling Card 20 to teach children how to identify and pronounce the /t/ sound in *short* and *tall.*

eBook Use digital material for vocabulary practice.

LESSON 2: Physical Characteristics

Set Purpose

- Tell children that today they will describe and compare family members. Display page 13 of the Newcomer Cards.

Teach/Model Vocabulary

- Elicit names of family members discussed in Lesson 1.
- Lead children through the song/chant on page T3.
- Display page 13 of the Newcomer Cards again. Say: *Look at the family. What do you see?* Then point to and describe the family members. Have children repeat. Help with pronunciation.
- Say these sentence frames as you point to a family member: **What does the mother look like? She has dark hair.** Then say the sentences again as you write them on the board. Have children repeat after you. Then say these sentence frames as you point to the father: **What does the father look like?** Have children answer chorally: **He has short hair.** Repeat for other people and characteristics shown on the card and in the vocabulary list.
- **Talk About It** Have partners discuss the physical characteristics of some family members on the card.
- Expand by teaching comparatives and superlatives with the sentence frames **She/He is short. She/He is taller than her/his sister** and **Grandfather is the tallest/ shortest**.

Practice/Apply

- **Talk About It** Have partners use the Newcomer Card and sentence frames they learned to talk about the physical characteristics of one person in their family.
- Guide children to complete the activity on page 81.
- Have partners sit back to back and describe the physical characteristics of two of their family members. One child describes and her/his partner draws what she/he hears. Then they switch roles. Have children share and discuss their drawings.

Make Connections

Have children share their own physical characteristics and say how they are different from those of a family member.

Name: ______________________

Use Newcomer Card, page 13

1. Label the pictures. Use words from the box.
2. Complete the sentences using the pictures.

short hair **long hair**

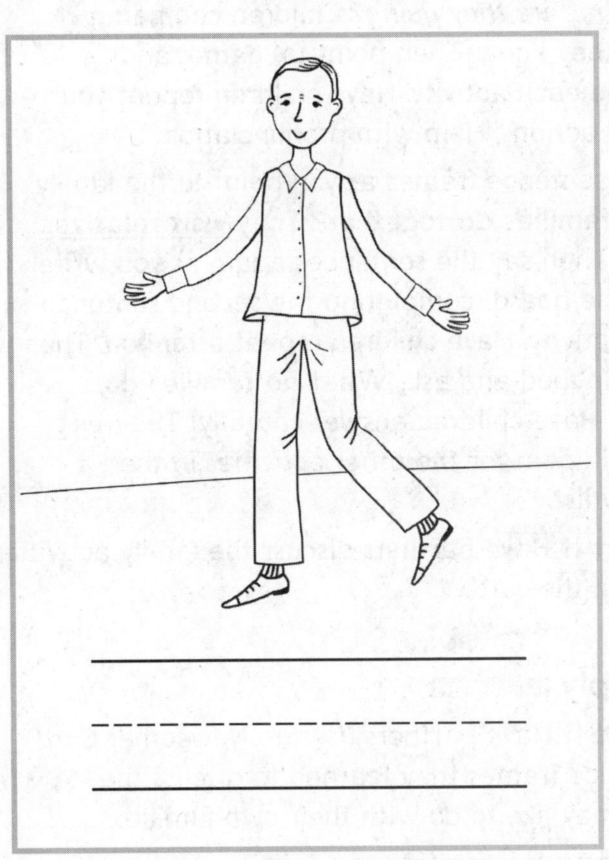

The father is ______________ than his daughter.

The daughter is ______________ than her father.

My Family

Language Objective:
Describe things families do together

Content Objective:
Identify things families do together

Sentence Frames:
What do families do together?
They ____ together.

VOCABULARY
visit relatives, go to the park, go shopping, eat, together
Cognates: visitar, parque

>> Go Digital

Language Transfers Handbook
See pages 16–19 for grammatical structures that do not transfer. Some Korean, Spanish, or Arabic speakers may struggle with the use of *in* and *on* with phrasal verbs.

Foundational Skills
Use Grade 1 High-Frequency Word Cards to practice saying *go, to, eat,* and *together*. Use Sound-Spelling Card 18 to teach children how to identify and pronounce the /r/ sound in *relatives* and *together.*

eBook and Games Provide audio support, interaction, and practice with the vocabulary.

LESSON 3: Family Activities

Set Purpose

- Tell children that today they will discuss family activities. Display page 13 of the Newcomer Cards.

Teach/Model Vocabulary

- Elicit family members and physical characteristics from Lessons 1 and 2.
- Lead children through the song/chant on page T3.
- Display the Newcomer Card again. Say: *Look at the family. What are they doing?* Children can name activities they know. Then point to, name, and pantomime each activity. Have children repeat your words and actions. Help with pronunciation.
- Say these sentence frames as you point to the family: **What do families do together? They visit relatives together.** Then say the sentences again as you write them on the board, completing the second sentence with the activity. Have children repeat after you. Then point to the food and ask: **What do families do together?** Have children answer chorally: **They eat together.** Repeat for the other activities in the vocabulary list.
- **Talk About It** Have partners discuss the family activities they see on the card.

Practice/Apply

- **Talk About It** Have partners use the Newcomer Card and sentence frames they learned to discuss the activities they like to do with their own families.
- Guide children to complete the activity on page 83.
- Display a variety of objects or pictures of objects related to family activities. Have children take turns selecting an object and telling how it relates to what families do together. Model before beginning. For example, select a ball and say: *They play together.*

Make Cultural Connections

Have children talk about what families do together in their home countries. Have children discuss with a partner, then share with the class.

Name: ______________________________

Family Activities

Use Newcomer Card, page 13

A. Talk about the pictures with a partner.

B. Draw something you do with your family. Label the activity.

My Home

Language Objective:
Name different kinds of homes

Content Objective:
Identify different kinds of homes

Sentence Frames:
What kind of home do you live in?
I live in a/an ____.

VOCABULARY
house, apartment building, mobile home
Cognates: apartamento, móvil

>> *Go Digital*

Language Transfers Handbook
See pages 16–19 for grammatical structures that do not transfer. Hmong, Vietnamese, Korean, Arabic, Tagalog, or Cantonese speakers may mistake *one* for *a/ an.*

Foundational Skills
Use the Grade 1 High-Frequency Word Cards to practice saying the words *do, live,* and *in.* Use Sound-Spelling Card 2 to teach children how to identify and pronounce the /b/ sound in *building* and *mobile.*

eBook Use digital material to practice vocabulary.

LESSON 1: Where We Live

Set Purpose

- Tell children that today they will discuss different kinds of homes. Display page 14 of the Newcomer Cards.

Teach/Model Vocabulary

- Lead children through the song/chant on page T4.
- Display the Newcomer Card again. Say: *Look at these homes. What do you see?* Children can name what they know. Then point to and name the kinds of homes. Have children repeat. Help with pronunciation.
- Say these sentence frames as you point to a home: **What kind of home do you live in? I live in an apartment building.** Then say the sentences again as you write them on the board, completing the second sentence with the kind of home. Have children repeat after you. Then point to the house and ask: **What kind of home do you live in?** Have children answer chorally: **I live in a house,** filling in the kind of home. Repeat for the mobile home.
- **Talk About It** Have partners describe the different homes on the card. Encourage them to talk about shapes, colors, and count the number of windows in each home.

Practice/Apply 

- **Talk About It** Have partners use the Newcomer Card and sentence frames to discuss what they now know about different kinds of homes.
- Guide children to complete the activity on page 85.
- Have children share the drawings of their homes with a partner. Then have children add their family to the drawing. Encourage children to use previously learned vocabulary to describe their home and family. Afterwards, have children present to the class.

Make Connections

Provide children with cutouts of squares, rectangles, triangles, and circles. Have children use the shapes to make a replica of their own home. Have partners ask and answer questions about their replica home. Be sure they use vocabulary from previous lessons.

Name: ______________________

Where We Live

Use Newcomer Card, page 14

Draw a picture of your home. Then write the kind of home it is.

My Home

Language Objective:
Describe the location of objects in a home

Content Objective:
Demonstrate knowledge of the names and locations of objects and rooms in a home

Sentence Frames:
Where is/are the ____?
The ____ is/are in/on the ____.

VOCABULARY

bedroom, bathroom, kitchen, living room, pillow, bed, dresser, sink, bathtub, toilet, table, chair, couch, television, desk, stove, pots, shower

>> Go Digital

Language Transfers Handbook
See pages 16–19 for grammatical structures that do not transfer. Cantonese or Hmong speakers may omit prepositions.

Foundational Skills
Use the Grade 1 High-Frequency Word Cards to practice saying the words *where, is, the,* and *in.* Use Sound-Spelling Card 29 to teach children how to identify and pronounce the /ch/ sound in *kitchen* and *chair.*

eBook Use digital material for vocabulary practice.

LESSON 2: Rooms in Our Home

Set Purpose

- Tell children that today they will discuss objects and rooms in a home. Show page 14 of the Newcomer Cards.

Teach/Model Vocabulary

- Review the kinds of homes discussed in Lesson 1.
- Lead children through the song/chant on page T4.
- Display the Newcomer Card again. Say: *Look at the rooms. What do you see?* Children can name things they know. Then point to and name each room and object. Have children repeat. Help with pronunciation.
- Say these sentence frames as you point to objects in the home: **Where is the <u>bed</u>? The <u>bed</u> is in the <u>bedroom</u>.** Then say the sentences again as you write them on the board. Have children repeat after you. Then point to the couch and ask: **Where is the <u>couch</u>?** Have children answer chorally: **The <u>couch</u> is in the <u>living room</u>.** Repeat for other objects and rooms on the card and in the vocabulary list.
- **Talk About It** Have partners discuss the different rooms and objects on the card.
- Expand by taking children on a quick tour of the school's kitchen and pointing to and naming objects. Children can ask and answer questions about what they see.

Practice/Apply COLLABORATIVE

- **Talk About It** Have partners use the Newcomer Card and sentence frames to discuss what they know about rooms and objects in a home.
- Guide children to complete the activity on page 87.
- In pairs, have each child pantomime something they do with one of the recently learned objects in a home. The partner guesses which object is being used. Have children choose their favorite object and share it with the class.

Make Connections

Ask children to think about their favorite room in their home. Have them share with a partner by drawing a picture and naming objects in the room. Encourage children to describe the room and objects using colors and other previously-learned vocabulary.

Name: ______________________

Use Newcomer Card, page 14

Write and say the names of objects in the home. Then complete the sentence.

bed chair couch dresser sink table

The ______________________ is in the bedroom.

My Home

Language Objective:
Name things people do to help around the house

Content Objective:
Identify things people do to help around the house

Sentence Frames:
What is the ____ doing?
She/He is ____ in the ____.

VOCABULARY
recycling, mopping, dusting, cooking, sweeping, making the bed
Cognates: reciclar

>> Go Digital

Language Transfers Handbook
See pages 16–19 for grammatical structures that do not transfer. Korean or Vietnamese speakers may avoid pronouns and repeat nouns.

Foundational Skills
Use the Grade 1 High-Frequency Word Cards to practice saying the words *what, is, he,* and *she.* Use Sound-Spelling Card 31 to teach children how to identify and pronounce the /o͝o/ sound in *cooking.*

eBook and Games Provide audio support, interaction, and practice with the vocabulary.

LESSON 3: Helping Around the House

Set Purpose

- Tell children that today they will discuss things people do to help at home. Display page 14 of the Newcomer Cards.

Teach/Model Vocabulary

- Elicit vocabulary from Lessons 1 and 2.
- Lead children through the song/chant on page T4.
- Display the Newcomer Card again. Ask: *What are the people doing?* Then point to, name, and pantomime each activity. Have children repeat. Help with pronunciation.
- Say these sentence frames as you point to an activity: **What is the mother doing? She is cooking in the kitchen.** Then say the sentences again as you write them on the board. Have children repeat after you. Then point to the father and ask: **What is the father doing?** Have children answer chorally: **He is mopping in the bathroom,** filling in the activity. Repeat for other activities on the vocabulary list.
- **Talk About It** Have partners discuss the things people do to help around the house.
- Expand the lesson by showing objects people use to help around the house, such as a mop or spatula.

Practice/Apply 

- **Talk About It** Have partners use the Newcomer Card and sentence frames they learned to discuss other ways people can help out in the kitchen.
- Guide children to complete the activity on page 89.
- Have children play charades. One child whispers a home activity to another child. That child acts it out while the other children try to guess the action. Ask children follow-up questions using previously learned vocabulary, such as: *Where is he mopping?*

Make Cultural Connections

Have partners discuss where they lived in their home country, including the kind of home, rooms and objects they had, and ways they helped around the house. Then they can share with you.

Use Newcomer Card, page 14

Name: ______________________________

Draw pictures of the things people do to help in your home. Then write words to describe the actions.

UNIT 3: Community OVERVIEW

My Community

Newcomer Card, p. 15

LESSONS	MATERIALS	LANGUAGE OBJECTIVES	LANGUAGE STRUCTURES/ GRAMMAR	VOCABULARY
Lesson 1: Community Places, p. 92–93	Newcomer Card p. 15 Sound-Spelling Card 37 Song/Chant p. T4	Describe the location of places in the community	Where is the ____? It is ____. ***Wh-* questions:** Where **Prepositions of place**	Community places **High-Frequency Words:** *is, it, the, school*
Lesson 2: Community Workers, p. 94–95	Newcomer Card p. 15 Sound-Spelling Card 38 Song/Chant p. T4	Tell the names of community workers and the places they work	Who works in/on a ____? A ____ works in/on a ____. **Verb:** to work ***Wh-* questions:** Who	Community workers **High-Frequency Words:** *who, in, on*
Lesson 3: Helping in My Community, p. 96–97	Newcomer Card p. 15 Sound-Spelling Card 45 Song/Chant p. T4	Describe ways people help in the community	What does she/he do in the community? She/He ____ in the ____. **Verb:** to do **Pronouns:** she, he	Jobs **High-Frequency Words:** *what, he, she, people*

Park

Newcomer Card, p. 16

LESSONS	MATERIALS	LANGUAGE OBJECTIVES	LANGUAGE STRUCTURES/ GRAMMAR	VOCABULARY
Lesson 1: Things in a Park, p. 98–99	Newcomer Card p. 16 Sound-Spelling Card 27 Song/Chant p. T4	Name things in a park	There is a/are ____. Let's ____ there. Let's ____ (on) them. **Verbs:** to be, to read, to swing, to ride, to eat **Adverb:** there	Things in a park **High-Frequency Words:** *there, are, eat, on*
Lesson 2: Park Activities, p. 100–101	Newcomer Card p. 16 Sound-Spelling Card 9 Song/Chant p. T4	Name common actions in a park	Can you ____? Yes, I can. Can you? No, I can't ____. I can ____. **Modal verb:** can **Yes/No questions**	Park activities **High-Frequency Words:** *yes, no, walk, run*
Lesson 3: Park Environment, p. 102–103	Newcomer Card p. 16 Sound-Spelling Card 17 Song/Chant p. T4	Name living things we see in a park	Where is the ____? It's on/in/ next to/near/by the ____. ***Wh-* questions:** Where **Prepositions of place**	Living things in a park **High-Frequency Words:** *where, is, on*

Transportation

Newcomer Card, p. 17

LESSONS	MATERIALS	LANGUAGE OBJECTIVES	LANGUAGE STRUCTURES/ GRAMMAR	VOCABULARY
Lesson 1: Signs, p. 104–105	Newcomer Card p. 17 Sound-Spelling Card 33 Song/Chant p. T5	Name signs in the community	What is this sign? This is a ____. What are those signs? **Verb:** to be **Pronouns:** this, those	Signs **High-Frequency Words:** *what, this, a*
Lesson 2: Getting Around Town, p. 106–107	Newcomer Card p. 17 Sound-Spelling Card 24 Song/Chant p. T5	Name different ways to get around town	How do you/they get to the ____? I/They (take a) ____. **Verb:** to take, to get ***How* questions**	Transportation **High-Frequency Words:** *how, do, to, the*
Lesson 3: Directions, p. 108–109	Newcomer Card p. 17 Sound-Spelling Card 15 Song/Chant p. T5	Use language to ask for and give directions	Where can I find the ____? The ____ is ____ the ____. **Verb:** to find **Modal verb:** can	Locations **High-Frequency Words:** *how, at, on*

Food and Meals

Newcomer Card, p. 18

LESSONS	MATERIALS	LANGUAGE OBJECTIVES	LANGUAGE STRUCTURES/ GRAMMAR	VOCABULARY
Lesson 1: At a Restaurant, p. 110–111	Newcomer Card p. 18 Sound-Spelling Card 27 Song/Chant p. T5	Ask and answer questions in a restaurant	May I see the menu, please? Can I have a/an/the ___, please? Thank you. **Verbs:** to see, to have **Modal verbs:** may, can	Ordering food **High-Frequency Words:** *have, I, you, and*
Lesson 2: Healthy Eating, p. 112–113	Newcomer Card p. 18 Sound-Spelling Card 43 Song/Chant p. T5	Express food likes and dislikes	What are you eating/drinking/ ordering? I'm eating/drinking/ ordering ___. Do you like ___? **Questions with *do*** **Contractions:** it's, I'm, don't	Food and drinks **High-Frequency Words:** *what, like, my*
Lesson 3: Lunchtime at School, p. 114–115	Newcomer Card p. 18 Sound-Spelling Card 16 Song/Chant p. T5	Name things we eat during lunch at school	What is/are she/he/you/they having for lunch? She's/He's/I'm/ They're having ___. ***Wh-* questions:** What **Present continuous verbs**	Lunches **High-Frequency Words:** *he, she, they, for*

Shopping

Newcomer Card, p. 19

LESSONS	MATERIALS	LANGUAGE OBJECTIVES	LANGUAGE STRUCTURES/ GRAMMAR	VOCABULARY
Lesson 1: Grocery Store, p. 116–117	Newcomer Card p. 19 Sound-Spelling Card 19 Song/Chant p. T5	Name where to buy different items in a grocery store	What do you need to buy? I need ___. Where is/are the ___? It's/They're in the ___. **Verb:** to need ***Wh-* questions:** What, Where	Grocery store items and departments **High-Frequency Words:** *what, where, do, in*
Lesson 2: Using Money, p. 118–119	Newcomer Card p. 19 Sound-Spelling Card 41 Song/Chant p. T5	Ask and answer questions about using money	What is this? This is a ___. A ___ is ___. How much are the ___? They cost ___ each. **Verb:** to be **Pronouns:** these, those ***How* questions**	Currency **High-Frequency Words:** *how, is, are, have*
Lesson 3: Grocery Shopping, p. 120–121	Newcomer Card p. 19 Sound-Spelling Card 42 Song/Chant p. T6	Ask and answer questions about what we do in the grocery store	Do you ___? Yes, I ___. No, I don't ___. **Questions with *do*** **Yes/No questions**	Activities in a grocery store **High-Frequency Words:** *do, make, you, or*

Progress Monitoring

Use the **Oral Language Proficiency Benchmark Assessment** on pages T40–T41 to monitor students' oral language proficiency growth.

Use the **Student Profile** on pages T43–T44 to record observations throughout the units.

My Community

Language Objective:
Describe the location of places in the community

Content Objective:
Identify the location of places in the community

Sentence Frames:
Where is the ____?
It is ____ the ____.

VOCABULARY
school, fire station, supermarket, park, hospital, post office, bank, police station
Cognates: supermercado, parque, hospital, oficina postal, banco, estación de policía

>> Go Digital

Language Transfers Handbook
See pages 16–19 for grammatical structures that do not transfer. Spanish, Vietnamese, or Hmong speakers may struggle with the gender-neutral pronoun *it*.

Foundational Skills
Use Grade 1 High-Frequency Word Cards to practice saying *is, it, the,* and *school.* Use Sound-Spelling Card 37 to teach how to identify and pronounce the /är/ sound in *supermarket* and *park.*

eBook Use digital material for vocabulary practice.

LESSON 1: Community Places

Set Purpose

- Tell children that today they will discuss places in the community. Display page 15 of the Newcomer Cards.
- If possible, show children a map or pictures of places in your community.

Teach/Model Vocabulary

- Lead children through the song/chant on page T4.
- Display the Newcomer Card. Ask: *What do you see?* Children can name things and places they know. Then point to and name each place in the community. Have children repeat. Help with pronunciation.
- Say these sentence frames as you point to community places: **Where is the fire station? It is next to the post office.** Then say the sentences again as you write them on the board, completing the sentences with the name of each place. Have children repeat after you. Then point to the fire station and ask: **Where is the fire station?** Have children answer chorally: **It is near the park.** Repeat for the other community places on the card, in the vocabulary list, and those children provide.
- **Talk About It** Have partners discuss different places on the card and in their own community.

Practice/Apply INTERPRETIVE

- **Talk About It** Have partners use the Newcomer Cards and sentence frames they learned to discuss what they know about community places.
- Guide children to complete the activity on page 93.
- Create an imaginary community in the classroom. Move desks to make a "street." Have children stand in groups along either side of this street, holding pictures of places in their community. Then ask children use prepositions to describe where each place in the community is located.

Make Connections

Have children respond to this prompt: *Tell me more about one place in your community.* Have partners discuss with each other and then present to the class. Children can ask follow-up questions.

Community Places

Use Newcomer Card, page 15

Name: ______________________________

Draw a place in your community. Then write the name of the place.

____

____

My Community

Language Objective:
Tell the names of community workers and the places they work

Content Objective:
Demonstrate understanding about community workers and the places they work

Sentence Frames:
Who works in/on a ____?
A ____ works in a ____.

VOCABULARY
teacher, fire fighter, nurse, doctor, mail carrier, bus driver, police officer, works
Cognates: doctor, policía

>> Go Digital

Language Transfers Handbook
See pages 16–19 for grammatical structures that do not transfer. Some Vietnamese speakers may overuse pronouns with nouns.

Foundational Skills
Use Grade 1 High-Frequency Word Cards to practice saying *who, in,* and *on.* Use Sound-Spelling Card 38 to teach how to identify and pronounce the /ûr/ sound in *works, nurse,* and *teacher.*

eBook Use digital material for vocabulary practice.

LESSON 2: Community Workers

Set Purpose

- Tell children that today they will discuss community workers. Display page 15 of the Newcomer Cards.
- If possible, invite community workers to visit your class.

Teach/Model Vocabulary

- Elicit names of community places from Lesson 1.
- Lead children through the song/chant on page T4.
- Display the Newcomer Card again. Ask: *What people do you see?* Then point to and name each community worker. Have children repeat. Help with pronunciation.
- Say these sentence frames as you point to the workers: **Who works in a fire station? A fire fighter works in a fire station.** Then say the sentences again as you write them on the board, completing the sentences with the name of the place and worker. Have children repeat after you. Then point to yourself and ask: **Who works in a school?** Have the children answer chorally: **A teacher works in a school.** Repeat for the other community workers on the Newcomer Card, listed in the vocabulary, and those children provide.
- **Talk About It** Have partners talk about and act out the roles of different workers they see on the card and know from their own community.
- Extend instruction with the sentence frame using the word *on*: **Who works on a bus? A bus driver works on a bus.**

Practice/Apply COLLABORATIVE

- **Talk About It** Have partners use the Newcomer Card and sentence frames they learned to discuss what they know about community workers.
- Have children draw pictures of different community workers. Then have children tell their partner where each community worker works.
- Guide children to complete the activity on page 95.

Make Connections

Have children choose one community worker. Then have them tell a partner more about where that person works and what the person does for his or her job.

Name: ______________________

Use Newcomer Card, page 15

A. Match the worker to the correct place in the community.

1. 

a. 

2. 

b. 

B. Write a sentence telling where the doctor works.

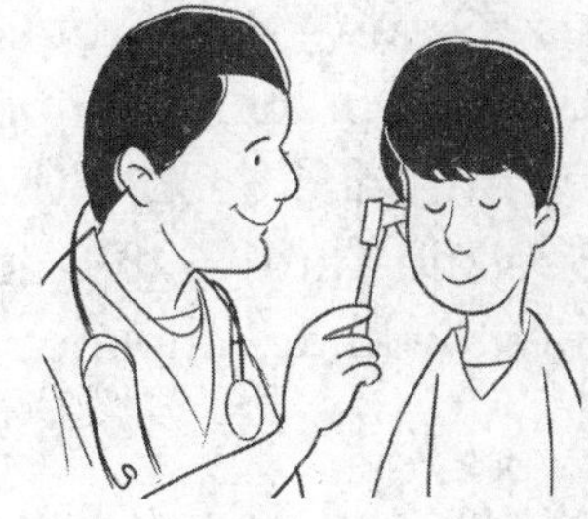

____

____

____

My Community

Language Objective:
Describe ways people help in the community

Content Objective:
Understand ways different people help in the community

Sentence Frames:
What does she/he do in the community?
She/He ____ the ____.

VOCABULARY
cares for, protects, teaches, delivers, cleans, drives, mail, bus, people, park, fire truck
Cognates: protege, autobús, parque

>> Go Digital

Language Transfers Handbook
See pages 16–19 for grammatical structures that do not transfer. Cantonese, Hmong, Korean, Vietnamese, Arabic, or Tagalog speakers may omit the *-s* in third person, present tense.

Foundational Skills
Use Grade 1 High-Frequency Word Cards to practice saying *what, he, she,* and *people.* Use Sound-Spelling Card 45 to teach how to identify and pronounce the /âr/ sound in *care.*

eBook and Games Provide audio support, interaction, and practice with the vocabulary.

LESSON 3: Helping in My Community

Set Purpose

- Tell children that today they will discuss helping in the community. Display page 15 of the Newcomer Cards.

Teach/Model Vocabulary

- Elicit vocabulary from Lessons 1 and 2.
- Lead children through the song/chant on page T4.
- Display the Newcomer Card again. Ask: *What are people doing?* Children can name activities they know. Then point to and name what the workers are doing. Have children repeat. Help with pronunciation.
- Say these sentence frames as you point to the people: **What does he do in the community? He delivers the mail.** Then say the sentences again as you write them on the board. Have children repeat after you. Then point to the doctor and ask: **What does she do in the community?** Have children answer chorally: **She cares for the people.** Repeat for the other ways to help in the community shown on the card and in vocabulary list.
- **Talk About It** Have partners talk about the ways people help in their own community.

Practice/Apply COLLABORATIVE

- **Talk About It** Have partners use the Newcomer Card and sentence frames they learned to discuss the ways a police officer helps in the community.
- Have children work together to make a scrapbook of community workers. Assign a worker to each pair of children. Have partners draw a picture of their assigned worker. Then help them write the sentence: **She/He ____ the ____.** Afterwards, put the pages together and have partners take turns reading the pages to each other.
- Guide children to complete the activity on page 97.

Make Cultural Connections

Have children tell a partner the name of a community place they used to go to in their home country. Have them describe things they did or people they saw there. Then have them share with the class.

Helping in My Community

Use Newcomer Card, page 15

Name: ______________________________

Complete each sentence. Use words from the box.

cares for	protects	drives	delivers

1. She ____________ the bus.

2. He ____________ the mail.

3. She ____________ the community.

4. She ____________ people.

Park

Language Objective:
Names things in a park

Content Objective:
Identify the names of things in a park

Language Function:
Identifying things in a park

Sentence Frames:
There is a ____.
There are ____.
Let's ____ there.
Let's ____ (on) them.

VOCABULARY
benches, swings, bicycles, path, picnic table, signs, eat, ride, swing, read
Cognate: bicicleta

>> Go Digital

Language Transfers Handbook
See pages 16–19 for grammatical structures that do not transfer. Cantonese, Korean, Hmong, or Vietnamese speakers may struggle with object pronouns.

Foundational Skills
Use Grade 1 High-Frequency Word Cards to practice saying *there, are, eat,* and *on;* Sound-Spelling Card 27 to teach how to identify and pronounce the /th/ sounds in *path* and *them.*

eBook Use digital material for vocabulary practice.

LESSON 1: Things in a Park

Set Purpose

- Tell children that today they will discuss things in a park. Display page 16 of the Newcomer Cards.
- If possible, take children on a tour of the playground, pointing to and naming things.

Teach/Model Vocabulary

- Lead children through the song/chant on page T4.
- Display the Newcomer Card again. Ask: *What do you see?* Children can name objects and activities they know. Then point to and name each object and activity. Pantomime the activities as you name them. Have children repeat. Help children with pronunciation.
- Say these sentence frames as you point to objects: **There is a picnic table. Let's eat there.** Then say the sentences again as you write them on the board, completing the sentences with the name of the object and activity. Have children repeat after you. Then point to the swings and say: **There are swings.** Have children respond chorally: **Let's swing on them.** Repeat for the other objects and activities on the card, in the vocabulary list, and others children provide.
- **Talk About It** Have children talk about their favorite things and activities in a park.
- Expand by introducing the sentence frames: **There are ____. Let's ____ there.**

Practice/Apply INTERPRETIVE

- **Talk About It** Have partners use the Newcomer Card and sentence frames they learned to tell what they know about objects and activities in a park.
- Guide children to complete the activity on page 99.
- Play a game of charades. Have a volunteer whisper the name of an object and activity to a child and have her/him act it out for the class. Have others guess the park-related object and activity using complete sentences.

Make Connections

Have partners discuss their drawings on page 99. Have them read the label on the drawing and describe what they like to do at a park. Then have children present to the class.

Name: ______________________

Things in a Park

Use Newcomer Card, page 16

A. Talk about the pictures.

B. Draw yourself in a park. Label one thing.

Park

Language Objective:
Name common actions in a park

Content Objective:
Distinguish between actions in a park

Sentence Frames:
Can you ____?
Yes, I can. (Can you?)
I can ____. (Can you?)
No, I can't ____. I can ____.

VOCABULARY

walk, run, kick, throw, skip, fly a kite, catch

>> Go Digital

Language Transfers Handbook
See pages 16–19 for grammatical structures that do not transfer. Korean, Spanish, or Vietnamese speakers may omit subject pronouns.

Foundational Skills
Use Grade 1 High-Frequency Word Cards to practice saying *yes, no, walk,* and *run*; Sound-Spelling Card 9 to teach how to identify and pronounce the /i/ sound in *skip* and *kick.*

eBook Use digital material for vocabulary practice.

LESSON 2: Park Activities

Set Purpose

- Tell children that today they will discuss things we do in a park. Display page 16 of the Newcomer Cards.

Teach/Model Vocabulary

- Elicit objects and activities in a park from Lesson 1.
- Lead children through the song/chant on page T4.
- Display the Newcomer Card again. Ask: *What are the people doing?* Children can name activities they know. Then point to, name, and pantomime each activity. Have children repeat. Help with pronunciation.
- Say these sentence frames as you point to the activities: **Can you fly a kite? Yes, I can. Can you?** Then say the sentences again as you write them on the board, completing the first sentence with a park activity. Then point to the man running and ask: **Can you run?** Have the children answer chorally: **Yes, I can.** Repeat for other actions on the card and in the vocabulary list.
- **Talk About It** Have children talk about their favorite park-related activities. Have them ask and answer each other's questions about these activities.
- Extend by introducing the sentence frames: **I can catch. Can you? No, I can't catch. I can throw.**

Practice/Apply

- **Talk About It** Have partners use the card and sentence frames they learned to discuss park activities. Encourage children to share activities they like that haven't yet been mentioned in class. If a child's partner doesn't know about the activity then have the child explain it to the class.
- Play a game of charades. Have volunteers act out a park-related activity while the other children guess the action, using complete sentences.
- Guide children to complete the activity on page 101.

Make Connections

Have a volunteer ask questions, such as: **Can you throw a ball?** Have children respond: **Yes, I can!** When children answer they also pretend to do that activity. Be sure the questions vary and that they use previously learned vocabulary.

Name: ________________________________

Park Activities

Use Newcomer Card, page 16

Read each word. Then spell and trace the word. Then draw a line from to the word to the picture it names.

1. 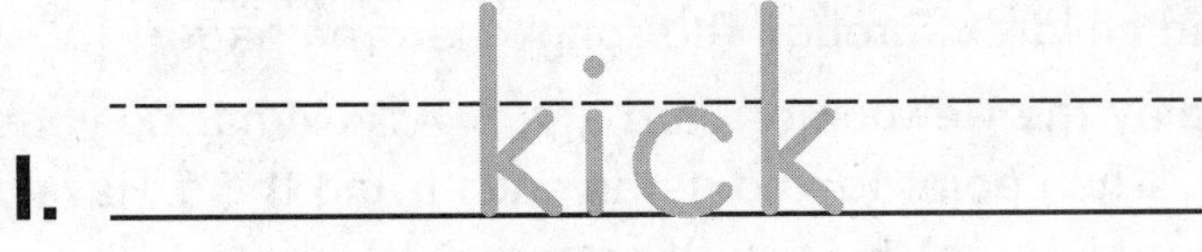
kick

2. 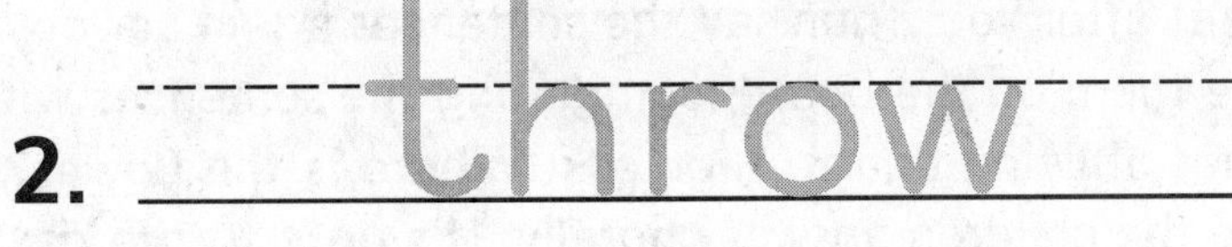
throw

3. 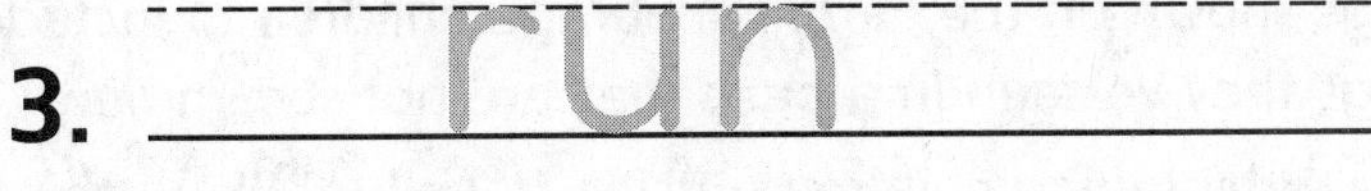
run

4. 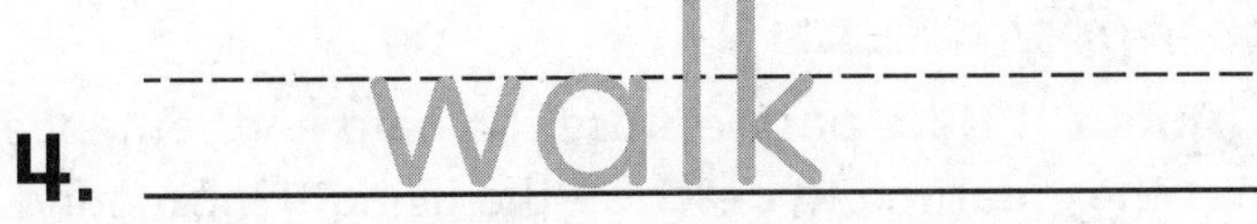
walk

5. 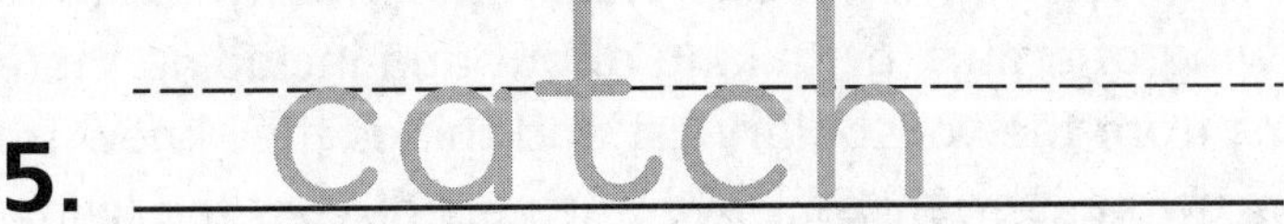
catch

6. 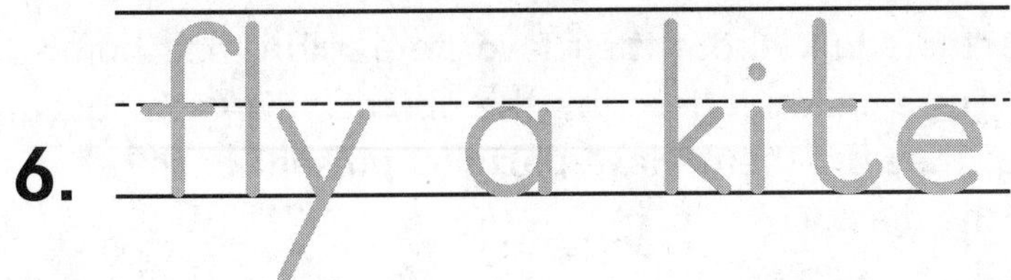
fly a kite

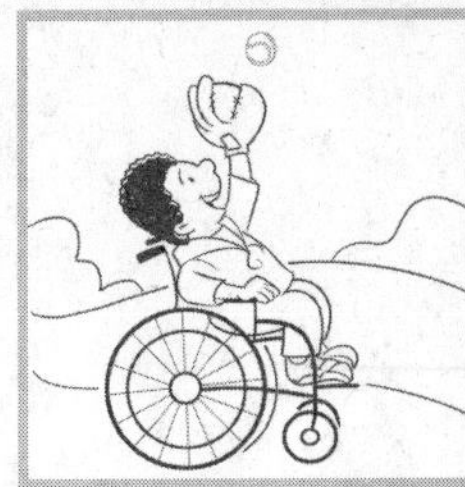

Park

Language Objective:
Name living things we see in a park

Content Objective:
Identify the location of living things we see in a park

Sentence Frames:
Where is the ____?
It's on/in/next to/near/by the ____.

VOCABULARY
garden, plant, flower, tree, bird, squirrel, dog, branch, insect, bush
Cognates: planta, flor, insecto

>> Go Digital

Language Transfers Handbook
See pages 16–19 for grammatical structures that do not transfer. Cantonese or Hmong speakers may omit prepositions.

Foundational Skills
Use Grade 1 High-Frequency Word Cards to practice saying *where, is,* and *on;* Sound-Spelling Card 17 to teach how to identify and pronounce the /kw/ sound in *squirrel.*

eBook and Games Provide audio support, interaction, and practice with the vocabulary.

LESSON 3: Park Environment

Set Purpose

- Tell children that today they will discuss living things we see in a park. Display page 16 of the Newcomer Cards.

Teach/Model Vocabulary

- Elicit the names of objects and park activities from Lessons 1 and 2.
- Lead children through the song/chant on page T4.
- Display the Newcomer Card again. Ask: *What do you see?* Then point to and name each living thing. Have children repeat. Help with pronunciation.
- Say these sentence frames as you point to a living thing: **Where is the dog? It's on the path.** Have children repeat after you. Then say the sentences again as you write them on the board, completing the sentences with names of living things. Then ask: **Where is the flower?** Have the children answer chorally: **It's next to the path.** Repeat for other living things on the card and vocabulary list.
- **Talk About It** Have partners talk about different living things shown on the card. Encourage children to include things they've seen in a park that are not shown here.
- Expand by taking children outside to look at living things. Point to and name those you see and their locations.

Practice/Apply

- **Talk About It** Have partners use the card and sentence frames they learned to describe the living things found in a park. Elicit action and descriptive words.
- Guide children to complete the activity on page 103.
- Have children work in pairs. Have them add to their drawing of a park by talking about and including more items from the vocabulary list and things they know from their own experiences. Have partners discuss the living things in the picture with the class.

Make Cultural Connections

Have partners talk about their favorite park in their home country. Have children describe the objects, living things, and activities they did there. Have partners present each other's park to the class.

Name: ______________________________

Park Environment

Use Newcomer Card, page 16

Draw a picture of animals in a park. Write a sentence about it.

Transportation

Language Objective:
Name signs in the community

Content Objective:
Identify signs in the community

Sentence Frames:
What is this sign?
This is a ____.
What are those signs?
Those are ____.

VOCABULARY
police station sign, bank sign, school sign, mall sign, crosswalk sign, walk sign, don't walk sign, stop sign, street sign, exit sign, bus stop sign
Cognates: signo de hospital

>> Go Digital

Language Transfers Handbook
See pages 16–19 for grammatical structures that do not transfer. Some Vietnamese speakers may overuse pronouns with nouns.

Foundational Skills
Use Grade 1 High-Frequency Word Cards to practice saying *what, this,* and *a*. Use Sound-Spelling Card 33 to teach how to identify and pronounce the /ī/ sound in *sign*.

eBook Use digital material for vocabulary practice.

LESSON 1: Signs

Set Purpose

- Tell children that today they will discuss signs we see in our community. Display page 17 of the Newcomer Cards.
- If possible, take children on a quick tour of the school, pointing to and identifying signs.

Teach/Model Vocabulary

- Lead children through the song/chant on page T5.
- Display the Newcomer Card again. Ask: *What signs do you see?* Then point to and name each sign. Use gestures to show what each sign represents. Have children repeat. Help with pronunciation.
- Say these sentence frames as you point to the signs: **What is this sign? This is a stop sign.** Then say the sentences again as you write them on the board, completing the second sentence with the name of the sign. Have children repeat after you. Then point to the walk sign and ask: **What is this sign?** Have children answer chorally: **This is a walk sign.** Repeat for the other signs on the Newcomer Card, on the vocabulary list, and those children provide.
- **Talk About It** Have partners discuss signs they see in their community.
- Expand by introducing the sentence frames for multiple signs: **What are those signs? Those are street signs.**

Practice/Apply 

- **Talk About It** Have partners use the Newcomer Card and sentence frames they learned to discuss why they think stop signs are important in the community.
- Guide children to complete the activity on page 105.
- Have children make and display signs around the classroom. Have partners line up behind you and walk two-by-two as if walking down the street on a field trip. Point to a sign and ask: *What is this sign? What do we do when we see this sign?* Have children answer chorally.

Make Connections

Have children make a street sign for their street and then read the sign to a partner. Afterwards have them talk about other signs they see in their neighborhood or community.

Name: ______________________________

Signs

Use Newcomer Card, page 17

A. Talk about the pictures with a partner.

B. Draw a sign you see every day. Write the name.

Transportation

Language Objective:
Name different ways to get around town

Content Objective:
Identify different ways to get around town

Sentence Frames:
How do you get to the ____?
I (take a) ____.
How do they get to the ____?
They (take a) ____.
How does she/he get to the ____?
She/He (takes a) ____.

VOCABULARY
car, truck, airplane, bus, train, taxi, walk
Cognates: tren, carro, bus

>> Go Digital

Language Transfers Handbook
See pages 16–19 for grammatical structures that do not transfer. Some Cantonese, Hmong, Korean, Vietnamese, Arabic, or Tagalog speakers may struggle with third-person agreement in present tense verbs.

Foundational Skills
Use Grade 1 High-Frequency Word Cards to practice saying *how, do, to,* and *the.* Use Sound-Spelling Card 24 to teach how to identify and pronounce the /ks/ sound in *taxi.*

eBook Use digital material for vocabulary practice.

LESSON 2: Getting Around Town

Set Purpose

- Tell children that today they will discuss ways to get around town. Display page 17 of the Newcomer Cards.
- If possible, take children to a window that overlooks a street. Point to and name the vehicles as they pass.

Teach/Model Vocabulary

- Elicit names of signs from Lesson 1.
- Lead children through the song/chant on page T5.
- Display the Newcomer Card again. Ask children to name modes of transportation they recognize. Then point to and name each one, using gestures and sounds. Have children repeat. Help with pronunciation.
- Say these sentence frames as you point to the vehicles: **How do you get to school? I take a bus.** Then say the sentences again as you write them on the board. Then point to the car and ask: **How do you get to the park?** Have children answer chorally: **I take a car.** Repeat for the other ways to get around shown on the Newcomer Card, in the vocabulary list, and those children provide.
- **Talk About It** Have partners talk about the different ways they get around in their own community.
- Extend by using the sentence frames with the pronouns *he, she,* and *they.* Then expand the sentence frames with the word *walks.* Have partners discuss different places that they walk to in their community.

Practice/Apply

- **Talk About It** Have partners use the Newcomer Card and sentence frames they learned to discuss when or why a person takes a plane to get somewhere.
- Guide children to complete the activity on page 107.
- Have partners talk about their favorite way to get around town. Children should tell why it's their favorite mode of transportation. Provide the sentence frame **I like ____ because ____** for support, as necessary.

Make Connections

Ask children to discuss with a partner how they get to school each day. Then have partners share with the class.

Name: ___________________________

Getting Around Town

Use Newcomer Card, page 17

Write the word from the box that names a way of getting around town.

train	bus	car	truck	airplane

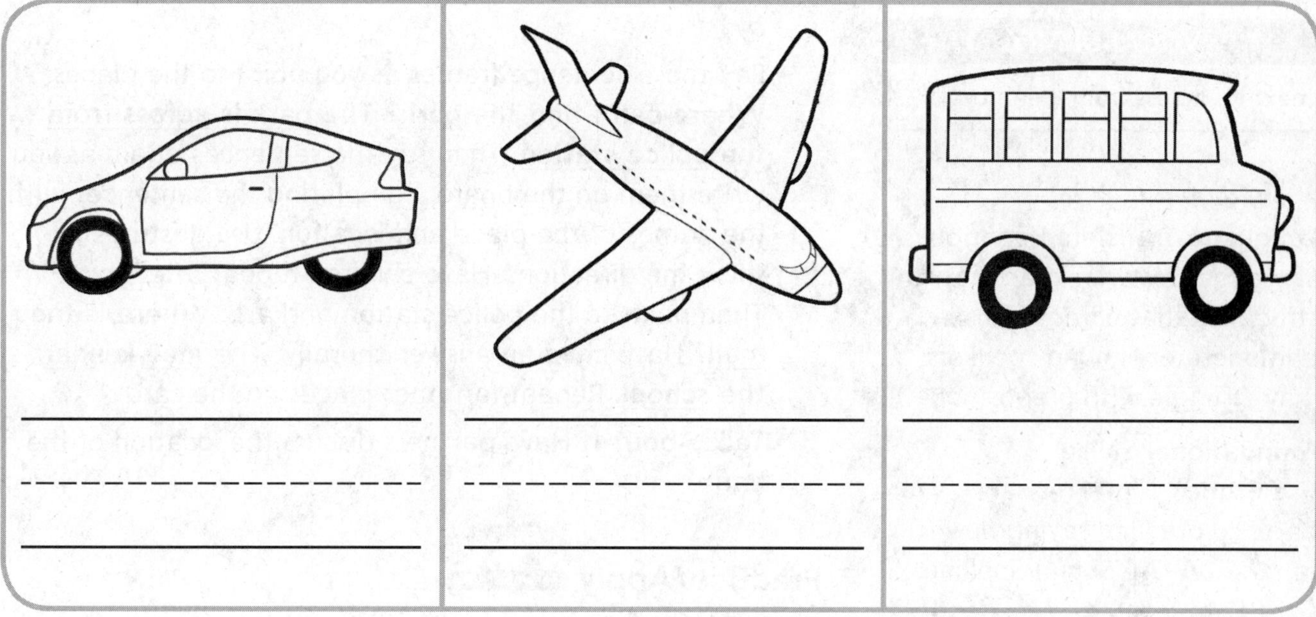

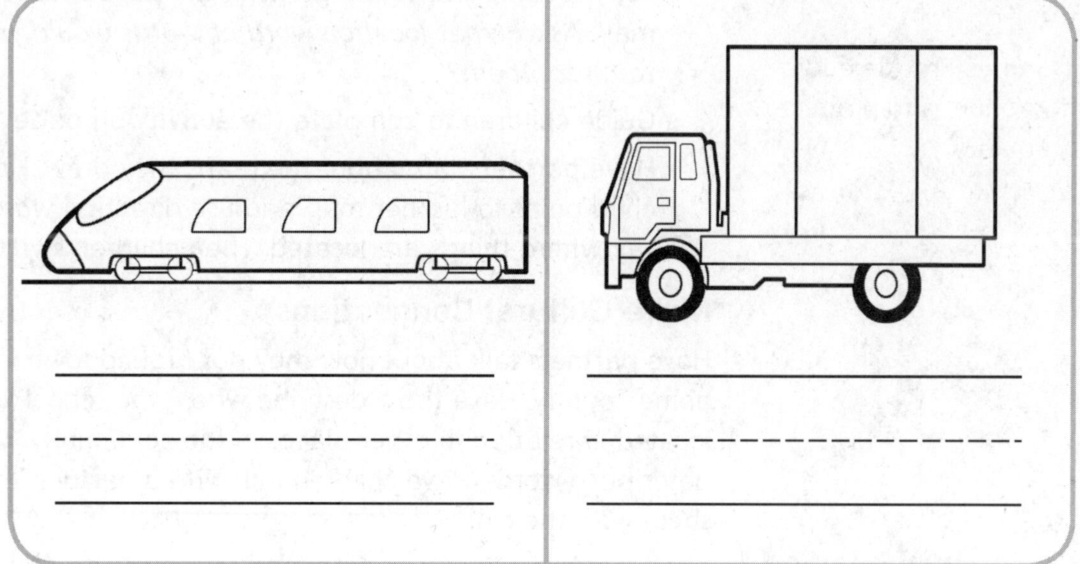

Transportation

Language Objective:
Use language to ask for and give directions

Content Objective:
Identify the location of places in the community

Sentence Frames:
Where can I find the ____?
The ____ is ____ the ____.

VOCABULARY
next to, across from, near, by

>> Go Digital

Language Transfers Handbook
See pages 16–19 for grammatical structures that do not transfer. Cantonese or Hmong speakers may struggle with prepositions.

Foundational Skills
Use Grade 1 High-Frequency Word Cards to practice saying *how, at,* and *on.* Use Sound-Spelling Card 19 to teach how to identify and pronounce the /s/ sound in *across.*

eBook and Games Provide audio support, interaction, and practice with the vocabulary.

LESSON 3: Directions

Set Purpose

- Tell children that today they will discuss directions. Display page 17 of the Newcomer Cards.

Teach/Model Vocabulary

- Elicit vocabulary from Lessons 1 and 2.
- Lead children through the song/chant on page T5.
- Display the Newcomer Card again. Ask: *What places in the community are near each other?* Review location words children have learned. Use props in the classroom to do a quick review of *next to, across from, near,* and *by.*
- Say these sentence frames as you point to the places: **Where can I find the park? The park is across from the police station.** Then say the sentences again as you write them on the board, completing the sentences with the names of the place and location. Use gestures to show the directions. Have children repeat after you. Then point to the police station and ask: **Where is the mall?** Have children answer chorally: **The mall is near the school.** Repeat for other places on the card.
- **Talk About It** Have partners discuss the location of the bank.

Practice/Apply PRODUCTIVE

- **Talk About It** Have partners discuss what they would say if people wanted to go from the police station to the mall. Ask: *What location word or words would you use to direct them?*
- Guide children to complete the activity on page 109.
- Have partners talk about the maps they drew. Have one child point to his/her map and use direction words to say where things are located. Then children switch roles.

Make Cultural Connections

Have partners talk about how they got around town in their home country. Have them describe where the school was located in relation to other places in the community. Elicit descriptive words. Have children talk with a partner and then share with the class.

Name: ____________________

Directions

Use Newcomer Card, page I7

Draw a map of your street. Include homes and other places you know. Then write a sentence about the location of your home.

Food and Meals

Language Objective:
Ask and answer questions in a restaurant

Content Objective:
Understand how to order in a restaurant

Sentence Frames:
May I see the menu, please?
Can I have a/an/the ____, please?
Thank you.
May I have the bill, please?

VOCABULARY
menu, order, bill, may I, please, thank you, sandwich, drink
Cognate: menú

>> Go Digital

Language Transfers Handbook
See pages 16–19 for grammatical structures that do not transfer. Hmong, Vietnamese, Korean, Arabic, Tagalog, or Cantonese speakers may confuse *a/an* with *one*.

Foundational Skills
Use Grade 1 High-Frequency Word Cards to practice saying *have, I, you,* and *and*; Sound-Spelling Card 27 to teach how to identify and pronounce the /th/ sound in *thank*.

eBook Use digital material for vocabulary practice.

LESSON 1: At a Restaurant

Set Purpose

- Tell children that today they will discuss ordering at a restaurant. Display page 18 of the Newcomer Cards.
- If possible, show pictures of restaurants in your community.

Teach/Model Vocabulary

- Lead children through the song/chant on page T5.
- Display the Newcomer Card again. Ask: *What do you see?* Point to and name some things in the restaurant. Have children repeat. Help with pronunciation.
- Say each of the sentence frames from the sidebar, in a natural order, as you gesture and point to the card: **May I see the menu, please? Can I have the fruit salad, please?** And so on. Then say the sentences again as you write them on the board, completing the sentences with the vocabulary words. Have children repeat after you. Then point to the soup on the menu and prompt children to say chorally: **Can I have the soup, please?** Repeat for the other items on the menu.
- Expand by having children talk about the kinds of sandwiches, soups, vegetables, noodles, and drinks that they like.
- **Talk About It** Have partners talk about different things people say in a restaurant.

Practice/Apply COLLABORATIVE

- **Talk About It** Have partners use the Newcomer Card and sentence frames they learned to discuss what they know about going to a restaurant.
- Guide children to complete the activity on page 111.
- Have children help you write a restaurant menu on the board using vocabulary from previous lessons and foods and drinks that they like. Then have partners take turns pretending to be the server and the patron. Children can use the Speech Balloons on page T26 to write dialogue for their role-play. Provide support, as needed.

Make Connections

Have partners talk about their favorite restaurant, what they order there, and why they like the restaurant and the food.

Name: ______________________________

Use the words from the box to label the items.

menu	drink

1. ______________________

2. ______________________

Food and Meals

Language Objective:
Express food likes and dislikes

Content Objective:
Identify food likes and dislikes

Sentence Frames:
What are you eating/drinking?
I'm eating/drinking ____.
What are you ordering?
I'm ordering ____.
Do you like ____?
Yes, I like ____.
No, I don't like ____.
I like ____.
It's my favorite.

VOCABULARY
noodles, cereal, eggs, cheese, soup, fish, vegetables, carrots, potatoes, rice, bread, milk, tea, water, orange juice, fruit, yogurt, sandwich, favorite, meals, drinks, sides
Cognates: cereal, sopa, vegetales, fruta, favorito

>> Go Digital

Language Transfers Handbook
See pages 16–19 for grammatical structures that do not transfer. Cantonese, Vietnamese, Arabic, or Hmong speakers may omit the helping verb in the passive voice.

Foundational Skills
Use Grade 1 High-Frequency Word Cards to practice saying *what, like,* and *my;* Sound-Spelling Card 43 to teach how to identify and pronounce the long /o͞o/ sound in *noodles* and *soup.*

eBook Use digital material for vocabulary practice.

LESSON 2: Healthy Eating

Set Purpose

- Tell children that today they will discuss healthy eating. Display page 18 of the Newcomer Cards.

Teach/Model Vocabulary

- Elicit the restaurant vocabulary from Lesson 1.
- Lead children through the song/chant on page T5.
- Display the Newcomer Card again. Ask: *What foods and drinks do you see?* Children can name what they know. Then point to and name each kind of food or drink. Have children repeat. Help with pronunciation.
- Say these sentence frames as you point to the food and drinks: **What are you eating? I'm eating noodles.** Then say the sentences again as you write them on the board, completing the second sentence with the name of each food. Then, point to the glass of milk and ask: **What are you drinking?** Have children answer chorally: **I'm drinking milk.** Repeat for the other foods and drinks on the card, the vocabulary list, and those provided by children.
- Extend with the sentence frames: **What are you ordering? I'm ordering ____. Do you like ____? Yes, I like ____. No, I don't like ____. I like ____. It's my favorite.** Use these frames to review likes and dislikes.
- **Talk About It** Have children pretend they are eating their favorite meal. Have them use the Conversation Starters on page T30.

Practice/Apply COLLABORATIVE

- **Talk About It** Have partners discuss the healthy foods they like. Have them explain why they like these foods.
- Guide children to complete the activity on page 113.
- Have partners talk about the information in their graphic organizers. Have partners present the similarities and differences in their graphic organizers to the class.

Make Connections

Have children tell a partner more about the foods that they like and don't like. Then have partners share with the class. Have children ask follow-up questions to the presentations.

Name: ______________________________

Healthy Eating

Use Newcomer Card, page 18

Draw pictures of healthy foods you like and don't like. Write why you like one food.

I like	I don't like

____

____

Food and Meals

Language Objective:
Name things we eat during lunch at school

Content Objective:
Identify things we eat during lunch at school

Sentence Frames:
What is/are she/he/you having for lunch?
I'm having ____.
She's/He's having ____.
They're having ____.
They're sharing ____.

VOCABULARY
lunch, sandwich, fruit, soup, noodles, apple, orange
Cognates: fruta, sopa

>> Go Digital

Language Transfers Handbook
See pages 16–19 for grammatical structures that do not transfer. Tagalog or Spanish speakers may struggle with countable and uncountable nouns.

Foundational Skills
Use Grade 1 High-Frequency Word Cards to practice saying *he, she, they,* and *for;* Sound-Spelling Card 16 to teach how to identify and pronounce the /p/ sound in *soup* and *apple*.

eBook and Games Provide audio support, interaction, and practice with the vocabulary.

LESSON 3: Lunchtime at School

Set Purpose

- Tell children that today they will discuss lunchtime at school. Display page 18 of the Newcomer Cards.
- If possible, take children to visit the school cafeteria and have a cafeteria worker show them different foods.

Teach/Model Vocabulary

- Elicit the restaurant and healthy eating vocabulary.
- Lead children through the song/chant on page T5.
- Display the Newcomer Card again. Ask: *What foods do you eat?* Then point to and name the foods on the card. Have children repeat. Help with pronunciation.
- Say these sentence frames as you point to the foods: **What is she having for lunch? She's having soup.** Then say the sentences again as you write them on the board, completing them with the names of foods. Have children repeat after you. Then point to the noodles and ask: **What is she having for lunch?** Have children answer chorally: **She's having noodles.** Repeat for other food on the card, in the vocabulary list, and provided by children.
- **Talk About It** Have partners discuss the food people are having on the card.
- Extend by using the sentence frames with *I'm, they're,* and *he's.* Then expand by with the word *sharing.*

Practice/Apply COLLABORATIVE

- **Talk About It** Have partners use the card and sentence frames to guess and talk about what other children in the class are having for lunch.
- Guide children to complete the activity on page 115.
- Have children pretend to be at a cafeteria table with their favorite meal. Have them work clockwise as they go around the circle asking and telling each other what they are "eating." Have children use the Conversation Starters on page T30. Ask some children: **What is she/ he having for lunch?** Have other children help if needed.

Make Cultural Connections

Have partners talk about their favorite foods from their home country. Elicit descriptive words. Then have children present to the class. Have other children ask follow-up questions.

Use Newcomer Card, page 18

Name: ______________________________

Draw the foods you eat for lunch. Then write their names.

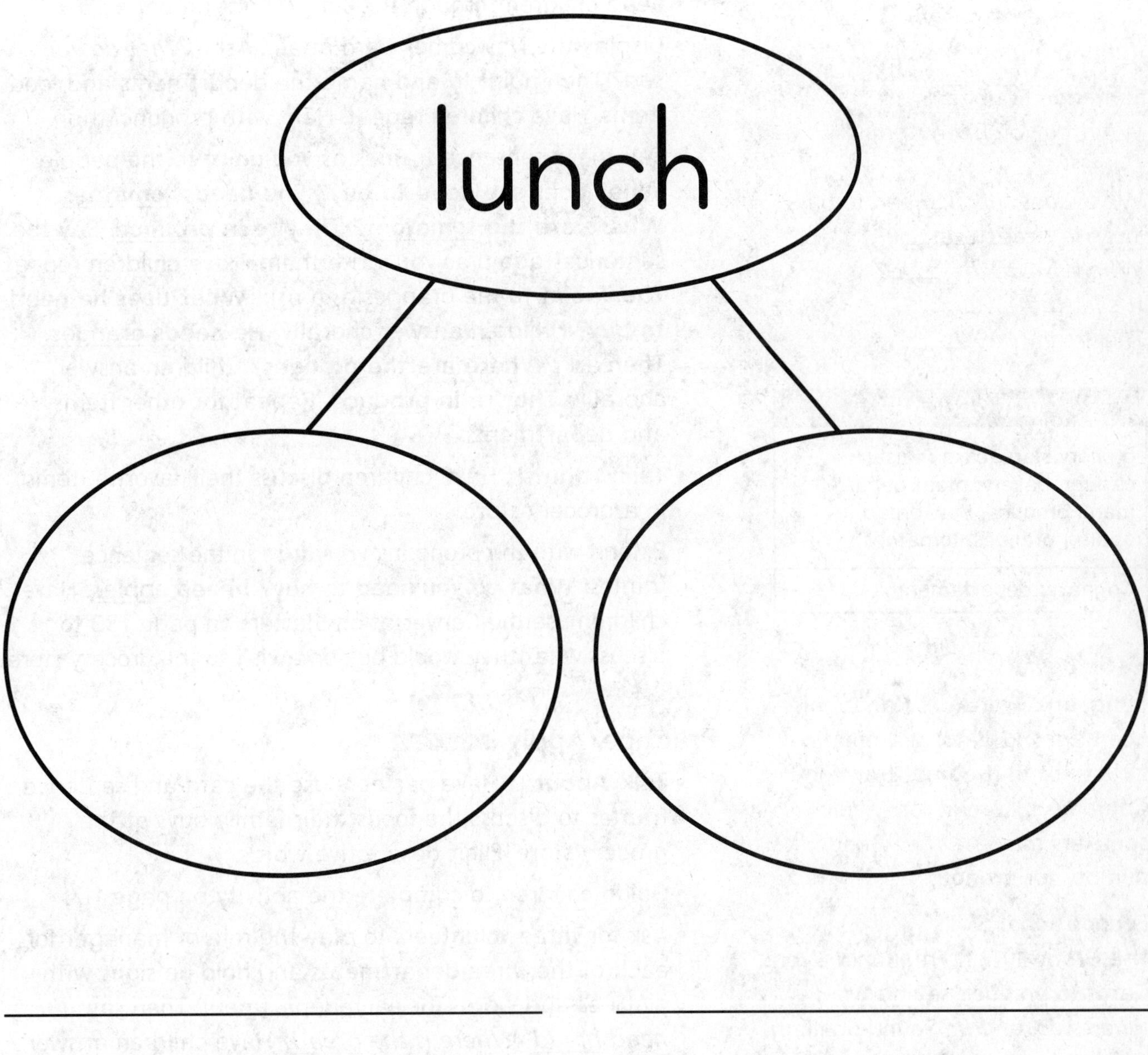

Shopping

Language Objective:
Name where to buy different items in a grocery store

Content Objective:
Determine names and locations of items in a grocery store

Sentence Frames:
What do you need to buy?
I need ____.
What does she/he need to buy?
She/He needs ____.
Where is/are the ____?
It's in (the) ____.
They're in (the) ____.

VOCABULARY
grocery store, cash register, cashier, bakery, meat department, produce, buy, bread, apples, oranges, tomatoes
Cognate: departamento

>> Go Digital

Language Transfers Handbook
See pages 16–19 for grammatical structures that do not transfer. Cantonese, Korean, or Arabic speakers may use the wrong number for pronouns.

Foundational Skills
Use Grade 1 High-Frequency Word Cards to practice saying *what, where, do,* and *in;* Sound-Spelling Card 19 to teach children how to identify and pronounce /s/ in *store* and *produce.*

eBook Use digital material for vocabulary practice.

LESSON 1: Grocery Store

Set Purpose

- Tell children that today they will discuss things found in a grocery store. Display page 19 of the Newcomer Cards.

Teach/Model Vocabulary

- Lead children through the song/chant on page T5.
- Display the Newcomer Card again. Ask: *What do you see?* Then point to and name the departments and food items. Have children repeat. Help with pronunciation.
- Say these sentence frames as you point to the people: **What does she need to buy? She needs <u>tomatoes</u>. Where are the <u>tomatoes</u>? They're in <u>produce</u>.** Say the sentences again as you write them. Have children repeat. Then point to the oranges and ask: **What does he need to buy?** Children answer chorally: **He needs <u>oranges</u>.** Then ask: **Where are the <u>oranges</u>?** Children answer chorally: **They're in <u>produce</u>.** Repeat for other items and departments.
- **Talk About It** Have children discuss their favorite items in a grocery store.
- Extend with the pronouns *you* and *I* in the sentence frames: **What do you need to buy? I need <u>apples</u>.** Have children use the Conversation Starters on page T30 to discuss what they would buy on a visit to the grocery store.

Practice/Apply COLLABORATIVE

- **Talk About It** Have partners use the card and sentence frames to discuss the foods their family buys at the grocery store. Elicit descriptive words.
- Guide children to complete the activity on page 117.
- Ask for three volunteers to play the role of manager for each of the three departments and hold up signs with pictures and words for each department. Then say: *I need <u>bread</u>. Where is the <u>bread</u>?* Have children answer chorally and point to the bakery. Have children take turns asking the questions.

Make Connections

Ask: *What other food or items do you buy at a grocery store?* Have partners discuss with each other and then present their most interesting findings to the class.

Name: ____________________

A. Talk about the pictures with a partner.

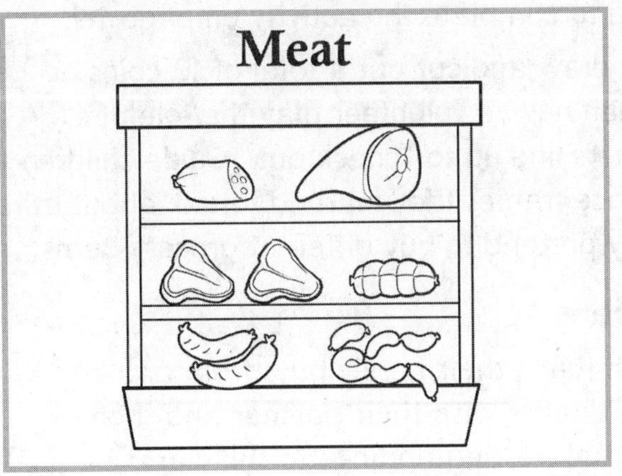

B. Draw yourself in a grocery store. Write one thing you need to buy.

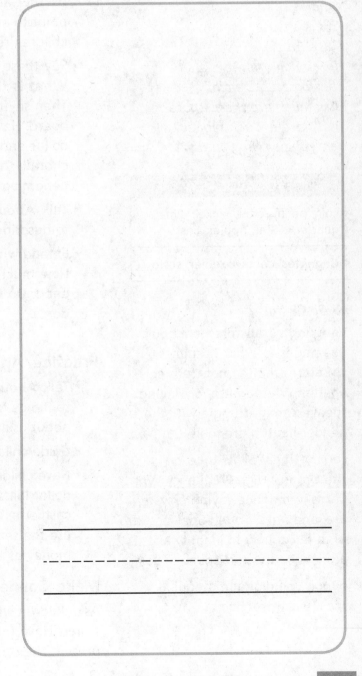

Shopping

Language Objective:
Ask and answer questions about using money

Content Objective:
Demonstrate understanding of the different denominations of money

Sentence Frames:
What is this?
This is a ____.
A ____ is ____.
How much are the ____?
They cost ____ each.
How much are these/those?
Do I have enough money?
Yes, you do./No, you don't.

VOCABULARY
coin, penny, cent, nickel, dime, quarter, dollar, apples, cost
Cognates: centavo, dólar, costo

>> Go Digital

Language Transfers Handbook
See pages 16–19 for grammatical structures that do not transfer. Spanish, Vietnamese, or Hmong speakers may struggle with the gender-neutral pronoun *it*.

Foundational Skills
Use Grade 1 High-Frequency Word Cards to practice saying *how, is, are,* and *have*; Sound-Spelling Card 41 to teach how to identify and pronounce the /oi/ sound in *coin*.

eBook Use digital material for vocabulary practice.

LESSON 2: Using Money

Set Purpose

- Tell children that today they will discuss buying items at a grocery store. Display page 19 of the Newcomer Cards.

Teach/Model Vocabulary

- Elicit grocery store items and departments from Lesson 1.
- Lead children through the song/chant on page T5.
- Display the Newcomer Card again and point to the money. Ask: *What are these?* Have children turn to a partner and talk about the money they know of. Then point to and name the denominations of money. Have children repeat. Help with pronunciation.
- Say these sentence frames as you point to the money: **What is this? This is a quarter. A quarter is 25 cents.** Then say the sentences again as you write them on the board. Have children repeat after you. Then point to the dollar and say: **What is this?** Have children answer chorally: **This is a dollar.** Repeat for other denominations of money on the Newcomer Card.
- **Talk About It** Have partners use color and shape words to describe the bill and coins to each other.
- Extend with the sentence frames to discuss using money **How much are these/those apples? They cost 50 cents each. Do I have enough money? Yes, you do. No, you don't.**

Practice/Apply COLLABORATIVE

- **Talk About It** Have partners use the Newcomer Card and sentence frames they learned to discuss what they know about using money.
- Guide children to complete the activity on page 119.
- Have children draw and cut out a total of 10 coins or dollar bills. Then have a volunteer play the role of a cashier as others line up to "check out." Guide children to use the sentence frames they learned to talk about using money as they pretend to buy different grocery items.

Make Connections

Ask children which items their family buys from grocery stores. Have them discuss with their partner and then present their most interesting findings to the class.

Name: ______________________________

Use Newcomer Card, page 19

Complete the sentences. Use words from the box.

quarter	penny	dime	dollar

1. This is a ______________.

2. This is a ______________.

3. This is a ______________.

4. This is a ______________.

Shopping

Language Objective:
Ask and answer questions about what we do in the grocery store

Content Objective:
Identify what people do in the grocery store

Sentence Frames:
Do you ____?
Yes, I ____.
No, I don't ____.
Do you ____ or ____?

VOCABULARY
make a shopping list, compare prices, look for something, ask for help, push the cart, carry the basket
Cognates: lista, precios

>> Go Digital

Language Transfers Handbook
See pages 16–19 for grammatical structures that do not transfer. Cantonese, Korean, Spanish, or Arabic speakers may omit helping verbs in negative statements.

Foundational Skills
Use Grade 1 High-Frequency Word Cards to practice saying *do, make, you,* and *or*; Sound-Spelling Card 42 to teach how to identify and pronounce the /oo/ sound in *look*.

eBook and Games Provides audio support, interaction, and practice with the vocabulary.

LESSON 3: Grocery Shopping

Set Purpose

- Tell children that today they will discuss grocery shopping. Display page 19 of the Newcomer Cards.

Teach/Model Vocabulary

- Elicit the names of money, grocery store departments, and grocery items from Lessons 1 and 2.
- Lead children through the song/chant on page T5.
- Display the Newcomer Card again. Ask: *What are people doing?* Then point to, name, and pantomime activities in a grocery store. Have children repeat your words and actions. Help with pronunciation. Have partners talk about other activities they know of.
- Say these sentence frames as you point to the people in the grocery store: **Do you carry the basket? Yes, I carry the basket. No, I don't carry the basket.** Then say the sentences again as you write them on the board, completing the sentences with the name of the shopping activity. Have children repeat after you. Then point to the shopping cart and ask: **Do you push the shopping cart?** Nod your head and have children answer chorally: **Yes, I push the shopping cart.** Repeat for grocery store activities on the card and in the vocabulary list.
- **Talk About It** Have partners talk about the things they do in a grocery store.
- Extend by introducing the sentence frames: **Do you ____ or do you ____? I ____.** Teach the conjunction *or.*

Practice/Apply COLLABORATIVE

- **Talk About It** Have partners use the Newcomer Card and sentence frames to discuss what they know about shopping in the grocery store.
- Guide children to complete the activity on page 121.
- Have small groups create displays for different departments in a grocery store. Then have children create shopping lists and pretend to go shopping.

Make Cultural Connections

Have children respond to the following prompt: *What did you do differently in grocery stores in your home country?* Have partners discuss their answers and then present to the class.

Name: ______________________

Grocery Shopping

Use Newcomer Card, page 19

A. Talk about the pictures.

B. Draw and write what you do in a grocery store.

____

____

Measurement	LESSONS	MATERIALS	LANGUAGE OBJECTIVES	LANGUAGE STRUCTURES/ GRAMMAR	VOCABULARY
Newcomer Card, p. 20	**Lesson 1:** Comparing Objects, p. 124–125	Newcomer Card p. 20 Sound-Spelling Card 27 Song/Chant p. T6	Ask and answer questions about different objects	How ____ is the/this ____? This ____ is ____ that ____. **Comparatives** ***How* questions** **Regular plurals**	Adjectives describing measurements **High-Frequency Words:** *how, is, this, the*
	Lesson 2: Same and Different, p. 136–127	Newcomer Card p. 20 Sound-Spelling Card 12 Song/Chant p. T6	Use language to compare and contrast objects	How are the ____ and the ____ the same/different? They are both ____. The ____ has ____. ***How* questions** **Conjunction:** and	Comparison words **High-Frequency Words:** *look, they, how*
	Lesson 3: Measuring in the Classroom, p. 128–129	Newcomer Card p. 20 Sound-Spelling Card 32 Song/Chant p. T6	Describe measurements of classroom objects	How ____ is (the) ____ ____? It's ____ ____ ____. **Verb:** to be ***How* questions**	Non-standard measurements **High-Frequency Words:** *is, it, how*

Animals	LESSONS	MATERIALS	LANGUAGE OBJECTIVES	LANGUAGE STRUCTURES/ GRAMMAR	VOCABULARY
Newcomer Card, p. 21	**Lesson 1:** Wild Animals and Insects, p. 130–131	Newcomer Card p. 21 Sound-Spelling Card 31 Song/Chant p. T6	Ask and answer questions about wild animals and insects	What is the ____ doing? The ____ is ____. **Verb:** to be **Article:** the	Wild animals and insects **High-Frequency Words:** *is, what, the*
	Lesson 2: Pets, p. 132–133	Newcomer Card p. 21 Sound-Spelling Card 33 Song/Chant p. T6	Name animals people keep as pets and tell what people do with them	Do you have a pet? Yes, I have a ____. No, I don't have a pet. **Questions with *do*** **Negatives**	Pets **High-Frequency Words:** *have, like, do, I*
	Lesson 3: Farm Animals, p. 134–135	Newcomer Card p. 21 Sound-Spelling Card 38 Song/Chant p. T6	Ask and answer questions about the sizes of farm animals	Which animal is ____? The ____ is ____ the ____. ***Wh-* questions:** Which **Comparatives**	Farm animals **High-Frequency Words:** *animal, the, is*

Growth and Change	LESSONS	MATERIALS	LANGUAGE OBJECTIVES	LANGUAGE STRUCTURES/ GRAMMAR	VOCABULARY
Newcomer Card, p. 22	**Lesson 1:** Animal Growth Cycle, p. 136–137	Newcomer Card p. 22 Sound-Spelling Card 9 Song/Chant p. T6	Name stages in a butterfly's growth cycle	____ it is a/an ____. **Verb:** to be **Sequence words**	Animal growth cycle **High-Frequency Words:** *it, is, a, an*
	Lesson 2: Plant Growth Cycle, p. 138–139	Newcomer Card p. 22 Sound-Spelling Card 36 Song/Chant p. T6	Ask and answer questions about the plant growth cycle	How does the ____ change? The ____ changes into a ____. **Verb:** to change ***How* questions**	Plant growth cycle **High-Frequency Words:** *how, does, into*
	Lesson 3: Human Growth, p. 140–141	Newcomer Card p. 22 Sound-Spelling Card 26 Song/Chant p. T6	Ask and answer questions about human growth	The ____ is ____ than the ____. Is the ____ ____ than the ____? **Comparatives** **Regular and irregular plurals**	Stages of human growth **High-Frequency Words:** *yes, no, not*

United States	LESSONS	MATERIALS	LANGUAGE OBJECTIVES	LANGUAGE STRUCTURES/ GRAMMAR	VOCABULARY
Newcomer Card, p. 23	**Lesson 1:** States, p. 142–143	Newcomer Card p. 23 Sound-Spelling Card 10 Song/Chant p. T6	Ask and answer questions about your state and some land features	Where do you live? I live in/near ____. Do you live near ____? **Verb:** to live ***Wh-* questions:** Where	States **High-Frequency Words:** *live, near, to, do*
	Lesson 2: National Landmarks, p. 144–145	Newcomer Card p. 23 Sound-Spelling Card 7 Song/Chant p. T7	Ask and answer questions about different landmarks in the United States	Do you want to go to the ____? I do/do not want to go to the ____. I want to go to the ____. **Verbs:** to want, to go **Pronouns:** I, you	United States landmarks **High-Frequency Words:** *want, go, to, do*
	Lesson 3: Natural Features, p. 146-147	Newcomer Card p. 23 Sound-Spelling Card 22 Song/Chant p. T7	Ask and answer questions about natural features in the United States	Do you want to live near a/an ____? Yes/No, I want to live near a/an ____. **Verbs:** to want, to live **Yes/No questions**	Places in nature **High-Frequency Words:** *want, live, near*

My World	LESSONS	MATERIALS	LANGUAGE OBJECTIVES	LANGUAGE STRUCTURES/ GRAMMAR	VOCABULARY
Newcomer Card, p. 24	**Lesson 1:** Where I'm From, p. 148–149	Newcomer Card p. 24 Sound-Spelling Card 3 Song/Chant p. T7	Ask and answer questions about where you and your classmates are from	What country are you from? I'm from ____. ***Wh-* questions:** What **Past tense verb**	My country **High-Frequency Words:** *from, what, are*
	Lesson 2: Land and Water Animals, p. 150–151	Newcomer Card p. 24 Sound-Spelling Card 5 Song/Chant p. T7	Ask and answer questions about animals in your home country	What land/water animals live in your home country? ___ live on land/in the water in ___. ***Wh-* questions:** What **Prepositions of place**	Land and water animals **High-Frequency Words:** *live, water, other*
	Lesson 3: In My New Country, p. 152–153	Newcomer Card p. 24 Sound-Spelling Card 34 Song/Chant p. T7	Compare and contrast your home country and your new country	I'm from ____. We spoke ____ there. In ____, I ____. In the United States, we play ____. **Present and past tense verbs** **Pronouns:** I, we	Old/new country **High-Frequency Words:** *I, my, we, school*

Progress Monitoring

Use the **Oral Language Proficiency Benchmark Assessment** on pages T40–T41 to monitor students' oral language proficiency growth.

Use the **Student Profile** on pages T43–T44 to record observations throughout the units.

Measurement

Language Objective:
Ask and answer questions about different objects

Content Objective:
Compare objects

Sentence Frames:
How ____ is the/this ____?
This ____ is ____ that ____.
How heavy are the ____?
____ ____ are ____ ____ ____.

VOCABULARY
long, tall, short, heavy, light, longer than, taller than, shorter than, heavier than, lighter than, tomato plant, leaf, leaves, plant, scale
Cognate: planta de tomate

>> Go Digital

Language Transfers Handbook
See pages 16–19 for grammatical structures that do not transfer. Some Hmong, Korean, Spanish, or Tagalog speakers may struggle with comparative ending *-er*.

Foundational Skills
Use the Grade 1 High-Frequency Word Cards to practice saying *how, is, this,* and *the;* Sound-Spelling Card 27 to teach children how to identify and pronounce /ôr/ in *short* and *shorter.*

eBook Use digital material to practice vocabulary.

LESSON 1: Comparing Objects

Set Purpose

- Tell children that today they will discuss comparing objects. Display page 20 of the Newcomer Cards.
- Explain that when we compare things, we tell what is the same and different about them.

Teach/Model Vocabulary

- Lead children through the song/chant on page T6.
- Display page 20 of the Newcomer Cards again. Ask: *What do you see?* Children can name things they know. Then point to and name the different greenhouse objects. Have children repeat. Help with pronunciation. Explain that we can tell what is different about the objects by looking at how tall they are (their height), how long they are (their length), and how heavy they are (their weight).
- Say these sentence frames as you point to leaves: **How long is this leaf? This leaf is longer than that leaf.** Say the sentences again as you write them on the board. Children repeat. Then point to a short leaf and ask: **How long is this leaf?** Have children answer chorally: **This leaf is shorter than that leaf.** Repeat for other objects on the card and in the vocabulary list.
- **Talk About It** Have partners discuss the sizes of the different plants shown on the card.
- Extend by comparing weight with the sentence frames: **How heavy are the apples? Four apples are heavier than one apple.**

Practice/Apply

- **Talk About It** Have partners use the Newcomer Card and sentence frames to discuss and compare the height of the tomato plant and the little boy standing next to it.
- Guide children to complete the activity on page 125.
- In small groups, have children talk about who in the group is the tallest and shortest. Then have them use the sentence frames they learned to compare heights.

Make Connections

Have children cut out pictures from magazines showing different sizes of plants, flowers, and fruit. Then have pairs compare them by length, height, and even weight.

Name: ______________________

Comparing Objects

Use Newcomer Card, page 20

A. Talk about the pictures with a partner.

B. Draw a tall plant and a short plant. Label the taller one.

Measurement

Language Objective:
Use language to compare and contrast objects

Content Objective:
Understand things that are the same and different between two objects

Sentence Frames:
How are the ____ and the ____ the same/different?
They both have ____.
The ____ has ____.

VOCABULARY
same, different, both

>> Go Digital

Language Transfers Handbook
See pages 16–19 for grammatical structures that do not transfer. Some Cantonese, Korean, or Arabic speakers may use the wrong number for pronouns.

Foundational Skills
Use the Grade 1 High-Frequency Word Cards to practice saying *look, they,* and *how;* Sound-Spelling Card 12 to teach how to identify and pronounce /d/ in *different.*

eBook Use digital material to practice vocabulary.

LESSON 2: Same and Different

Set Purpose

- Tell children that today they will discuss similarities and differences. Display page 20 of the Newcomer Cards.

Teach/Model Vocabulary

- Elicit vocabulary from Lesson 1.
- Lead children through the song/chant on page T6.
- Display the Newcomer Card again. Ask: *What do you notice about the different plants?* Then have children take turns pointing to and describing the leaf shape, color, and size of each plant.
- Say these sentence frames as you point to first the tomato plant and then the hanging plant on the left: **How are the tomato plant and the hanging plant the same? They both have green leaves.** Say the sentences again as you write them on the board. Children repeat.
- **Talk About It** Point to the two tomato plants and ask: **How are the short plant and the tall plant the same?** Encourage children to study the two plants. Partners can discuss their answer and then share with the group.
- Introduce these sentence frames to talk about differences: **How are the blue plant and the orange plant different? The orange plant has orange leaves. The blue plant has blue leaves.**
- **Talk About It** Have partners take turns saying what is the same and different about the various plants and objects on the card.

Practice/Apply COLLABORATIVE

- **Talk About It** Have partners use the Newcomer Card and sentence frames to discuss what is the same and different about the watering can and spray bottle on the card.
- Have children compare the size, shape, and color of classroom objects.
- Guide children to complete the activity on page 127.

Make Connections

Have pairs talk about what is the same and different about each other, looking at hair color, eye color, and height.

Name: ___________________________

Study the two tomato plants on the card. Draw what is the same and different about them. Write a sentence telling how they're the same.

tall tomato plant	short tomato plant

____

Measurement

Language Objective:
Describe measurements of classroom objects

Content Objective:
Demonstrate understanding of measuring objects

Sentence Frames:
How ____ is (the) ____ ____?
It's ____ ____ ____.
____ ____ *is* ____ *than* ____ ____.

VOCABULARY
crayons, paper clip, pencils

>> Go Digital

Language Transfers Handbook See pages 16–19 for grammatical structures that do not transfer. Some Cantonese, Hmong, Korean, Vietnamese, Arabic, or Spanish speakers may forget to use the plural marker *-s*.

Foundational Skills Use the Grade 1 High-Frequency Word Cards to practice saying *is, it,* and *how*; Sound-Spelling Card 32 to teach children how to identify and pronounce /ā/ in *paper*.

eBook and Games Provide audio support, interaction, and practice with the vocabulary.

LESSON 3: Measuring in the Classroom

Set Purpose

- Tell children that today they will discuss measuring in the classroom. Display page 20 of the Newcomer Cards.

Teach/Model Vocabulary

- To review, elicit vocabulary from Lessons 1 and 2.
- Lead children through the song/chant on page T6.
- Display the Newcomer Card again. Ask: *What are the children measuring?*
- Say these sentence frames as you point to the boy measuring the tomato plant: **How tall is the tomato plant?** Point to the pencils he's using to measure the plant. Have a volunteer count and share the number: **It's two pencils tall.** Say the sentences again as you write them on the board. Have children repeat. Then point to a child's desk or table and ask: **How long is your desk?** Keep adding crayons until they are lined up from one end to the other. Have children count the crayons together and answer chorally: **It's ten crayons long.** Repeat by measuring the height and length of other classroom objects with crayons, pencils, or paper clips.
- **Talk About It** Have partners discuss the results of the measurements.
- Expand by reviewing comparisons with the sentence frames: **How heavy is the book? The book is heavier than the eraser** and **How tall is the easel? The easel is four crayons shorter than the door.**

Practice/Apply

INTERPRETIVE

- **Talk About It** Have partners use crayons and the sentence frames they learned to measure their backpacks and discuss the results.
- Have partners identify classroom objects that are *short, tall,* and *long*. Then have them measure and compare the objects using crayons as measuring tools.
- Guide children to complete the activity on page 129.

Make Cultural Connections

Have children choose two animals from their home country and draw them. They can use crayons to measure their height and length, and describe the results to a partner.

Name: ______________________________

Measuring in the Classroom

Use Newcomer Card, page 20

Draw a picture of an object you use every day. Use a crayon to measure it. Then complete the sentence.

The ______________ is ______________ crayons long.

Animals

Language Objective:
Ask and answer questions about wild animals and insects

Content Objective:
Identify the actions of wild animals and insects

Sentence Frames:
What is the ____ doing?
The ____ is ____.

VOCABULARY
elephant, lion, tiger, bear, deer, raccoon, snake, praying mantis, bee, ant, buzzing, walking, running, crawling
Cognates: *elefante, león, tigre*

>> Go Digital

Language Transfers Handbook
See pages 16–19 for grammatical structures that do not transfer. Cantonese, Hmong, or Vietnamese speakers may omit linking verbs.

Foundational Skills
Use Grade 1 High-Frequency Word Cards to practice saying *the, is,* and *what;* Sound-Spelling Card 31 to teach children how to identify and pronounce the */ng/* sound in *-ing* verbs.

eBook Use digital material for vocabulary practice.

LESSON 1: Wild Animals and Insects

Set Purpose

- Tell children that today they will discuss wild animals and insects. Display page 21 of the Newcomer Cards.
- If possible, take children to the library to look at books with pictures of wild animals and insects.

Teach/Model Vocabulary

- Lead children through the song/chant on page T6.
- Display page 21 of the Newcomer Cards again. Ask *What do you see?* Then point to and name the wild animals, insects, and describe how they're moving. Have children repeat. Help with pronunciation.
- Say these sentence frames as you point to each of the wild animals and insects: **What is the elephant doing? The elephant is walking.** Then say the sentences again as you write them on the board, completing the sentences with the name of the animal and how the animal is moving. Have children repeat after you. Then make a buzzing sound, point to the bee, and ask: **What is the bee doing?** Have children answer chorally: **The bee is buzzing.** Repeat for all wild animals and insects on the card, vocabulary list, and ones children provide.
- **Talk About It** Have partners talk about and pantomime the different ways wild animals and insects move.

Practice/Apply

- **Talk About It** Have partners use the Newcomer Card and sentence frames they learned to describe some wild animals and insects and how they move. Elicit action verbs and descriptive words.
- Guide children to complete the activity on page 131.
- Have children play charades. Whisper an animal or insect to a child and have her/him act out for the class how the animal moves. Other children guess the name of the wild animal or insect and what it is doing. Continue playing so that each child has a turn acting.

Make Connections

Ask the following question: *What else can you tell me about a wild animal or insect?* Have children talk to a partner and then share with the class.

Name: ______________________________

Write the word from the box to match each picture.

ant	bear	bee	deer	raccoon	praying mantis

1.  ____________________

2.  ____________________

3.  ____________________

4.  ____________________

5. ____________________

6.  ____________________

Animals

Language Objective:
Name animals that people keep as pets and tell what people do with them

Content Objective:
Identify different pets and what people do with them

Sentence Frames:
Do you have a pet?
Yes, I have a ____.
No, I don't have a pet.
My friend has a ____.
Do you like to ____ your (friend's) ____?
Yes/No, I like to ____ my (friend's) ____.

VOCABULARY
bird, cat, dog, fish, hamster, turtle, play with, brush, walk, feed

>> Go Digital

Language Transfers Handbook
See pages 16–19 for grammatical structures that do not transfer. Some Korean, Spanish, or Arabic speakers may struggle with the phrasal verb *play with*.

Foundational Skills
Use Grade 1 High-Frequency Word Cards to practice saying *have, like, do,* and *I;* Sound-Spelling Card 33 to teach /ī/ in *like*.

eBook Use digital material for vocabulary practice.

LESSON 2: Pets

Set Purpose

- Tell children that today they will discuss animals people have at home. Say: *They are called pets.* Display page 21 of the Newcomer Cards.
- If possible, take children to visit any pets in your school.

Teach/Model Vocabulary

- Elicit the names and actions of wild animals and insects discussed in Lesson 1.
- Lead children through the song/chant on page T6.
- Display the Newcomer Card. Ask: *What pets do you see?* Then point to and name each pet. Have children repeat. Help with pronunciation.
- Say these sentence frames as you point to the cat: **Do you have a pet? Yes, I have a cat.** Then say the sentences again as you write them on the board, completing the second sentence with the name of the pet. Have children repeat after you. Then point to the dog and ask: **Do you have a pet?** Have children answer chorally: **Yes, I have a dog**, filling in the name of the pet. Repeat for the other pets on the card and the vocabulary list.
- **Talk About It** Have partners discuss the pets on the card.
- Expand by introducing the frames: **No, I don't have a pet. My friend has a hamster. Do you like to feed your (friend's) hamster? Yes, I like to feed my (friend's) hamster. No, I like to play with my (friend's) hamster.**

Practice/Apply

- **Talk About It** Have partners use the card and sentence frames to discuss animals people have as pets and what they do with them. Elicit action and descriptive words.
- Guide children to complete the activity on page 133.
- Play a guessing game. Have children take turns orally describing their drawings to the class. As they present, other children guess the animal being described. For example: *It is brown. It likes to walk. It likes to play.*

Make Connections

Ask children to describe their favorite pet, why they like it, and what activities they can do with it.

Name: ________________________________

Pets

Use Newcomer Card, page 21

A. Talk to your partner about the pictures.

B. Draw and label what you can do with a pet.

Animals

Language Objective:
Ask and answer questions about the sizes of farm animals

Content Objective:
Demonstrate understanding about the different sizes of farm animals

Sentence Frames:
Which animal is ____?
The ____ is ____ than the ____.

VOCABULARY
goat, rooster, horse, sheep, smaller, smaller than, bigger, bigger than

>> Go Digital

Language Transfers Handbook
See pages 16–19 for grammatical structures that do not transfer. Some Hmong, Korean, Spanish, or Tagalog speakers may struggle with the comparative ending *-er*.

Foundational Skills
Use Grade 1 High-Frequency Word Cards to practice saying *animal, the,* and *is*; Sound-Spelling Card 38 to teach children how to identify and pronounce the /ûr/ sound in *-er* word endings.

eBook and Games Provide audio support, interaction, and practice with the vocabulary.

LESSON 3: Farm Animals

Set Purpose

- Tell children that today they will discuss the different sizes of farm animals. Display page 21 of the Newcomer Cards.
- Encourage children to play with toy farm animals.

Teach/Model Vocabulary

- Elicit names of animals and insects from Lessons 1 and 2.
- Lead children through the song/chant on page T6.
- Display the Newcomer Card. Say: *What do you see? Tell your partner about the farm animals you know.* Then point to and name each farm animal and say whether it is big or small. Have children repeat. Help with pronunciation.
- Say these sentence frames as you point to the farm animals: **Which animal is smaller? The rooster is smaller than the goat.** Then say the sentences again as you write them on the board, completing the sentences with the names of the animals and the comparative adjective. Have children repeat after you. Then point to the animals again and ask: **Which animal is bigger?** Have children answer chorally: **The goat is bigger than the rooster.** Repeat for other animals on the card, vocabulary list, and others children know.
- **Talk About It** Have pairs discuss some of the differences between wild animals, pets, insects, and farm animals.

Practice/Apply

- **Talk About It** Have partners use the card and sentence frames to discuss the sizes of animals on a farm. Elicit descriptive and comparative words.
- Guide children to complete the activity on page 135.
- Have children draw pictures of farm animals that are different sizes and colors. Have partners use previously learned vocabulary and sentence frames to ask and answer questions about each other's drawings.

Make Cultural Connections

Have children describe farm animals they saw in their home country. Encourage them to compare animal sizes as they share their descriptions with the class.

Name: ______________________________

Farm Animals

Use Newcomer Card, page 2I

Look at the pictures. Then complete the sentences.

big **small**

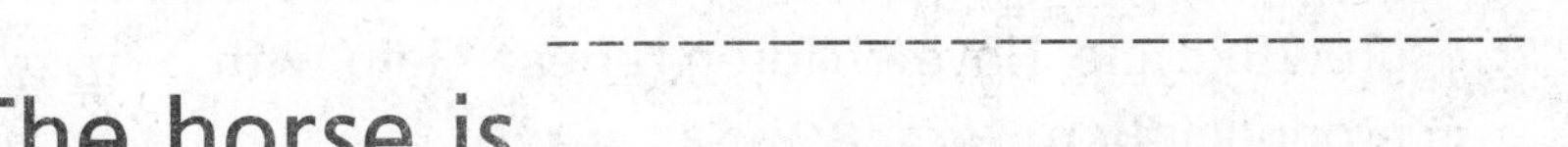

The horse is ____________ .

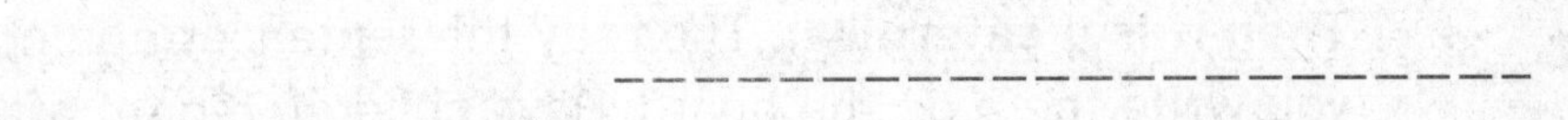

The rooster is ____________ .

goat **rooster** **horse**

The ____________ is smaller than the goat.

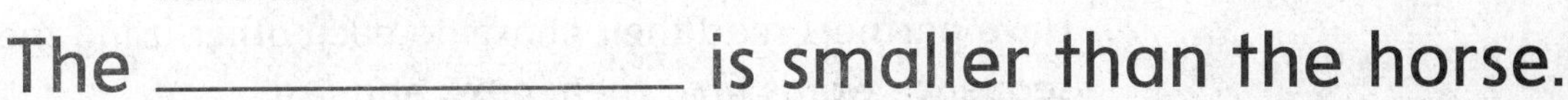

The ____________ is smaller than the horse.

The ____________ is bigger than the goat.

Growth and Change

Language Objective:
Name stages in a butterfly's growth cycle.

Content Objective:
Demonstrate understanding of a butterfly's growth cycle

Sentence Frames:
____ *it is a/an* ____.

VOCABULARY
egg, caterpillar, pupa, butterfly, first, then, next, last

>> Go Digital

Language Transfers Handbook
See pages 16–19 for grammatical structures that do not transfer. Some Spanish, Vietnamese, or Hmong speakers may use inappropriate gender-specific pronouns for neutral nouns.

Foundational Skills
Use the Grade 1 High-Frequency Word Cards to practice saying *it, is, a,* and *an;* Sound-Spelling Card 9 to teach children how to identify and pronounce */g/* in egg.

eBook Use digital material to practice vocabulary.

LESSON 1: Animal Growth Cycle

Set Purpose

- Tell children that today they will discuss the growth cycle of a butterfly. Display page 22 of the Newcomer Cards.
- If possible, have children observe an animal at a stage of their growth cycle. Have children talk about it.

Teach/Model Vocabulary

- Lead children through the song/chant on page T6.
- Display the Newcomer Card again. Say: *Tell me about the animal.* Then point to and name each stage of the growth cycle. Have children repeat. Help with pronunciation.
- Say these sentence frames as you point to the first two stages of the butterfly's growth cycle: **First it is an egg. Then it is a caterpillar.** Then say the sentences again as you write them on the board. Have children repeat after you. Then point to the next stage and say: **Next it is a pupa. Last it is a...** Then point to the last stage and have children chorally respond: **...butterfly**. Repeat for the other animal growth cycles the children may know, such as the frog.
- **Talk About It** Have partners work together to describe how the butterfly changes.

Practice/Apply

- **Talk About It** Have partners use the Newcomer Card and sentence frames to discuss what they now know about the butterfly growth cycle.
- Guide children to complete the activity on page 137. Have partners read their charts to each other using the sequence words *first, then, next,* and *last*.
- Have partners take turns acting out each stage of the butterfly growth cycle. The child watching has to guess and name the stage.

Make Connections

Ask the following question: *What else can you tell me about a butterfly's growth cycle?* Have partners discuss how the animal changes. Encourage children to use previously learned vocabulary. Then have them share with the class what they discussed.

Name: ______________________________

Animal Growth Cycle

Use Newcomer Card, page 22

Write the stages of a butterfly's growth cycle. Use words from the box.

pupa	butterfly	caterpillar	egg

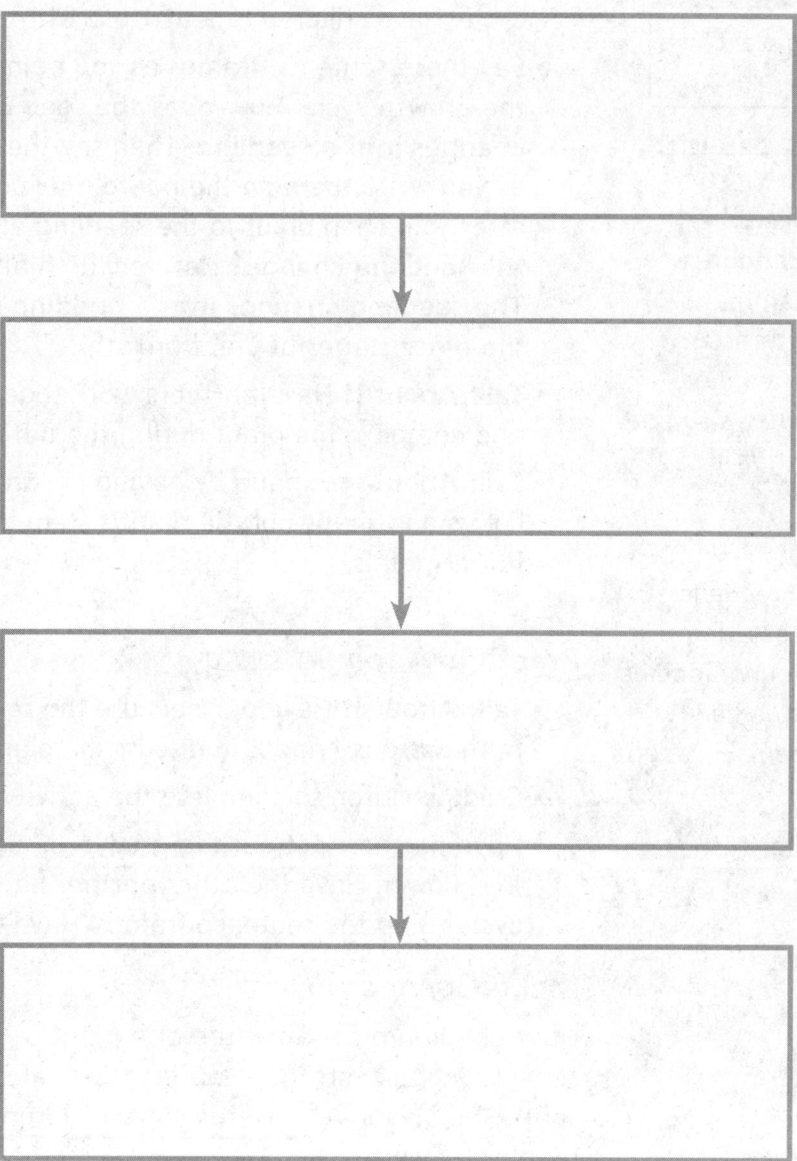

Growth and Change

Language Objective:
Ask and answer questions about the plant growth cycle

Content Objective:
Identify the stages of the plant growth cycle

Sentence Frames:
How does the ____ change?
A ____ changes into a ____.

VOCABULARY
seed, seedling, budding plant, flower
Cognate: *planta*

>> Go Digital

Language Transfers Handbook
See pages 16–19 for grammatical structures that do not transfer. Cantonese, Hmong, Korean, or Vietnamese speakers may struggle with inflectional ending *-s* in *changes.*

Foundational Skills
Use the Grade 1 High-Frequency Word Cards to practice saying *how, does,* and *into;* Sound-Spelling Card 36 to teach children how to identify and pronounce */ē/* in *seed* and *seedling.*

eBook Use digital material to practice vocabulary.

LESSON 2: Plant Growth Cycle

Set Purpose

- Tell children that today they will discuss the growth cycle of plants. Display page 22 of the Newcomer Cards.
- Take children on a tour to look at plants around the school. Have them make observations about the size, color, and shape of the plants.

Teach/Model Vocabulary

- To review, elicit sequence words learned in Lesson 1.
- Lead children through the song/chant on page T6.
- Display the Newcomer Card again. Say: *Tell me about the plants.* Point to and name each stage of the growth cycle. Have children repeat. Help with pronunciation.
- Say these sentence frames as you point to the stages of the growth cycle: **How does the seed change? The seed changes into a seedling.** Then say the sentences again as you write them on the board. Have children repeat after you. Then point to the seedling and ask: **How does the seedling change?** Have children answer chorally: **The seedling changes into a budding plant**. Repeat for the other stages of plant growth.
- **Talk About It** Have partners work together to describe and compare the plant during the different stages.
- **Talk About It** Expand by having children talk about the colors and shapes of the plant's stem, roots, leaves, and flower petals.

Practice/Apply

- **Talk About It** Have partners use the sentence frames from Lessons 1 and 2 to discuss the plant's growth cycle.
- Guide children to complete the activity on page 139.
- Have partners act out the growth of a plant from a seed to a flower. Have the other partner narrate the growth cycle using the sentence frames. Have them take turns.

Make Connections

Have children draw a picture of a plant or flower they have seen. Have partners make observations about the size, shape, and color. Afterwards, have children describe their plant or flower to the class.

Name: ______________________________

A. Circle the picture that shows the correct stage of the plant's growth cycle.

1. seed

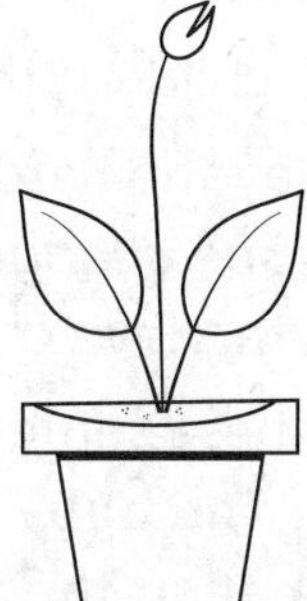

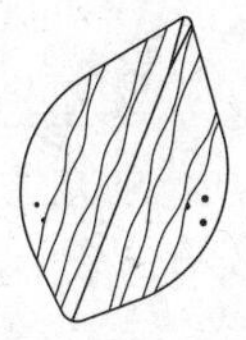

2. seedling

3. budding plant

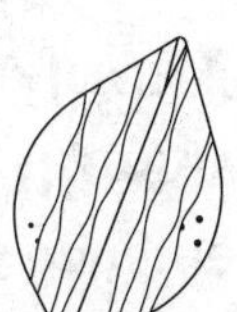

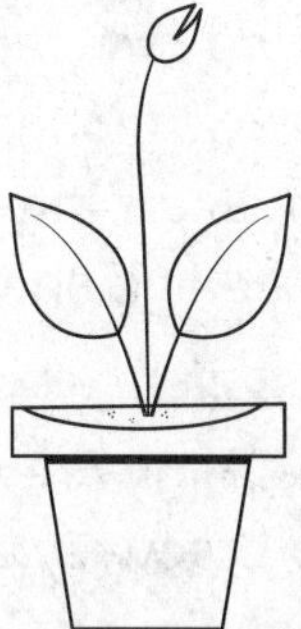

B. What stage of the plant growth cycle do you see?

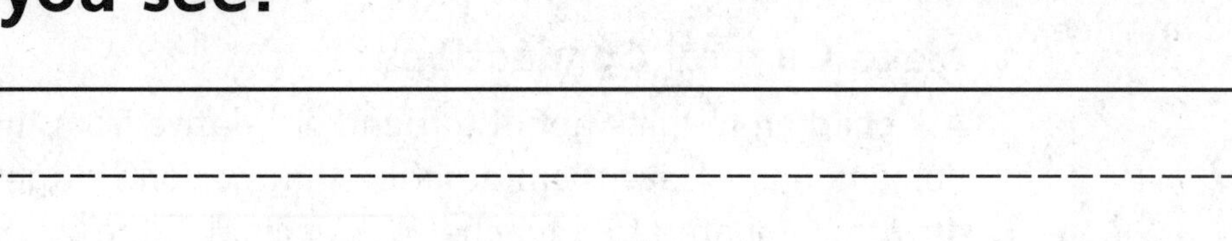

Growth and Change

Language Objective:
Ask and answer questions about human growth

Content Objective:
Understand the different stages of human growth

Sentence Frames:
The ____ is ____ the ____.
____ are ____ than ____.
Is the ____ ____ than the ____?
Yes/No, the ____ is/is not ____ than the ____.

VOCABULARY
baby, babies, child, children, teenager, adult, older than, younger than
Cognates: bebé, adulto

>> Go Digital

Language Transfers Handbook See pages 16–19 for grammatical structures that do not transfer. Some Cantonese, Hmong, or Vietnamese speakers may struggle with the linking verb *is*.

Foundational Skills Use the Grade 1 High-Frequency Word Cards to practice saying *yes, no,* and *not*; Sound-Spelling Card 26 to teach children how to identify and pronounce the /z/ sound in *babies*.

eBook and Games Provide audio support, interaction, and practice with the vocabulary.

LESSON 3: Human Growth

Set Purpose

- Tell children that today they will discuss the growth of people. Display page 22 of the Newcomer Cards.

Teach/Model Vocabulary

- Elicit vocabulary from Lessons 1 and 2.
- Lead children through the song/chant on page T6.
- Display the card again. Say: *Look at this person. How does she change?* Point to and name the stages of growth. Have children repeat. Help with pronunciation.
- Say these sentence frames as you point to stages on the card: **The baby is younger than the child. The adult is older than the teenager.** Then say the sentences again as you write them on the board. Have children repeat after you. Then point to the adult and the teenager and prompt children to say chorally: **The adult is older than the teenager**. Repeat for other stages on the card.
- Extend by reusing the sentence frame with plural nouns and the verb *are*. Expand with the sentence frames: **Is the child younger than the baby? No, the child is not younger than the baby.**
- **Talk About It** Have partners talk about their own stage of the human growth cycle. Have them compare themselves to their family members.

Practice/Apply

- **Talk About It** Have partners use the Newcomer Card and sentence frames they learned to discuss what they know about the stages of human growth.
- Guide children to complete the activity on page 141.
- Have children cut out pictures from magazines that show people at various stages of life. Then have partners put them in order and discuss the stages with the class. Have them describe other aspects of the photos, using previously learned vocabulary.

Make Cultural Connections

Ask children to think about a friend or relative from their home country. Have them describe that person's stage of growth compared to a teacher or principal in the school.

Name: ______________________________

Use Newcomer Card, page 22

A. Draw a picture of your family.

B. Use words from the box to compare two people in your drawing.

younger	baby	child
adult	teenager	

United States

Language Objective:
Ask and answer questions about your state and some land features

Content Objective:
Understand that there are different states and land features in the United States

Sentence Frames:
Where do you live?
I live in ____.
I live near ____.
Do you live near ____?
Yes, I live near ____.
No, I live closer to ____.

VOCABULARY
near, closer to, state, river, lake

>> Go Digital

Language Transfers Handbook
See pages 16–19 for grammatical structures that do not transfer. Some Cantonese and Hmong speakers may omit prepositions from sentences.

Foundational Skills
Use the Grade 1 High-Frequency Word Cards to practice saying *live, near, to* and *do*; Sound-Spelling Card 10 to teach children how to identify and pronounce the /j/ sound in *region.*

eBook Use digital material to practice vocabulary.

LESSON 1: States

Set Purpose

- Tell children that today they will discuss the states in the United States. Display page 23 of the Newcomer Cards.

Teach/Model Vocabulary

- Lead children through the song/chant on page T6.
- Display the Newcomer Card again. Say: *This is the United States. What do you see?* Children can tell what they know. Then point to and name the state you live in and other states close to your state. Have children repeat. Help with pronunciation.
- Say these sentence frames as you point to the states of the United States: **Where do you live? I live in (your state).** Then say the sentences again as you write them on the board. Have children repeat after you. Then teach the words *near* and *closer to* using your state as a focal point. Point to one of the states bordering your state and ask: **Do you live near (bordering state)?** Have children answer chorally: **Yes, I live near (bordering state).**
- **Talk About It** Have partners discuss their state's proximity to surrounding states.
- Extend with: **Do you live near (state name)? No, I live closer to (state name)**. Expand by having children look at other states on the map and use the sentence frames to ask and answer each other about their proximity to these states.

Practice/Apply

- **Talk About It** Have partners use the Newcomer Card and sentence frames to ask and answer questions about their own state's proximity to rivers and lakes.
- Guide children to complete the activity on page 143. Provide the card or another map for reference.
- Have partners discuss their state drawings. Then have them add more details, such as the name of the state and the city or town they live in.

Make Connections

Ask: *What else can you tell me about ____?* Fill in with the name of your state. Have partners use previously learned vocabulary to discuss. Then they can share with the class.

Name: ______________________________

States

Use Newcomer Card, page 23

Draw a picture of your state. Write a sentence about it.

United States

Language Objective:
Ask and answer questions about different landmarks in the United States

Content Objective:
Identify landmarks in the United States

Sentence Frames:
Do you want to go to the ____?
I do want to go to the ____.
I do not want to go to the ____.
I want to go to the ____.

VOCABULARY
Yosemite Park, Grand Canyon, Statue of Liberty, Mount Rushmore, Golden Gate Bridge, Gateway Arch, Everglades, White House

>> Go Digital

Language Transfers Handbook
See pages 16–19 for grammatical structures that do not transfer. Some Cantonese, Hmong, Korean, Spanish, Tagalog, or Vietnamese speakers may omit verbs from negative sentences.

Foundational Skills
Use Grade 1 High-Frequency Word Cards to practice saying *want, go, to,* and *do*; Sound-Spelling Card 7 to teach children how to identify and pronounce the /g/ sound in *Golden Gate Bridge* and *Grand Canyon.*

eBook Use digital material to practice vocabulary.

LESSON 2: National Landmarks

Set Purpose

- Tell children that today they will discuss national landmarks in the United States. Display page 23 of the Newcomer Cards.

Teach/Model Vocabulary

- Elicit vocabulary from Lesson 1.
- Lead children through the song/chant on page T7.
- Display the Newcomer Card again. Ask: *What can you tell me about these places in the photos?* Point to and name each landmark. Have children repeat. Help with pronunciation.
- Say these sentence frames as you point to a landmark: **Do you want to go to the White House? Yes, I do want to go to the White House.** Then say the sentences again as you write them on the board. Have children repeat after you. Then point to the Grand Canyon and ask: **Do you want to go to the Grand Canyon?** Have children answer chorally: **Yes, I do want to go to the Grand Canyon.** Repeat for other landmarks on the card, in the vocabulary list, and other well-known landmarks in your area.
- **Talk About It** Have partners talk about the national and local landmarks they have seen or heard about.
- Extend by introducing the negative response: **I do not want to go to the Grand Canyon. I want to go to the Golden Gate Bridge.**

Practice/Apply COLLABORATIVE

- **Talk About It** Have partners use the Newcomer Card to describe the White House and the Statue of Liberty. Have them use the sentence frames to state opinions.
- Guide children to complete the activity on page 145.
- Ask children to choose one landmark to draw. Have them add colors and shapes to their drawings. Then have partners describe their pictures to each other using descriptive words.

Make Connections

Have partners discuss which landmark they would like to visit with their family and why.

Name: ____________________

National Landmarks

Use Newcomer Card, page 23

A. Talk about the places with a partner.

B. Draw and label a landmark you want to visit.

United States

Language Objective:
Ask and answer questions about natural features in the United States

Content Objective:
Identify natural features in the United States

Sentence Frames:
Do you want to live near a/an ____?
Yes/No, I want to live near a/an ____.

VOCABULARY
mountain, valley, farm, pond, lake, ocean, river, prairie, plain, tree, live, near
Cognates: montaña, valle, lago, océano

>> Go Digital

Language Transfers Handbook
See pages 16–19 for grammatical structures that do not transfer. Some Korean, Spanish, or Vietnamese speakers may omit subject pronouns.

Foundational Skills
Use the Grade 1 High-Frequency Word Cards to practice saying *want, live,* and *near;* Sound-Spelling Card 22 to teach children how to identify and pronounce /v/ in *valley* and *live.*

eBook and Games Provide audio support, interaction, and practice with the vocabulary.

LESSON 3: Natural Features

Set Purpose

- Tell children that today they will discuss natural features in the United States. Explain that natural features are things that are part of the land and water all around us. Display page 23 of the Newcomer Cards.
- If possible, take children on a quick tour outside to name things in nature.

Teach/Model Vocabulary

- Elicit vocabulary from Lessons 1 and 2.
- Lead children through the song/chant on page T7.
- Display the Newcomer Card again. Ask: *What do you see?* Then point to and name the natural features. Have children repeat. Help with pronunciation.
- Say these sentence frames as you point to things in nature: **Do you want to live near a <u>river</u>? Yes, I want to live near a <u>river</u>. No, I want to live near a <u>mountain</u>.** Then say the sentences again as you write them on the board. Have children repeat after you. Then point to the ocean and ask: **Do you want to live near an <u>ocean</u>?** Nod your head *yes* and have children answer chorally: **Yes, I want to live near an <u>ocean</u>.** Repeat for the other features on the card, the vocabulary list, and near where you live. Remind children when to use *a* and *an.*
- **Talk About It** Have partners talk about different natural features and whether they want to live near them.

Practice/Apply 

- **Talk About It** Have partners use the Newcomer Card and sentence frames they learned to talk about which natural feature they would like to live near.
- Guide children to complete the activity on page 147.
- Have children cut pictures from magazines to make a collage of the natural features they like. Children can share their collages with the class.

Make Cultural Connections

Have children draw pictures of and describe natural features and landmarks in their home country. Have children discuss with a partner. Then have them present to the class.

Use Newcomer Card, page 23

Name: ______________________________

Fill in the graphic organizer with the correct natural features.

land features	water features

My World

Language Objective:
Ask and answer questions about where you and your classmates are from

Content Objective:
Identify the country you are from and activities done there

Sentence Frames:
What country are you from?
I'm from ____.
Did you live in/near a/the ____?
I lived in/near a/the ____.
What do people do in your home country?
In ____, people like to ________.

VOCABULARY
celebrate, play, sports, eat, country, city, town, big, small
Cognate: celebrar

>> Go Digital

Language Transfers Handbook
See pages 16–19 for grammatical structures that do not transfer. Cantonese and Hmong speakers may omit prepositions from sentences.

Foundational Skills
Use Grade 1 High-Frequency Word Cards to practice saying *from, what,* and *are.* Use Sound-Spelling Card 3 to teach children how to identify and pronounce the /s/ sound in *celebrate* and *sports.*

eBook Use digital material for vocabulary practice.

LESSON 1: Where I'm From

Set Purpose

- Tell children that today they will discuss where they are from. Display page 24 of the Newcomer Cards.

Teach/Model Vocabulary

- Lead children through the song/chant on page T7.
- Display the Newcomer Card and ask: *What do you see?*
- Review sentence frames for meeting a new friend: **Hello. I'm ____.** Introduce the sentence frames **What country are you from? I'm from ____.** Then read the text in the speech balloon: **Ni hao. I'm Ying. I'm from China.** Tell children that people can say "Ni hao" when they greet each other in China.
- **Talk About It** Have partners use the Conversation Starters on page T28 to practice exchanging greetings and telling where they're from.
- Point to the pictures and read the labels. Tell children that these pictures tell more about Ying's country. Say these sentence frames as you point to the noodles: **What do people like to do in your home country? In China, people like to eat noodles.** Have children repeat.
- **Talk About It** Partners can discuss food people like to eat in their home country.
- Repeat the instructional routine using the sentence frames in the sidebar. When discussing the city and town pictures, note that the city is Shanghai and the town is in Fenghuang County.

Practice/Apply COLLABORATIVE

- **Talk About It** Have partners use the Newcomer Card and sentence frames to discuss their favorite activities in their home country and why they like them.
- Guide children to complete the activity on page 149.
- Have partners take turns describing their home town or city. The listener draws the place and then the speaker describes it to the class. Elicit descriptive words.

Make Connections

Have partners answer the following prompt: *What else can you tell me about your home country?* Have children discuss their answers with a partner and then with you.

Name: ______________________________

Where I'm From

Use Newcomer Card, page 24

Draw a picture of where you lived in your home country. Describe it to a partner. Complete the sentence.

____

I'm from ______________________________.

My World

Language Objective:
Ask and answer questions about animals in your home country

Content Objective:
Identify which animals live on land and in the water

Sentence Frames:
What land animals live in your home country?
____ live on land in ____.
What water animals live in your home country?
____ live in the water in ____.

VOCABULARY
camel, panda, kangaroo, alligator, giraffe, dolphin, whale, octopus, crab, starfish, monkey, parrot
Cognates: camello, panda, canguro, jirafa, delfín

>> Go Digital

Language Transfers Handbook
See pages 16–19 for grammatical structures that do not transfer. Some Vietnamese speakers may overuse pronouns with nouns.

Foundational Skills
Use Grade 1 High-Frequency Word Cards to practice saying *live, water,* and *other.* Use Sound-Spelling Card 5 to teach children how to identify and pronounce the /f/ sound in *giraffe* and *starfish.*

eBook Use digital material for vocabulary practice.

LESSON 2: Land and Water Animals

Set Purpose

- Tell children that today they will discuss animals that live in their home countries. Display page 24 of the Newcomer Cards.
- If possible, show children pictures of animals from around the world.

Teach/Model Vocabulary

- Elicit country names and vocabulary from Lesson 1.
- Lead children through the song/chant on page T7.
- Display the Newcomer Card. Ask: *What animals do you see?* Then point to and name the animals. Have children repeat. Help with pronunciation.
- Say these sentence frames as you point to the animals: **What land animals live in your home country? Pandas live on land in China** and **What water animals live in your home country? Whales live in the water in China**. Then say the sentences again as you write them on the board, completing them with the names of animals and country. Have children repeat after you. Then repeat for the other animals from the vocabulary list and those that children provide.
- **Talk About It** Have partners talk about the animals they have seen in their home country.

Practice/Apply

- **Talk About It** Have partners use the Newcomer Card and sentence frames they learned to discuss the differences between the land animals and water animals they know.
- Guide children to complete the activity on page 151.
- Play charades. Have children sit in a circle and go clockwise as they whisper the name of an animal into a classmate's ear. That child acts out being that animal while the others try to guess the animal. The first child to name the animal uses the word in a sentence.

Make Connections

Ask children to describe, in detail, the animals that are special to their home country.

Name: ______________________

Use Newcomer Card, page 24

Draw land and sea animals from your home country. Write the names.

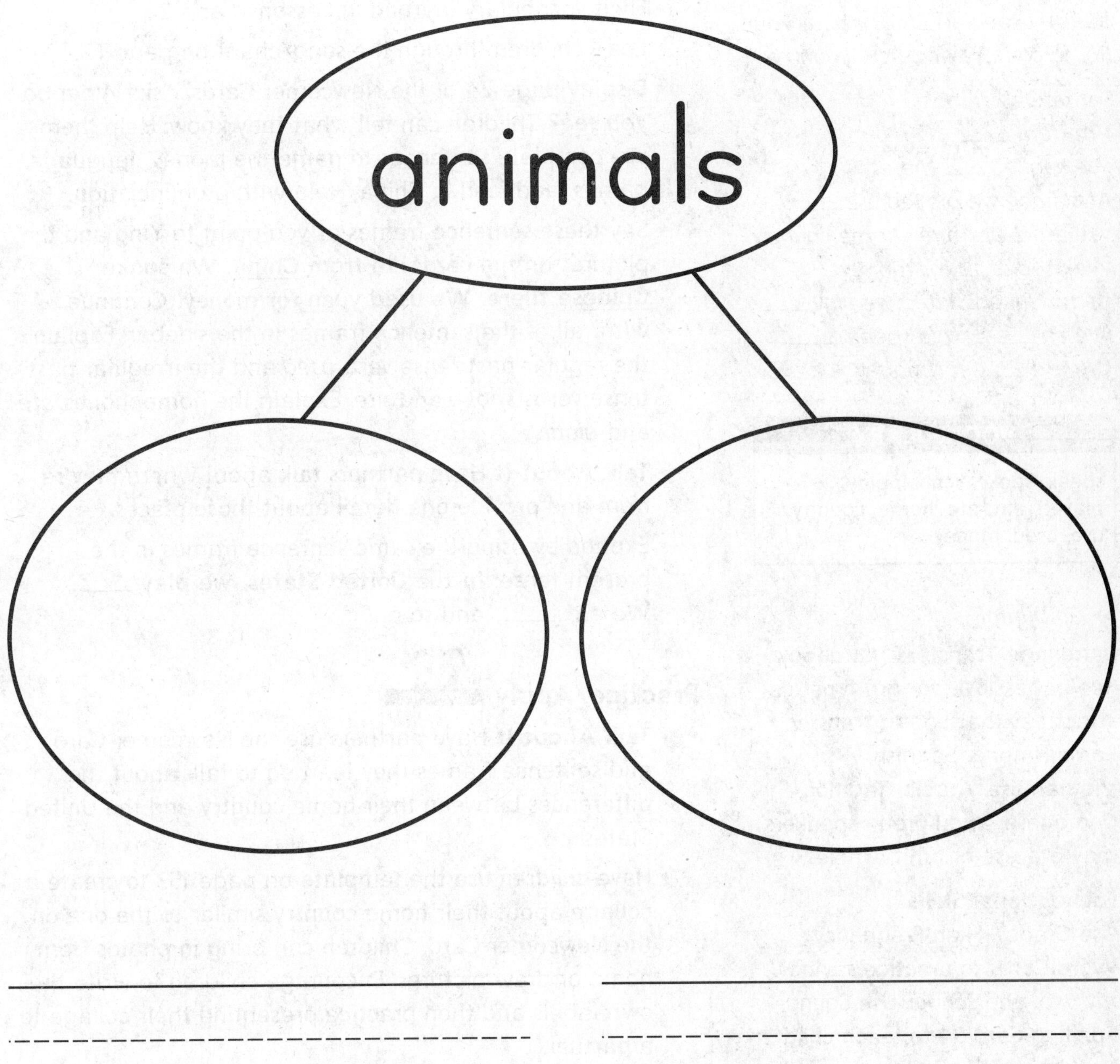

My World

Language Objective:
Compare and contrast your home country and your new country

Content Objective:
Identify special things about your home country and new country

Sentence Frames:
I'm from ____.
We spoke ____ there.
At school, we played ____.
We ate ____ in my home country.
We used ____ for money.
In the United States, we play ____.
We eat ____. We speak ____.
We use ____ for money.

VOCABULARY

speak, spoke, school, play, played, eat, ate, home, country, use, used, money

>> Go Digital

Language Transfers Handbook
See pages 16–19 for grammatical structures that do not transfer. Some Hmong, Spanish, Vietnamese, Arabic, Tagalog, Cantonese, and Korean speakers may overuse or omit articles.

Foundational Skills
Use Grade 1 High-Frequency Word Cards to practice saying *I, my, we,* and *school.* Use Sound-Spelling Card 34 to teach children how to identify and pronounce the /o/ sound in *spoke* and *home.*

eBook and Games Provide audio support, interaction, and practice with the vocabulary.

LESSON 3: In My New Country

Set Purpose

- Tell children that today they will compare things in their home country with things in their new country.

Teach/Model Vocabulary

- Elicit vocabulary learned in Lessons 1 and 2.
- Lead children through the song/chant on page T7.
- Display page 24 of the Newcomer Cards. Ask: *What do you see?* Children can tell what they know. Help them use complete sentences to name the money, language, games, and food in China. Help with pronunciation.
- Say these sentence frames as you point to Ying and the pictures on the card: **I'm from China. We spoke Chinese there. We used yuan for money.** Continue with all of the sentence frames in the sidebar. Explain the regular past tense verb *used* and the irregular past tense verbs *spoke* and *ate*. Explain the homophones *ate* and *eight*.
- **Talk About It** Have partners talk about where they're from and provide one detail about those places.
- Expand by using the same sentence frames in the present tense: **In the United States, we play ____. We eat ____,** and so on.

Practice/Apply INTERPRETIVE

- **Talk About It** Have partners use the Newcomer Card and sentence frames they learned to talk about the differences between their home country and the United States.
- Have children use the template on page 153 to create a collage about their home country similar to the one on the Newcomer Card. Children can bring in photos from home or draw pictures. Encourage children to write their own labels and then practice presenting their collage to a partner.

Make Cultural Connections

Have children bring in a special souvenir from their home country and use that and their collage to tell the class a few things about where they're from. Have children ask and answer questions after each presentation.

Name: ______________________

In My New Country

Use Newcomer Card, page 24

Draw or paste pictures that tell about your home country. Write a sentence about what you did there.

SONGS/CHANTS

START SMART: Alphabet, Lesson 1, p. 2

Let's all sing, let's all cheer:
The letters of the alphabet are all here!
A, B, C, D, E, F, G, H, I, J, K, L, M, N, O, P,
Q, R, S, T, U, V, W, X, Y, Z

START SMART: Alphabet, Lesson 2, p. 4

Uppercase letters, they are tall.
Lowercase letters, they are small.
Uppercase A, way up high.
Lowercase a, way down low.
How many uppercase and lowercase letters do you know?

[Repeat for other uppercase and lowercase letters.]

START SMART: Alphabet, Lesson 3, p. 6

My name is __________.
My name is __________.
I spell my name __________.
What is your name?
What is your name?

START SMART: Greetings, Lesson 1, p. 8

Hello, Hello.
I say hello.
I like to ask your name.

Hello, hello.
I say hello.
You smile and do the same.

START SMART: Greetings, Lesson 2, p. 10

Numbers, numbers everywhere.
Numbers here and numbers there.
My address has a number, too:
4 or 5 or even 2!

START SMART: Greetings, Lesson 3, p. 12

I like fruit. It's good to eat.
Crunchy, juicy, and very sweet.
Apples, bananas, grapes, and a plum.
Fruit to eat! Yum, yum, yum.

START SMART: Shapes and Colors, L1, p. 14

Circle, triangle,
Square, and rectangle.
Look at all the shapes.
Circle, triangle,
Square, and rectangle.
What's your favorite shape?

START SMART: Shapes and Colors, L2, p. 16

Clap for red.
Clap, clap!
Knock for blue.
Knock, knock!
Tap for green.
Tap, tap!

Sing with me!
Clap, clap... red!
Knock, knock... blue!
Tap, tap... green!

START SMART: Shapes and Colors, L3, p. 18

Tick-tock, tick-tock.
I have a present for you.
What is it? What is it?
Is it green? Is it blue?

Tick-tock, tick-tock.
I have a circle for you.
What is it? What is it?
Is it green? Is it blue?

START SMART: Numbers, Lesson 1, p. 20

1, 2, 3.
Count with me!
4, 5, 6.
Now repeat!

1, 2, 3.
Count with me!
4, 5, 6.
Now repeat!

START SMART: Numbers, Lesson 2, p. 22

Happy Birthday!
How old are you?

I'm __________ years old.
You are __________ years old!

Happy Birthday!
I have something for you.
A cake with __________ candles
Is a present for you!

START SMART: Numbers, Lesson 3, p. 24

1 apple, 2 apples, 3 apples.
We have three!
4 apples, 5 apples, 6 apples.
We have six!

UNIT 1: In the Classroom, Lesson 1, p. 28

Books, crayons, and glue.
Three books, two crayons, one glue.
One glue, two crayons, three books.

Books, crayons, and glue.
Two books, two crayons, one glue.
One glue, two crayons, two books.

UNIT 1: In the Classroom, Lesson 2, p. 30

Reading and writing all day long.
Counting and counting: so much fun.
Matching and talking: blah, blah, blah.
Playing and singing: fa, la, la.

Reading and writing all day long.
Counting and counting: it's a snap.
Talking and listening: shh, shh, shh.
Singing and playing: clap, clap, clap.

UNIT 1: In the Classroom, Lesson 3, p. 32

I say hello.
Then I sit down.
I take a crayon
And write my name.

I raise my hand.
Then talk and listen.
I say goodbye
When I am leaving.

UNIT 1: Computers, Lesson 1, p. 34

We use many things in school.
Sometimes they are hard to find.
Where is my pen?
It is on your desk!
Where is my book?
It is by the glue!
Where are my things?
They are near you!

UNIT 1: Computers, Lesson 2, p. 36

Sometimes I don't know.
I don't understand.
I think I need help.
Please say it again.

Yes, I can help you.
My teacher says yes.
What is your question?
I say it again.

UNIT 1: Computers, Lesson 3, p. 38

Computer, computer, how do we use it?
First turn it on and look at the screen.
Computer, computer, how do we use it?
Type on the keyboard, move the mouse, and click.
Computer, computer, I know how to use it!

UNIT 1: A Day at School, Lesson 1, p. 40

School, school,
We are in school.
A gym, a library are all in school.

The hallway, the office,
The restrooms, and more
Are places we go
When we come in the door.

UNIT 1: A Day at School, Lesson 2, p. 42

I write in school.
I read in school.
I play in school all day.

I walk in school.
I talk in school.
There is a lot to say!

UNIT 1: A Day at School, Lesson 3, p. 44

The gym teacher is in the gym.
Is this the nurse's office?
What do you see?
This is the nurse's office.
She can help you and me!

UNIT 1: Calendar, Lesson 1, p. 46

There are seven days in a week.
Knock, clap for Sunday.
Clap, clap for Monday.

Knock, knock for Tuesday.
Thumbs up for Wednesday.
High five for Thursday.

Did we miss anything?
Knock, clap for Friday.
Tap, clap for Saturday.
There are seven days in a week.

UNIT 1: Calendar, Lesson 2, p. 48

Get up.
Brush my hair.
Finding something good to wear.

Read in school.
Play, play, play.
This is what I did today!

UNIT 1: Calendar, Lesson 3, p. 50

It's morning,
It's early,
I'm ready for school.

It's evening,
It's late,
I'm ready for bed.

UNIT 1: Weather, Lesson 1, p. 52

Sunny days, sunny days, lots of sun.
Cloudy days, cloudy days, bye-bye sun.
Rainy days, rainy days, it's drip and drop.
Snowy days, snowy days, the snow never stops.

UNIT 1: Weather, Lesson 2, p. 54

Four seasons, four seasons,
I like them all.
Winter, spring, summer, fall.

Winter snow.
Spring and flowers.
Summer sun.
Fall is leaves and showers.

UNIT 1: Weather, Lesson 3, p. 56

Look at the night sky:
So many stars.
Look at the day sky:
There is the sun!

Look at the night sky:
I see the moon.
Look at the day sky:
It's all bright and blue.

UNIT 2: My Body, Lesson 1, p. 60

One head, one face,
One mouth, two eyes, two ears,
Two arms, two legs, and don't forget two feet!

UNIT 2: My Body, Lesson 2, p. 62

How do I stay healthy? I...
Brush, brush, brush my teeth.
Wash, wash, wash my face.
Brush, brush, brush my hair.
Wash, wash, wash my hands.
I also take a bath!

UNIT 2: My Body, Lesson 3, p. 64

I feel, I hear, I taste, I smell, I see!
I feel with my hands, soft, soft, soft.
I hear with my ears, dong, dong, dong.
I taste with my mouth, yum, yum, yum.
I smell with my nose, sniff, sniff, sniff.
I see with my eyes, look, look, look.
Five senses for you and me!

UNIT 2: Clothing, Lesson 1, p. 66

Hmmm... I like this blue shirt and blue pants. Lots of blue!
Hmmm... I like this red dress and white boots, too.
I know! I'll wear this black shirt, shorts, and these shoes!

UNIT 2: Clothing, Lesson 2, p. 68

Spring, summer, winter, fall:
What do you wear for them all?
Spring is warm. I can wear shorts.
Summer is hot! Wear a bathing suit.
Winter is cold! Wear mittens and boots.
Fall is cool, don't forget your hat!

UNIT 2: Clothing, Lesson 3, p. 70

I'm going to swim, I'm going to swim.
Wear a bathing suit!

I'm going to hike, I'm going to hike.
Wear sneakers or boots!

[Repeat for other actions.]

UNIT 2: Feelings, Lesson 1, p. 72

I'm happy! Hahaha!
I'm scared. Ahhhh!
I'm sad. Waaaa!
I'm mad. Grrrr!
I'm sleepy. Zzz...
Happy, scared, sad, mad, and sleepy
With these words we talk about feelings.

UNIT 2: Feelings, Lesson 2, p. 74

What do we like to do with friends?
We laugh and we play.
We work and we eat.
Being with friends is such a treat!

UNIT 2: Feelings, Lesson 3, p. 76

Help, help! My friend needs help!
What do I do?
You care for your friend.
You share with your friend.
You listen to your friend.
You talk to your friend, too.

UNIT 2: My Family, Lesson 1, p. 78

Here is a family. Here is another.
Families stay with each other.
There's a father and mother,
And a son and a daughter,
Who are also a sister and brother.
That's the grandfather and grandmother.
Happy or sad they stay together!

UNIT 2: My Family, Lesson 2, p. 80

Long or short,
Shorter or shortest?
Dark or light,
Lighter or lightest?
Short or tall,
Taller or tallest?

UNIT 2: My Family, Lesson 3, p. 82

Families eat, laugh, visit, and play.
That's what they do together.
They laugh together all day.
And go to the park in the sun.
They visit relatives and stay,
Go shopping for clothes,
Then eat together, hooray!

UNIT 2: My Home, Lesson 1, p. 84

We all live in different places,
We all live in different spaces.
What kind of home do you live in?
Some of us live in apartment buildings
With other people next door.
Some of us live in mobile homes
Which have one floor.
And some of us live in houses
With two rooms or more.

UNIT 2: My Home, Lesson 2, p. 86

Where does the couch go?
In the living room? Yes!
Where does the bed go?
In the bathroom? No!
That goes in the bedroom.
And where does the sink go?
In the kitchen? Yes!

UNIT 2: My Home, Lesson 3, p. 88

In the kitchen, someone is cooking.
Can you smell the food?
Yum, yum, yum.
And someone else is recycling.
Clank, clank, clank!
In the living room, someone is sweeping.
Sweep, sweep, sweep!

UNIT 3: My Community, Lesson 1, p. 92

Where's the school?
Help me look!
Next to a bank?
Or across from the park?

Where's the school?
Help me look!
Is it right there, next to you?
It's down the street. I see it, too!

UNIT 3: My Community, Lesson 2, p. 94

Who works in a hospital?
I'm a nurse.
I do, I do!

Who works on a bus?
I'm a bus driver.
I do, I do!

Who carries mail?
I'm a mail carrier.
I do, I do!

UNIT 3: My Community, Lesson 3, p. 96

What does she do?
What does she do?
She teaches about the sun and the moon.

What does he do?
What does he do?
He drives a bus and takes us to school.

UNIT 3: Park, Lesson 1, p. 98

Let's go to the park!
Sit on the benches. Sit, sit, sit.
Swing on the swings. Swing, swing, swing.
Eat at the picnic tables. Eat, eat, eat.
And ride on a bicycle. Ride, ride, ride.

UNIT 3: Park, Lesson 2, p. 100

At the park with family and friends,
The fun never ends.
I walk. Step! I run. Hop!
I skip. Skip! I kick. Whoop!
I throw. Whoosh! I play soccer. Whoop!
And I fly a kite! Wee!

UNIT 3: Park, Lesson 3, p. 102

The park is full of living things,
And if you look closely
You'll see something growing.
There's a flower! There's a tree!
You'll see something with wings.

There's a bird. There's an insect.
You'll see something moving.
There's a squirrel. There's a dog.

UNIT 3: Transportation, Lesson 1, p. 104

Walk signs, stop signs,
Street signs all around!
Crosswalk, bus stop,
Street signs all around!

Stop or walk?
Come or go?
See the signs
So you will know.

UNIT 3: Transportation, Lesson 2, p. 106

How do we get from here to there?
A car can take us anywhere!
We take a bus around the town.
Going uptown, going down.
To get from Park Street over to Main,
We pay our fare and take the train.

UNIT 3: Transportation, Lesson 3, p. 108

Make a left turn, make a right.
The school is almost right in sight.
Look for the parks, look for the mall,
The school is right between them all!
Cross the street, one block away.
There's the mall. You found the way!

UNIT 3: Food and Meals, Lesson 1, p. 110

I'm hungry, I'm hungry.
Let's order! Let's eat!
I'd like something sweet!
Or maybe salty, too.
A sandwich? A drink? Or a soup?
The menu will tell us what is there
To crunch or munch or offer to share.

UNIT 3: Food and Meals, Lesson 2, p. 112

Oodles of noodles,
Eggs and cheese,
Carrots, carrots.
I'd like more please.

Yogurt, yogurt,
Rice and peas,
Cereal, cereal.
I'd like more please.

UNIT 3: Food and Meals, Lesson 3, p. 114

Lunch at school, lunch at school.
What are you having
For lunch at school?

Are you having soup?
I'm having some carrots.
He's having some soup.

Are you having fruit?
I'm having some noodles.
He's having some fruit.

UNIT 3: Shopping, Lesson 1, p. 116

At the store, at the store.
It's time to shop at the grocery store.
I need some bread. Where do I go?
Go to the bakery.
Go, go, go.

I need some apples. Where do I go?
Go to produce.
Go, go, go.

UNIT 3: Shopping, Lesson 2, p. 118

I have a dollar, I have a dime,
What can I buy, what can I buy?
Three apples, three apples, I can buy
three apples.
I have a quarter, I have a nickel.
What can I buy, what can I buy?
One orange, one orange, I can buy
one orange.

UNIT 3: Shopping, Lesson 3, p. 120

At the grocery store, we can
Make a list and have a plan
Of what to buy, what we need.
We need a list, yes indeed.
At the grocery store, we can
Push a cart, with our hand.
We pick up fruit and veggies, too.
It's a good day at the store for you!

UNIT 4: Measurement, Lesson 1, p. 124

If something's long,
We measure the length.
The rose bush is two pencils tall.

If something's heavy
We measure the weight.
Three tomatoes are heavier than one!

UNIT 4: Measurement, Lesson 2, p. 126

How are these leaves the same?
The leaves are both green.
How are these leaves different?
This is a tomato plant leaf

And this is a rose bush leaf.

UNIT 4: Measurement, Lesson 3, p. 128

How long is this desk?
Let's find out.
Let's use this crayon to figure it out.
How long is this book?
Let's find out.
Let's use this crayon to figure it out.

UNIT 4: Animals, Lesson 1, p. 130

Shhh! Watch closely and you'll see
Wild animals and insects roaming free:
There's a bear running: crash, crash, crash.
There's a snake crawling: hiss, hiss, hiss.
There's a tiger jumping: scratch,
scratch, scratch.
And there's a bee flying: buzzzzzzzzzz!

UNIT 4: Animals, Lesson 2, p. 132

Do you have a pet to play with? Some of
us do!
Some have a bird that tweets and sings, too.
Some have a dog that likes to catch.
Some have a cat that likes to scratch.
Some have a fish that swims all day.
Some have a hamster that likes to play.

Unit 4: Animals, Lesson 3, p. 134

On the farm, the animals run around,
Eating and jumping up and down.
The rooster clucks, runs, and flies.
The horse watches as he goes by.
The sheep baa and eat the grass,
And the goats jump as they all pass.

UNIT 4: Growth and Change, Lesson 1, p. 136

First, there is an egg, very small.
Then, a caterpillar that will crawl.
Next, it turns into a pupa and hides.
Finally, it turns into a butterfly and flies!

UNIT 4: Growth and Change, Lesson 2, p. 138

First, you plant a seed in the ground
And water until a seedling is found.
Then, a budding plant will start to grow.
Finally, a flower will start to show.

UNIT 4: Growth and Change, Lesson 3, p. 140

First, you were a baby and cried a lot.
Now you are a child and like to play.
Next, you'll be a teenager, you'll learn a lot.
Then, you'll be an adult and work all day.
Every stage is lots of fun.
Which will be your favorite one?

UNIT 4: United States, Lesson 1, p. 142

Welcome to the USA,
USA, USA
50 states in the USA, USA, USA

States are here and everywhere.
Here is my state, yours is there.
From sea to sea
and north to south
There's so much here
to smile about.

UNIT 4: United States, Lesson 2, p. 144

So many national landmarks.
Which ones do you want to see?
The Statue of Liberty,
The Grand Canyon
Or the White House for me!
Mount Rushmore,
The Golden Gate Bridge,
Or maybe Yosemite!

UNIT 4: United States, Lesson 3, p. 146

I want to live somewhere
Where I can see the water in motion:
Near a river, a lake, or the ocean.

I want to live somewhere
Where there's no one else but me:
Near a mountain, a farm, or a prairie.

UNIT 4: My World, Lesson 1, p. 148

Where are you from?
A big city or a small town?
Tell me what people eat and what they play.
And what money you used, every day.
What animals could you see in a tree?
What animals liked to swim in the sea?

UNIT 4: My World, Lesson 2, p. 150

What animals do you see?
Do you see pandas?
I don't see pandas.
Do you see camels? Please tell!
I don't see camels.
What animals do you see?
I see starfish. I live by the sea.

UNIT 4: My World, Lesson 3, p. 152

Where are you from?
How do you pay?
In the United States we use dollars,
That's how we pay!
Where are you from?
What do you play?
In the United States we play baseball,
That's what we play!

ANSWER KEY

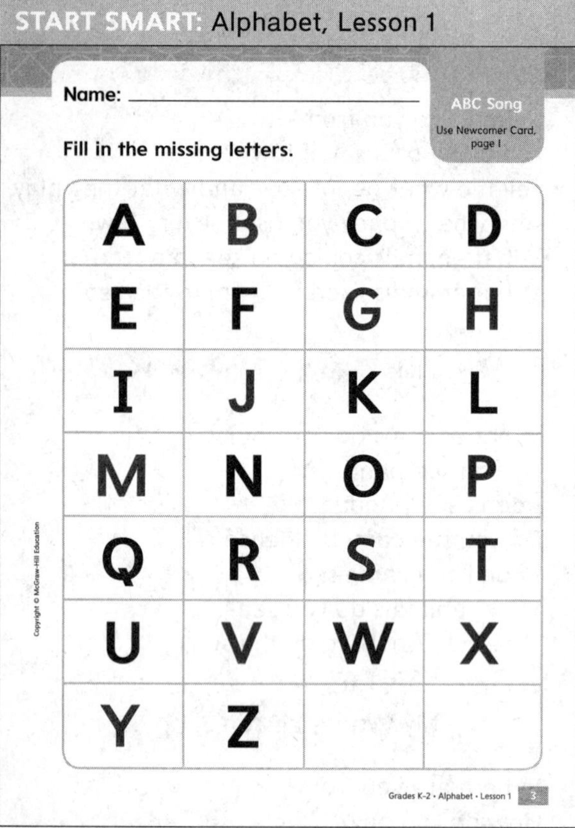

START SMART: Alphabet, Lesson 1

Name: ______________________

ABC Song

Use Newcomer Card, page 1

Fill in the missing letters.

A	B	C	D
E	F	G	H
I	J	K	L
M	N	O	P
Q	R	S	T
U	V	W	X
Y	Z		

Copyright © McGraw-Hill Education

Grades K-2 • Alphabet • Lesson 1 3

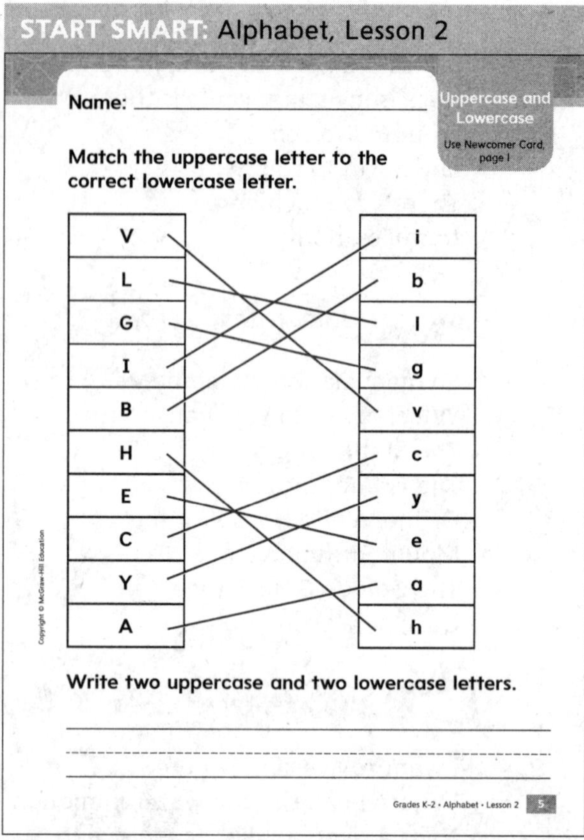

START SMART: Alphabet, Lesson 2

Name: ______________________

Uppercase and Lowercase

Use Newcomer Card, page 1

Match the uppercase letter to the correct lowercase letter.

V	i
L	b
G	l
I	g
B	v
H	c
E	y
C	e
Y	a
A	h

Write two uppercase and two lowercase letters.

Copyright © McGraw-Hill Education

Grades K-2 • Alphabet • Lesson 2 5

START SMART: Alphabet, Lesson 3

Name: ______________________

Spelling My Name

Use Newcomer Card, page 1

Draw a picture of yourself. Then complete the sentence.

My name is Answers will vary.

Copyright © McGraw-Hill Education

Grades K-2 • Alphabet • Lesson 3 7

START SMART: Greetings, Lesson 1

Name: ______________________

Hello and Goodbye

Use Newcomer Card, page 2

Draw a picture of yourself meeting new friends in class. Then write their names.

Drawings will vary.

Answers will vary.

Copyright © McGraw-Hill Education

Grades K-2 • Greetings • Lesson 1 9

START SMART: Greetings, Lesson 2

Talking About You and Me

Use Newcomer Card, page 2

Name: ____________________

Circle the numbers in your phone number. Then write your phone number on the line.

1 2 3
4 5 6
7 8 9
0

Answers will vary.

Copyright © McGraw-Hill Education

Grades K-2 • Greetings • Lesson 2 11

START SMART: Greetings, Lesson 3

Likes and Dislikes

Use Newcomer Card, page 2

Name: ____________________

Write or draw fruits you like. Then write or draw fruits you don't like. Talk to a partner about them.

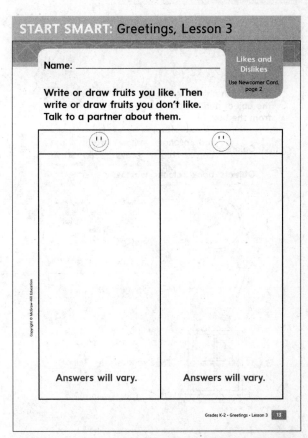

☺	☹
Answers will vary.	Answers will vary.

Copyright © McGraw-Hill Education

Grades K-2 • Greetings • Lesson 3 13

START SMART: Shapes and Colors, Lesson 1

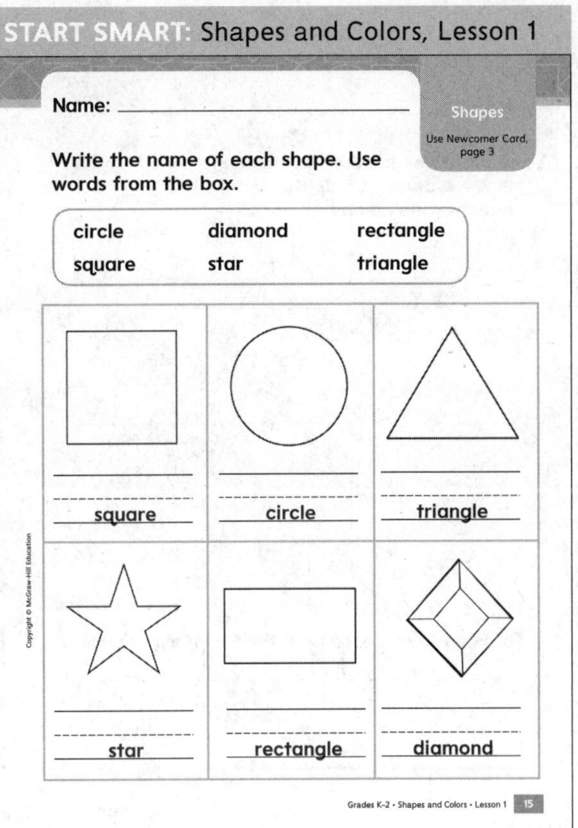

Shapes

Use Newcomer Card, page 3

Name: ____________________

Write the name of each shape. Use words from the box.

circle	diamond	rectangle
square	star	triangle

square	circle	triangle
star	rectangle	diamond

Copyright © McGraw-Hill Education

Grades K-2 • Shapes and Colors • Lesson 1 15

START SMART: Shapes and Colors, Lesson 2

Colors

Use Newcomer Card, page 3

Name: ____________________

Say and trace the words. Then fill in each shape with the correct color.

1. blue diamond
2. red triangle
3. orange rectangle
4. green star
5. yellow circle
6. purple square

Copyright © McGraw-Hill Education

Grades K-2 • Shapes and Colors • Lesson 2 17

ANSWER KEY

START SMART: Shapes and Colors, Lesson 3

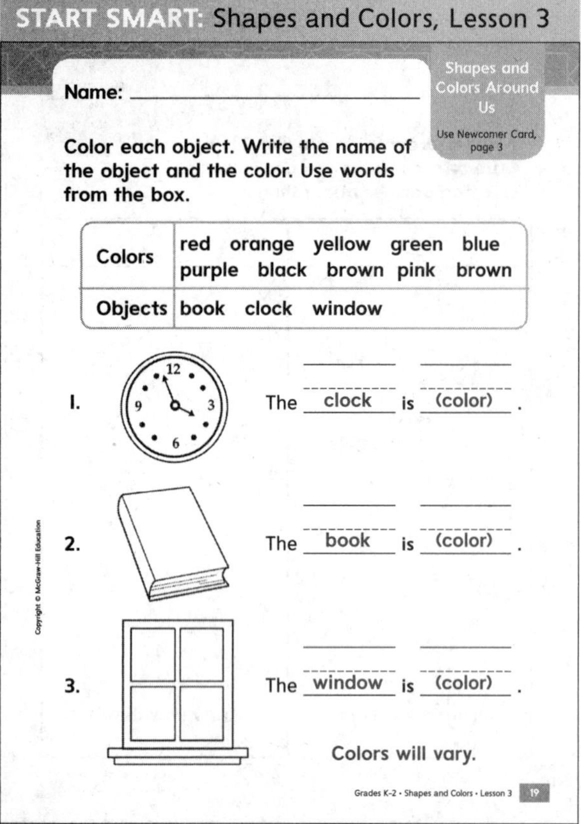

Shapes and Colors Around Us

Use Newcomer Card, page 3

Name: ______________________

Color each object. Write the name of the object and the color. Use words from the box.

Colors	red orange yellow green blue purple black brown pink brown
Objects	book clock window

1. The clock is (color).

2. The book is (color).

3. The window is (color).

Colors will vary.

Grades K-2 • Shapes and Colors • Lesson 3 19

START SMART: Numbers, Lesson 1

Numbers 1-20

Use Newcomer Card, page 4

Name: ______________________

Fill in the missing numbers. Then write the missing numbers on the line.

1	2	__
4	5	6
__	8	__
10	__	12
13	14	15
__	17	__
19	20	

3 7 9 11 16 17 18

Grades K-2 • Numbers • Lesson 1 21

START SMART: Numbers, Lesson 2

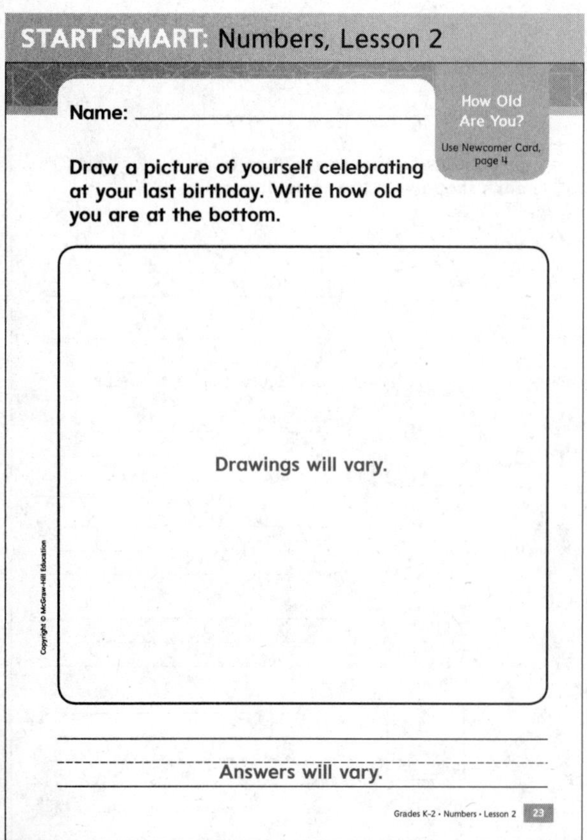

How Old Are You?

Use Newcomer Card, page 4

Name: ______________________

Draw a picture of yourself celebrating at your last birthday. Write how old you are at the bottom.

Drawings will vary.

Answers will vary.

Grades K-2 • Numbers • Lesson 2 23

START SMART: Numbers, Lesson 3

How Many?

Use Newcomer Card, page 4

Name: ______________________

A. Read the number. Count the items in the pictures. Circle the picture that matches the number.

7

3

B. Write a sentence about the number of gifts.

Grades K-2 • Numbers • Lesson 3 25

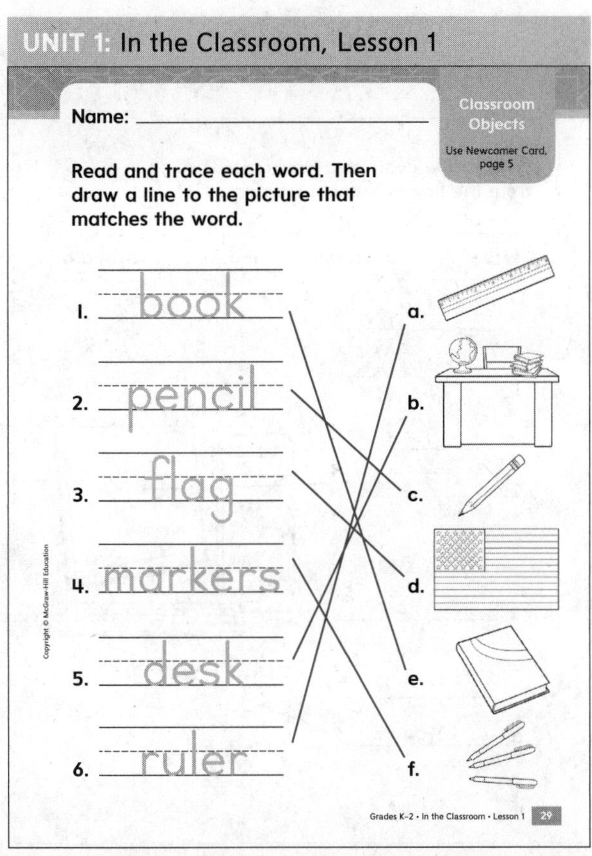

UNIT 1: In the Classroom, Lesson 1

Classroom Objects

Use Newcomer Card, page 5

Name: ______________________

Read and trace each word. Then draw a line to the picture that matches the word.

1. book — a.
2. pencil — b.
3. flag — c.
4. markers — d.
5. desk — e.
6. ruler — f.

Copyright © McGraw-Hill Education

Grades K–2 • In the Classroom • Lesson 1 29

UNIT 1: In the Classroom, Lesson 2

Classroom Activities

Use Newcomer Card, page 5

Name: ______________________

A. Read each word. Circle the picture that matches the classroom activity.

1. reading
2. writing
3. counting

B. What classroom activity do you see?

Answers may vary.

Copyright © McGraw-Hill Education

Grades K–2 • In the Classroom • Lesson 2 31

UNIT 1: In the Classroom, Lesson 3

Classroom Commands

Use Newcomer Card, page 5

Name: ______________________

A. Talk with a partner about the pictures.

B. Draw something your teacher tells you to do. Write the command.

Copyright © McGraw-Hill Education

Grades K–2 • In the Classroom • Lesson 3 33

UNIT 1: Computers, Lesson 1

Location of Objects

Use Newcomer Card, page 6

Name: ______________________

A. Read the word. Circle the picture that the word describes.

1. in
2. on
3. by

B. Where is the girl?

She is ___on___ the chair.

Copyright © McGraw-Hill Education

Grades K–2 • Computers • Lesson 1 35

ANSWER KEY

UNIT 1: Computers, Lesson 2

Name:
Asking for Help
Use Newcomer Card, page 6
A. Talk with a partner about the pictures.
B. Draw what happens next.
Grades K-2 • Computers • Lesson 2 37

UNIT 1: Computers, Lesson 3

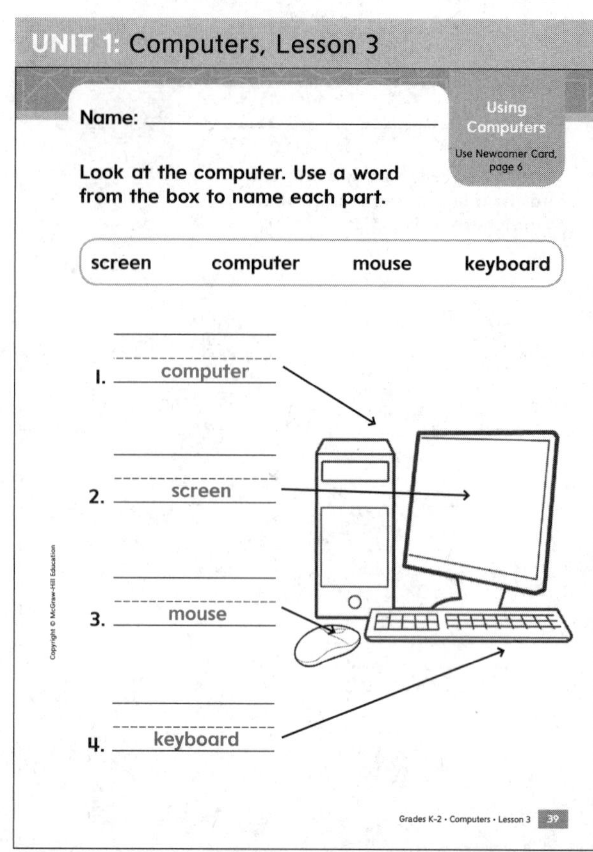

Name:
Using Computers
Use Newcomer Card, page 6
Look at the computer. Use a word from the box to name each part.
screen computer mouse keyboard
1. computer
2. screen
3. mouse
4. keyboard
Grades K-2 • Computers • Lesson 3 39

UNIT 1: A Day at School, Lesson 1

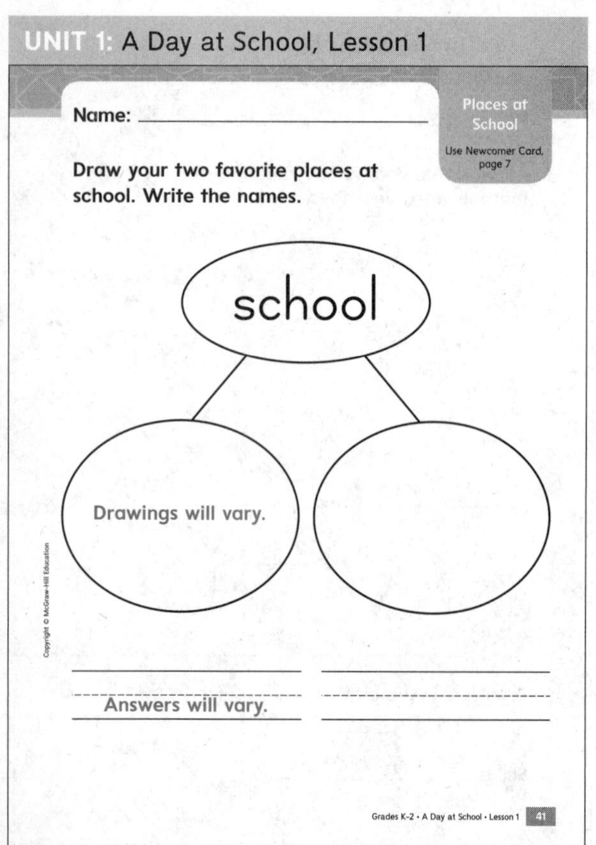

Name:
Places at School
Use Newcomer Card, page 7
Draw your two favorite places at school. Write the names.
school
Drawings will vary.
Answers will vary.
Grades K-2 • A Day at School • Lesson 1 41

UNIT 1: A Day at School, Lesson 2

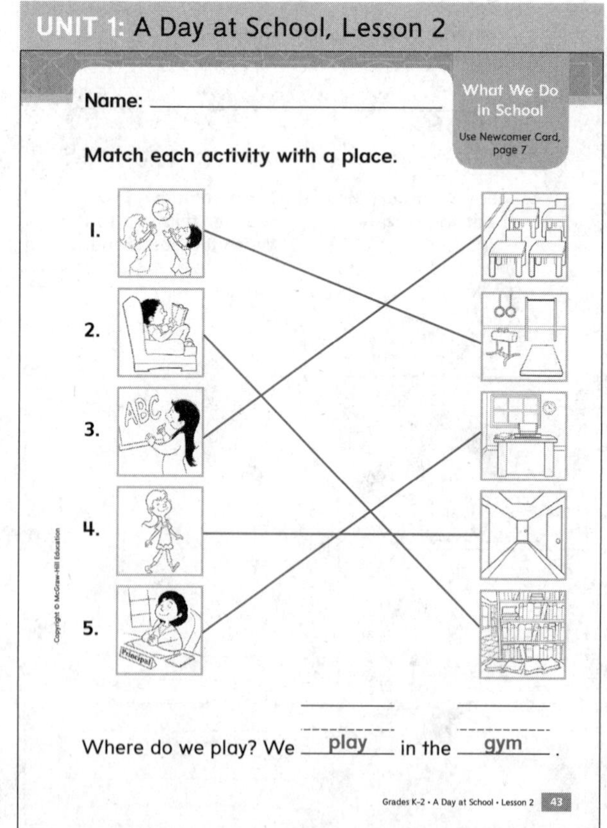

Where do we play? We play in the gym.

UNIT 1: A Day at School, Lesson 3

People in School
Use Newcomer Card, page 7

Name: ______

Draw a person in school and where you see that person. Then complete the sentence.

Drawings will vary.

The **Answers vary.** is in the ______.

UNIT 1: Calendar, Lesson 1

Days and Months
Use Newcomer Card, page 8

Name: ______

A. Read the days of the week.

Put a ◯ around today.
Put a □ around yesterday.
Put a △ around tomorrow.

Sunday	Monday	Tuesday	Wednesday	Thursday	Friday	Saturday
			Answers will vary.			

B. Write the name of one day you don't go to school.

Saturday Sunday

C. Write the month of your birthday.

Answers will vary.

UNIT 1: Calendar, Lesson 2

School-Day Routine
Use Newcomer Card, page 8

Name: ______

Draw a picture in each box to show what you do *First, Then, Next,* and *Finally* in the morning.

First

Then

Next

Finally

Answers will vary.

UNIT 1: Calendar, Lesson 3

Times of the Day
Use Newcomer Card, page 8

Name: ______

Use the words from the box to tell when each activity takes place.

morning afternoon night

1. It's **morning**.
2. It's **morning**.
3. It's **afternoon**.
4. It's **night**.
5. It's **afternoon**.

ANSWER KEY

UNIT 1: Weather, Lesson 1

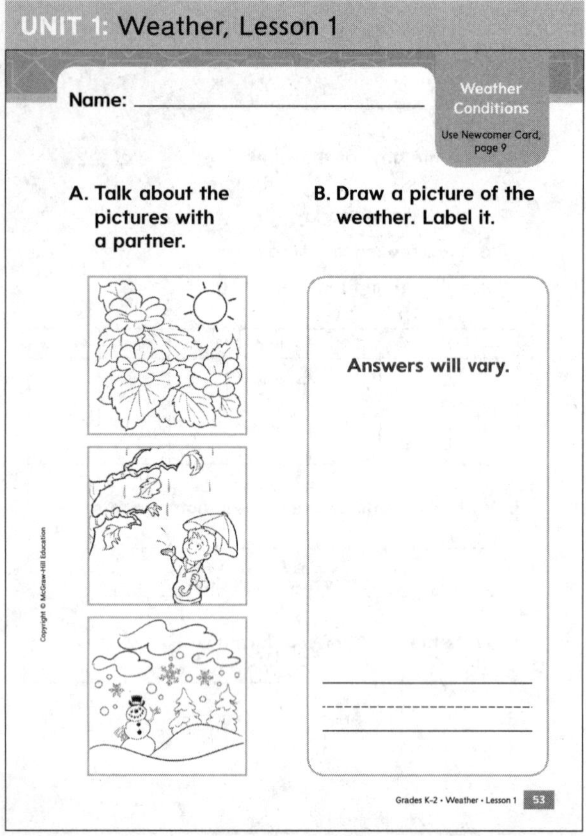

Name: ____________

Weather Conditions

Use Newcomer Card, page 9

A. Talk about the pictures with a partner.

B. Draw a picture of the weather. Label it.

Answers will vary.

Copyright © McGraw-Hill Education

Grades K-2 • Weather • Lesson 1 53

UNIT 1: Weather, Lesson 2

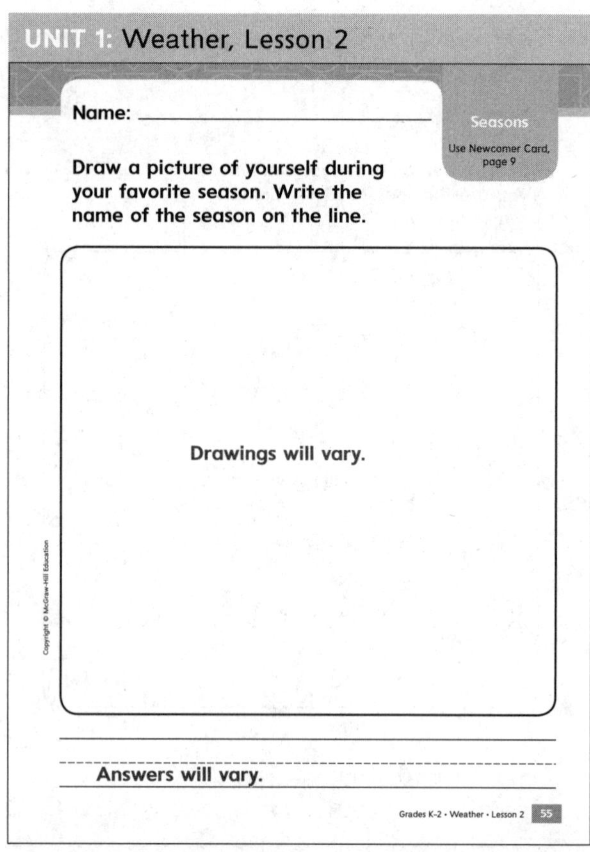

Name: ____________

Seasons

Use Newcomer Card, page 9

Draw a picture of yourself during your favorite season. Write the name of the season on the line.

Drawings will vary.

Answers will vary.

Copyright © McGraw-Hill Education

Grades K-2 • Weather • Lesson 2 55

UNIT 1: Weather, Lesson 3

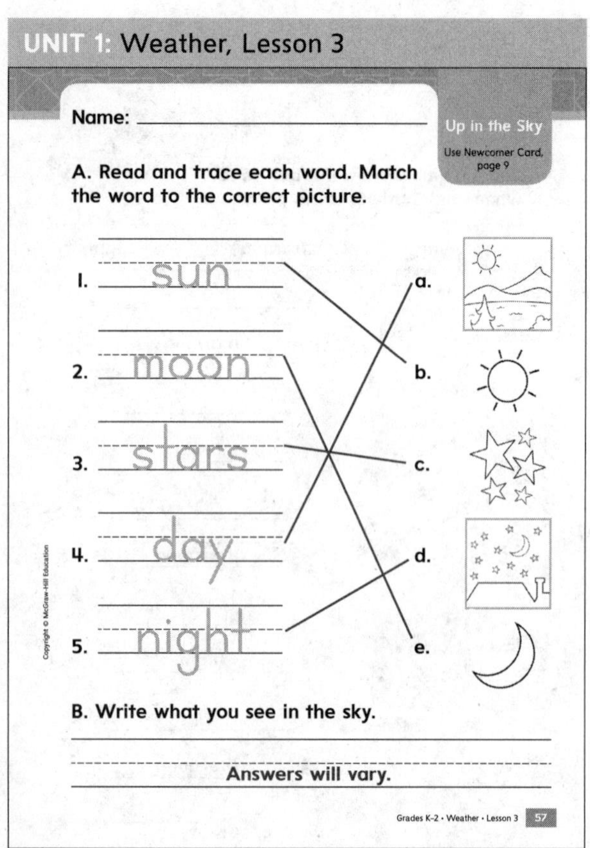

Name: ____________

Up in the Sky

Use Newcomer Card, page 9

A. Read and trace each word. Match the word to the correct picture.

1. sun
2. moon
3. stars
4. day
5. night

a.
b.
c.
d.
e.

B. Write what you see in the sky.

Answers will vary.

Copyright © McGraw-Hill Education

Grades K-2 • Weather • Lesson 3 57

UNIT 2: My Body, Lesson 1

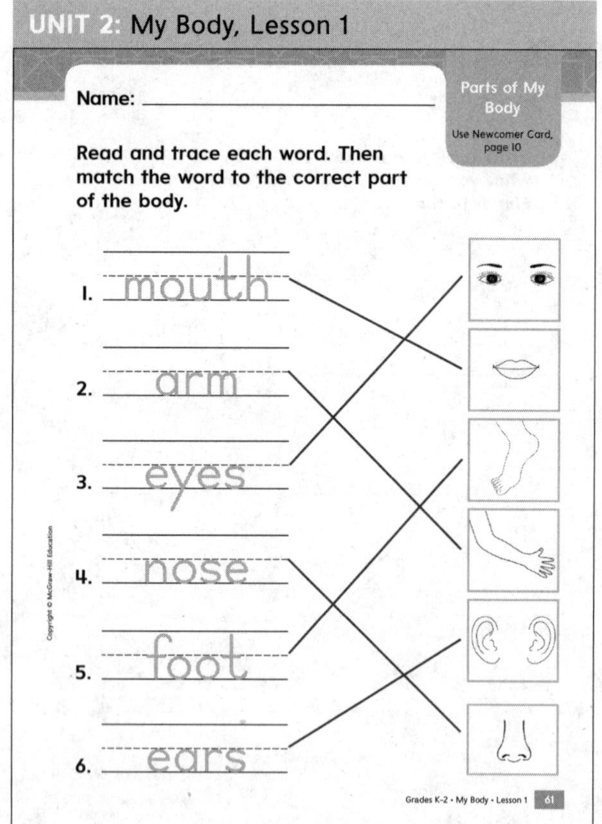

Name: ____________

Parts of My Body

Use Newcomer Card, page 10

Read and trace each word. Then match the word to the correct part of the body.

1. mouth
2. arm
3. eyes
4. nose
5. foot
6. ears

Copyright © McGraw-Hill Education

Grades K-2 • My Body • Lesson 1 61

UNIT 2: My Body, Lesson 2

Name: ______

Healthy Routines

Use Newcomer Card, page 10

Draw two ways to stay healthy. Write the actions on the lines.

stay healthy

Drawings will vary.

Answers may vary. Answers may vary.

UNIT 2: My Body, Lesson 3

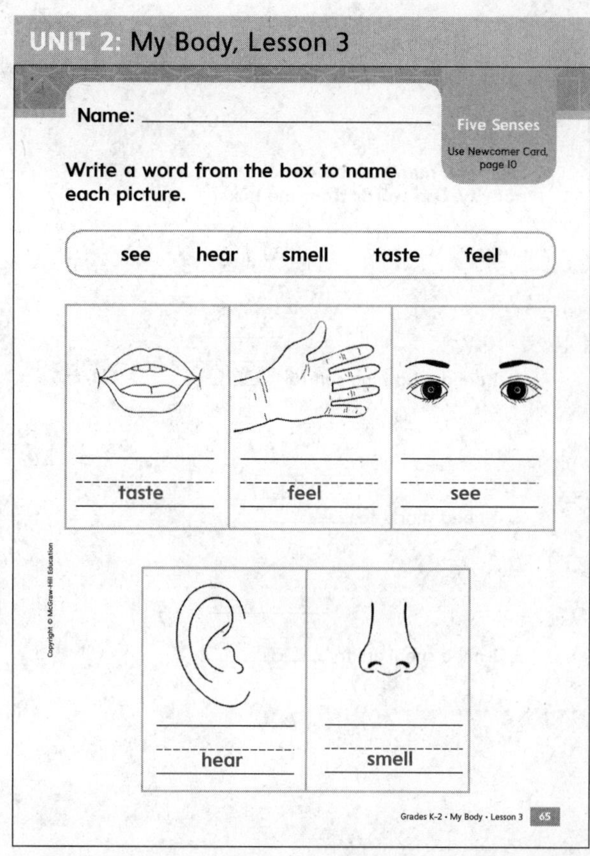
Name: ______

Five Senses

Use Newcomer Card, page 10

Write a word from the box to name each picture.

see hear smell taste feel

taste feel see

hear smell

UNIT 2: Clothing, Lesson 1

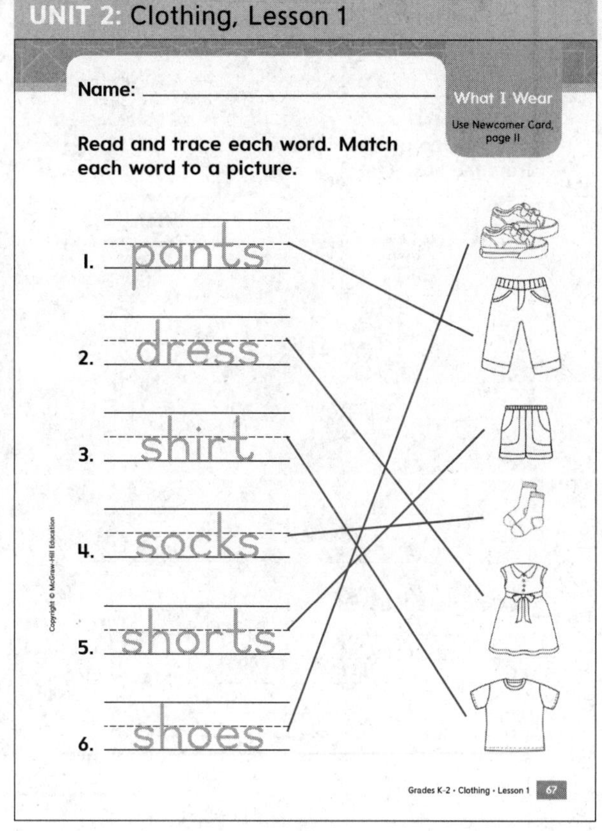
Name: ______

What I Wear

Use Newcomer Card, page 11

Read and trace each word. Match each word to a picture.

1. pants
2. dress
3. shirt
4. socks
5. shorts
6. shoes

UNIT 2: Clothing, Lesson 2

Name: ______

Clothing and Seasons

Use Newcomer Card, page 11

A. Talk about the clothing with a partner. Circle the correct season.

1. winter (summer)
2. (winter) spring
3. summer (spring)
4. spring (fall)

B. Write what you wear during your favorite season.

Answers will vary.

ANSWER KEY

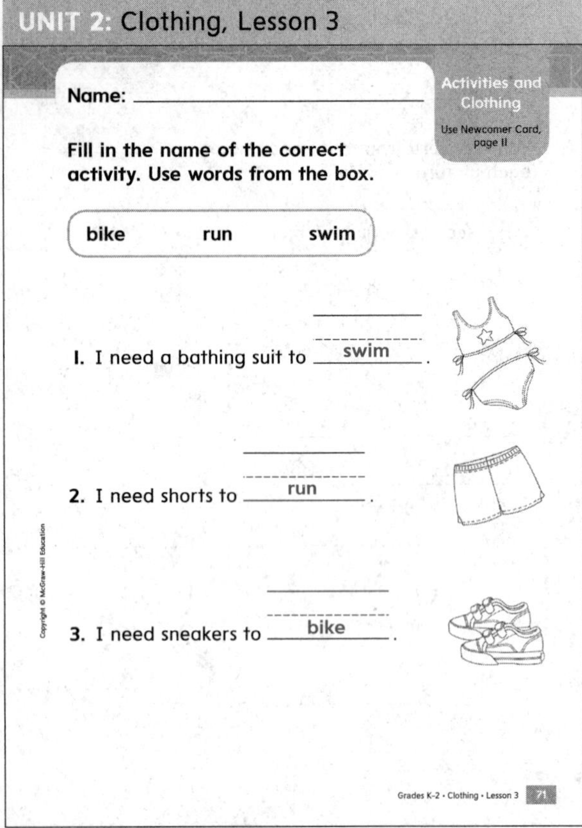

UNIT 2: Clothing, Lesson 3

Name: ____________

Activities and Clothing
Use Newcomer Card, page 11

Fill in the name of the correct activity. Use words from the box.

bike run swim

1. I need a bathing suit to swim.
2. I need shorts to run.
3. I need sneakers to bike.

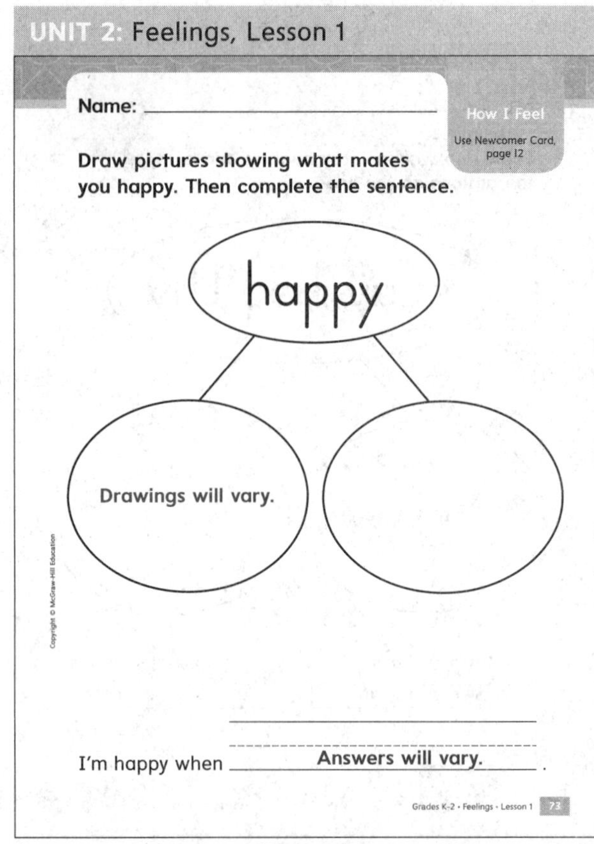

UNIT 2: Feelings, Lesson 1

Name: ____________

How I Feel
Use Newcomer Card, page 12

Draw pictures showing what makes you happy. Then complete the sentence.

happy

Drawings will vary.

I'm happy when Answers will vary.

UNIT 2: Feelings, Lesson 2

Name: ____________

Friendship
Use Newcomer Card, page 12

A. Talk about the pictures with a partner.

B. Draw and label what you like to do with friends.

Answers may vary.

UNIT 2: Feelings, Lesson 3

Name: ____________

Helping Others
Use Newcomer Card, page 12

A. Label the pictures with words from the box.

share listen

listen share

B. Complete the sentences.

I listen to my friend.

I share with my friend.

UNIT 2: My Family, Lesson 1

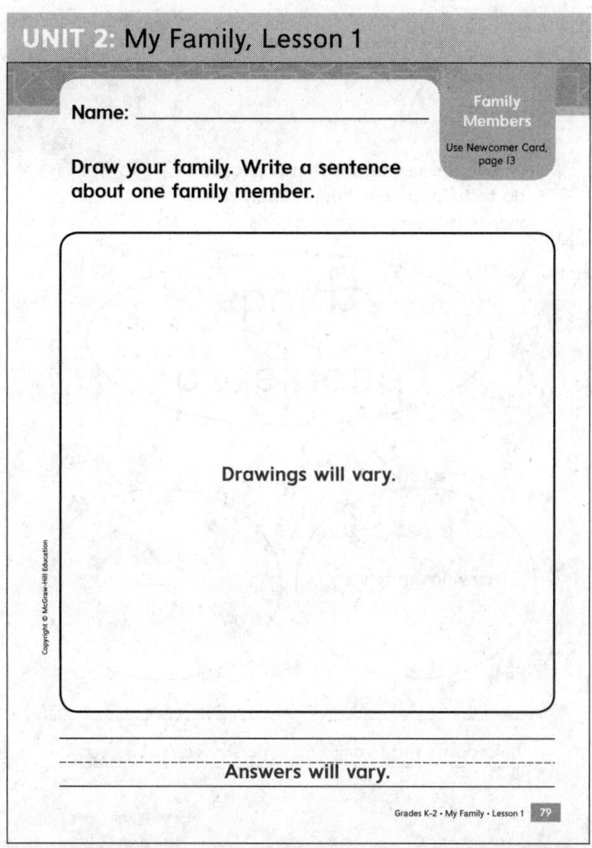

Name: ________________

Family Members

Use Newcomer Card, page 13

Draw your family. Write a sentence about one family member.

Drawings will vary.

Answers will vary.

UNIT 2: My Family, Lesson 2

Name: ________________

Physical Characteristics

Use Newcomer Card, page 13

1. Label the pictures. Use words from the box.
2. Complete the sentences using the pictures.

short hair	long hair

short hair

long hair

The father is **taller** than his daughter.

The daughter is **shorter** than her father.

UNIT 2: My Family, Lesson 3

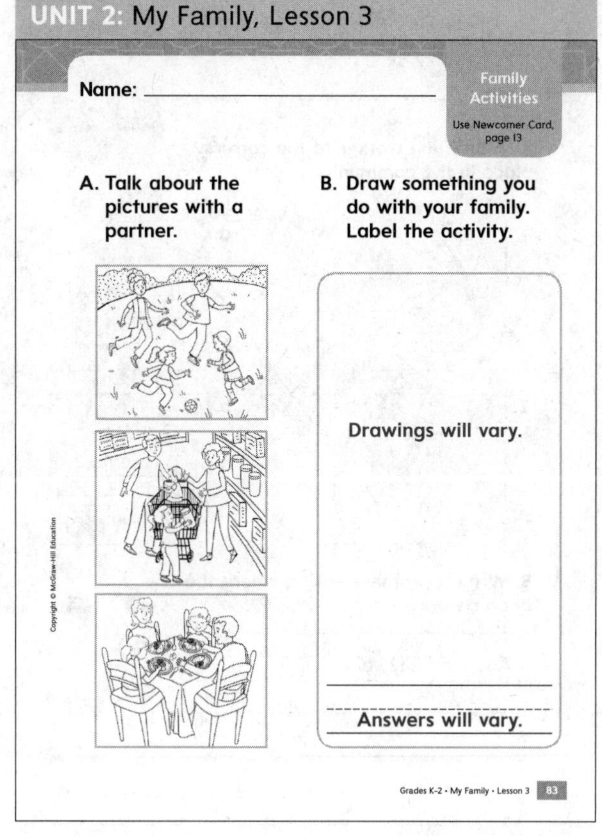

Name: ________________

Family Activities

Use Newcomer Card, page 13

A. Talk about the pictures with a partner.

B. Draw something you do with your family. Label the activity.

Drawings will vary.

Answers will vary.

UNIT 2: My Home, Lesson 1

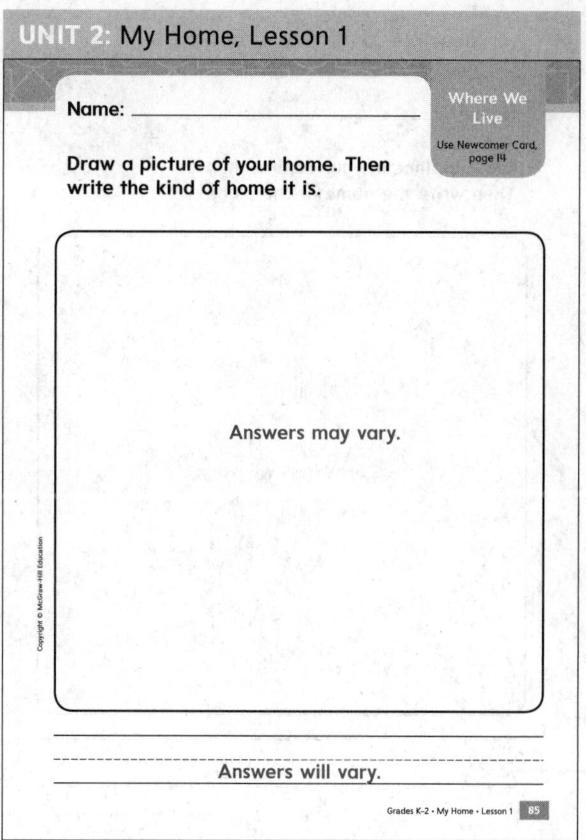

Name: ________________

Where We Live

Use Newcomer Card, page 14

Draw a picture of your home. Then write the kind of home it is.

Answers may vary.

Answers will vary.

ANSWER KEY

UNIT 2: My Home, Lesson 2

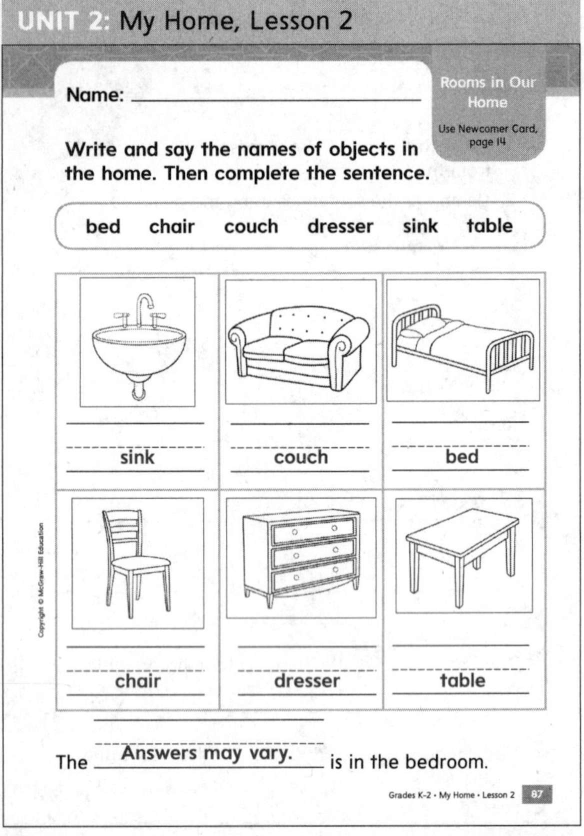

Rooms in Our Home

Use Newcomer Card, page 14

Name: ____________________

Write and say the names of objects in the home. Then complete the sentence.

bed chair couch dresser sink table

sink	couch	bed
chair	dresser	table

The Answers may vary. is in the bedroom.

Copyright © McGraw-Hill Education

Grades K-2 • My Home • Lesson 2 87

UNIT 2: My Home, Lesson 3

Helping Around the House

Use Newcomer Card, page 14

Name: ____________________

Draw pictures of the things people do to help in your home. Then write words to describe the actions.

Answers may vary. Answers may vary.

Copyright © McGraw-Hill Education

Grades K-2 • My Home • Lesson 3 89

UNIT 3: My Community, Lesson 1

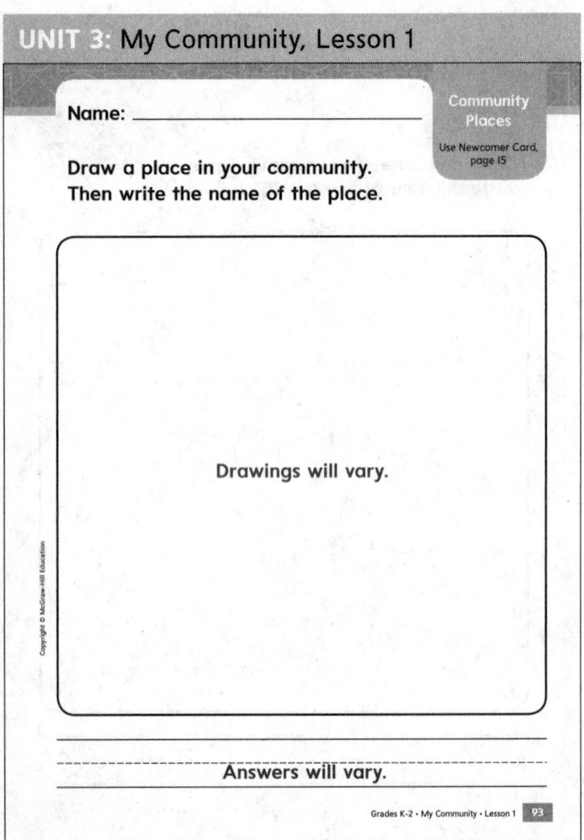

Community Places

Use Newcomer Card, page 15

Name: ____________________

Draw a place in your community. Then write the name of the place.

Drawings will vary.

Answers will vary.

Copyright © McGraw-Hill Education

Grades K-2 • My Community • Lesson 1 93

UNIT 3: My Community, Lesson 2

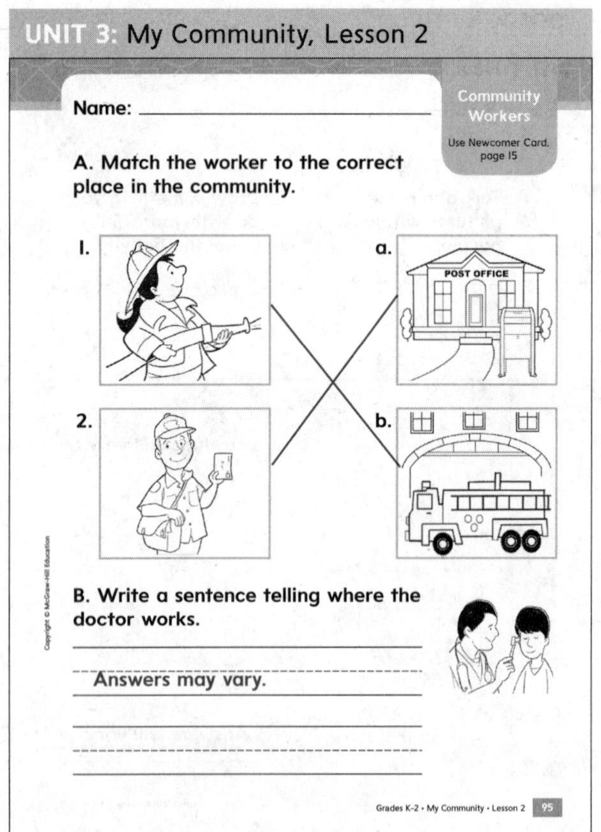

Community Workers

Use Newcomer Card, page 15

Name: ____________________

A. Match the worker to the correct place in the community.

B. Write a sentence telling where the doctor works.

Answers may vary.

Copyright © McGraw-Hill Education

Grades K-2 • My Community • Lesson 2 95

UNIT 3: My Community, Lesson 3

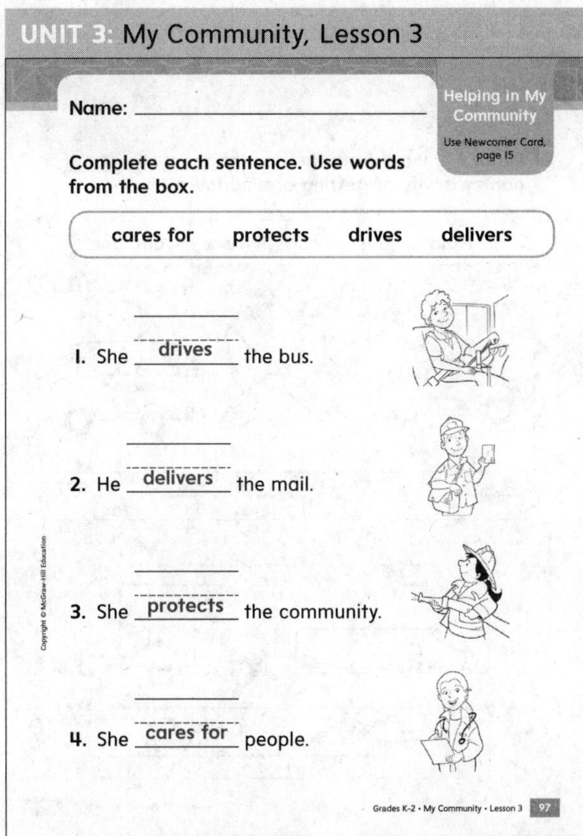

Name:
Helping in My Community
Use Newcomer Card, page 15
Complete each sentence. Use words from the box.
cares for protects drives delivers
1. She drives the bus.
2. He delivers the mail.
3. She protects the community.
4. She cares for people.
Copyright © McGraw-Hill Education
Grades K-2 • My Community • Lesson 3 97

UNIT 3: Park, Lesson 1

Name:
Things in a Park
Use Newcomer Card, page 16
A. Talk about the pictures.
B. Draw yourself in a park. Label one thing.
Drawings will vary.
Answers will vary.
Copyright © McGraw-Hill Education
Grades K-2 • Park • Lesson 1 99

UNIT 3: Park, Lesson 2

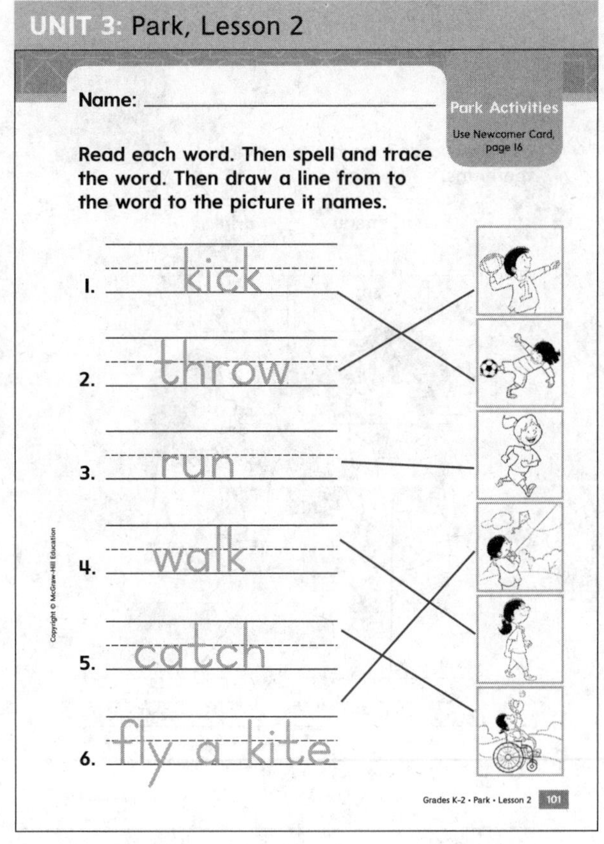

Name:
Park Activities
Use Newcomer Card, page 16
Read each word. Then spell and trace the word. Then draw a line from to the word to the picture it names.
1. kick
2. throw
3. run
4. walk
5. catch
6. fly a kite
Copyright © McGraw-Hill Education
Grades K-2 • Park • Lesson 2 101

UNIT 3: Park, Lesson 3

Name:
Park Environment
Use Newcomer Card, page 16
Draw a picture of animals in a park. Write a sentence about it.
Drawings will vary.
Answers will vary.
Copyright © McGraw-Hill Education
Grades K-2 • Park • Lesson 3 103

ANSWER KEY

UNIT 3: Transportation, Lesson 1

Name:
Signs
Use Newcomer Card, page 17
A. Talk about the pictures with a partner.
B. Draw a sign you see every day. Write the name.
MAIN ST.
EXIT
BUS STOP
Drawings will vary.
Answers will vary.
Grades K-2 • Transportation • Lesson 1 105

UNIT 3: Transportation, Lesson 2

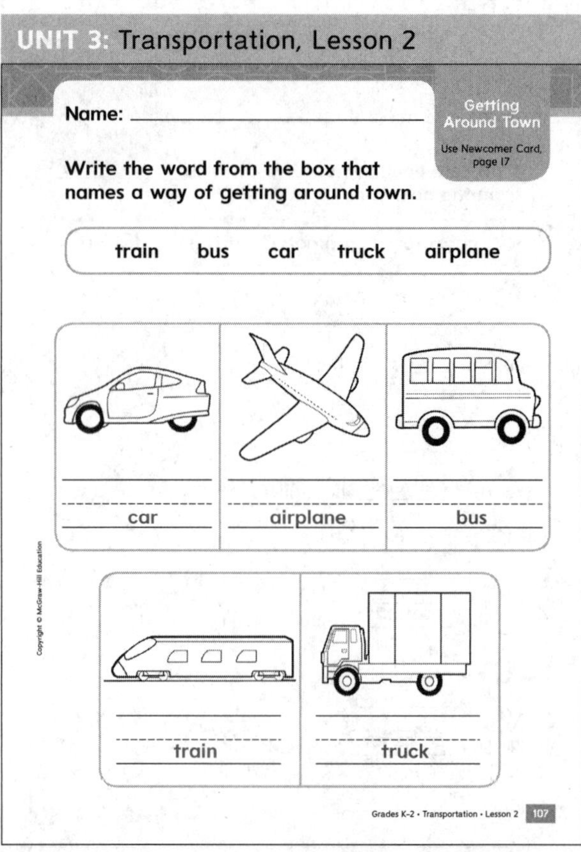

Name:
Getting Around Town
Use Newcomer Card, page 17
Write the word from the box that names a way of getting around town.
train bus car truck airplane
car
airplane
bus
train
truck
Grades K-2 • Transportation • Lesson 2 107

UNIT 3: Transportation, Lesson 3

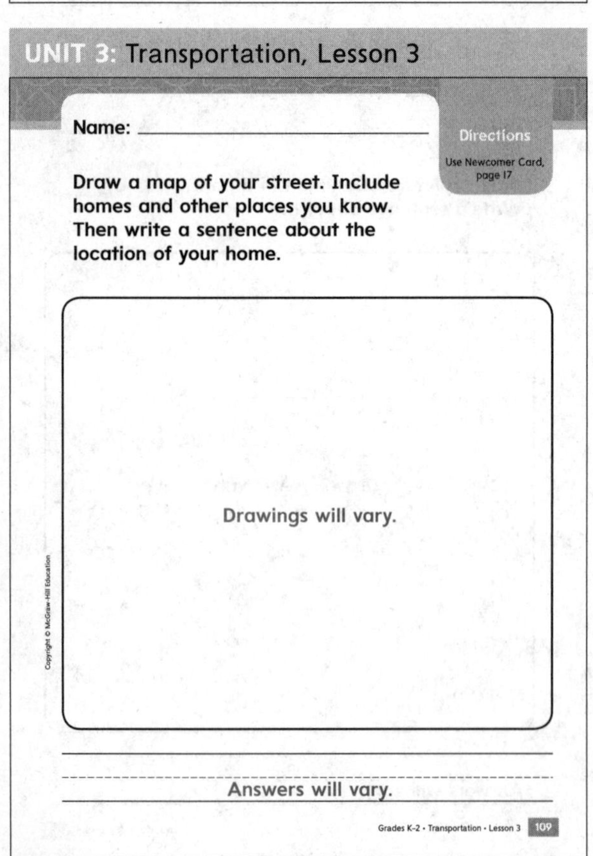

Name:
Directions
Use Newcomer Card, page 17
Draw a map of your street. Include homes and other places you know. Then write a sentence about the location of your home.
Drawings will vary.
Answers will vary.
Grades K-2 • Transportation • Lesson 3 109

UNIT 3: Food and Meals, Lesson 1

Name:
At a Restaurant
Use Newcomer Card, page 18
Use the words from the box to label the items.
menu drink
1. menu
2. drink
Grades K-2 • Food and Meals • Lesson 1 111

UNIT 3: Food and Meals, Lesson 2

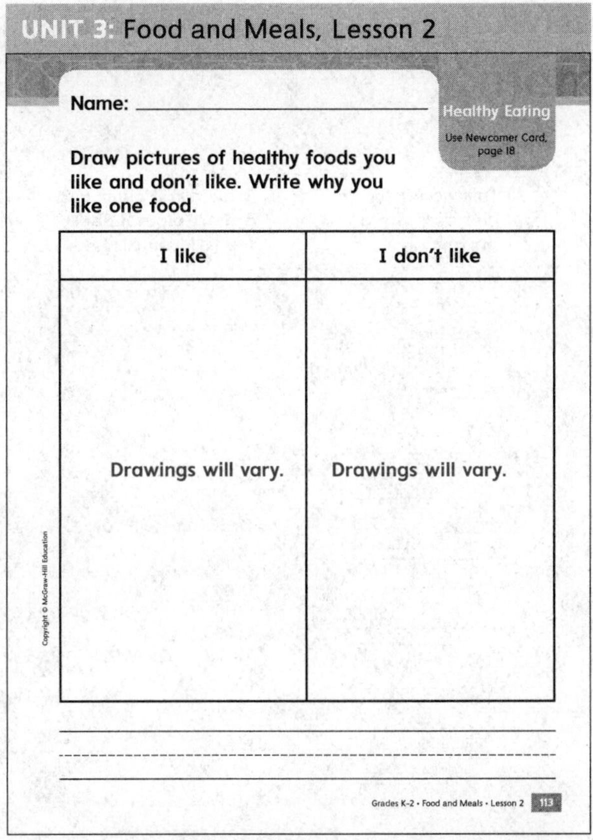

Name: ______________________

Healthy Eating

Use Newcomer Card, page 18

Draw pictures of healthy foods you like and don't like. Write why you like one food.

I like	I don't like
Drawings will vary.	Drawings will vary.

Copyright © McGraw-Hill Education

Grades K-2 • Food and Meals • Lesson 2 113

UNIT 3: Food and Meals, Lesson 3

Name: ______________________

Lunchtime at School

Use Newcomer Card, page 18

Draw the foods you eat for lunch. Then write their names.

lunch

Drawings will vary.

Answers will vary. Answers will vary.

Copyright © McGraw-Hill Education

Grades K-2 • Food and Meals • Lesson 3 115

UNIT 3: Shopping, Lesson 1

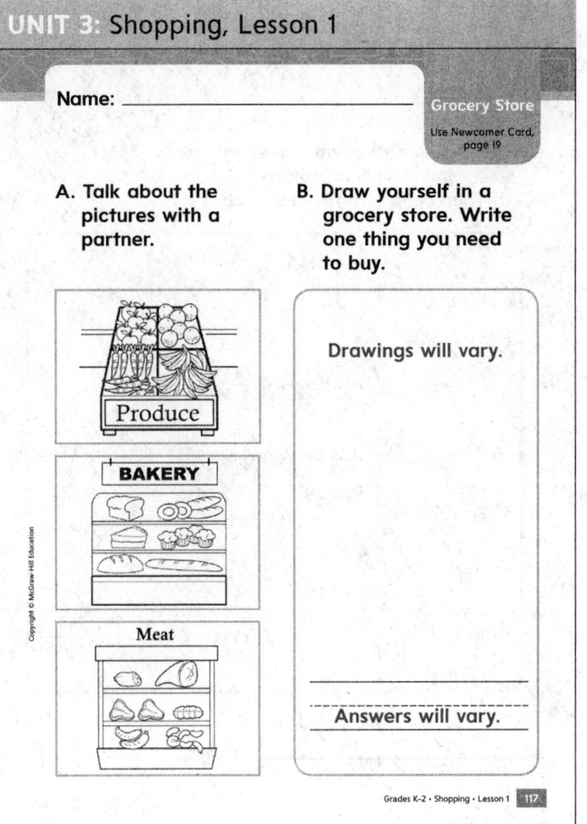

Name: ______________________

Grocery Store

Use Newcomer Card, page 19

A. Talk about the pictures with a partner.

B. Draw yourself in a grocery store. Write one thing you need to buy.

Drawings will vary.

Answers will vary.

Copyright © McGraw-Hill Education

Grades K-2 • Shopping • Lesson 1 117

UNIT 3: Shopping, Lesson 2

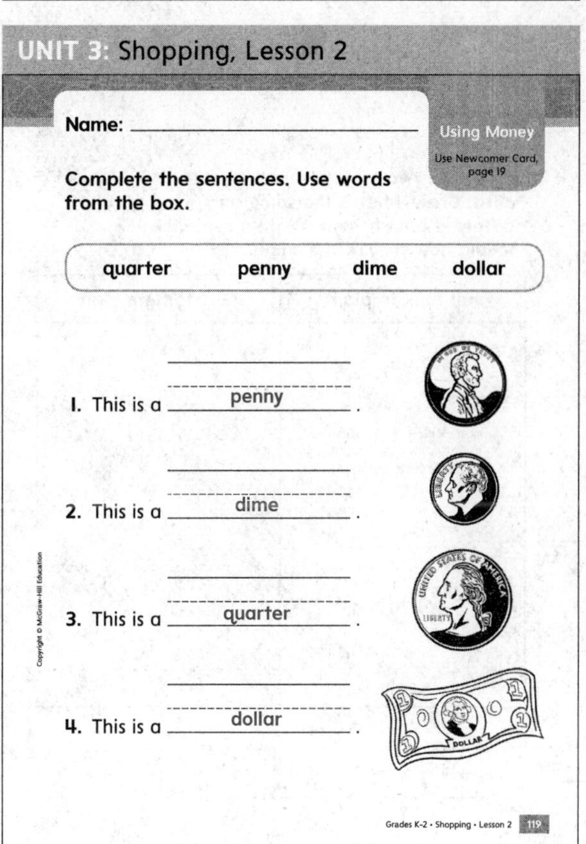

Name: ______________________

Using Money

Use Newcomer Card, page 19

Complete the sentences. Use words from the box.

quarter penny dime dollar

1. This is a penny.
2. This is a dime.
3. This is a quarter.
4. This is a dollar.

Copyright © McGraw-Hill Education

Grades K-2 • Shopping • Lesson 2 119

ANSWER KEY

UNIT 3: Shopping, Lesson 3

Name:
Grocery Shopping
Use Newcomer Card, page 19
A. Talk about the pictures.
B. Draw and write what you do in a grocery store.
Shopping List
Apples
Oranges
Bananas
Carrots
Strawberries
CEREAL
$5.00
$6.00
Drawings will vary.
Answers will vary.
Copyright © McGraw-Hill Education
Grades K-2 • Shopping • Lesson 3
121

UNIT 4: Measurement, Lesson 1

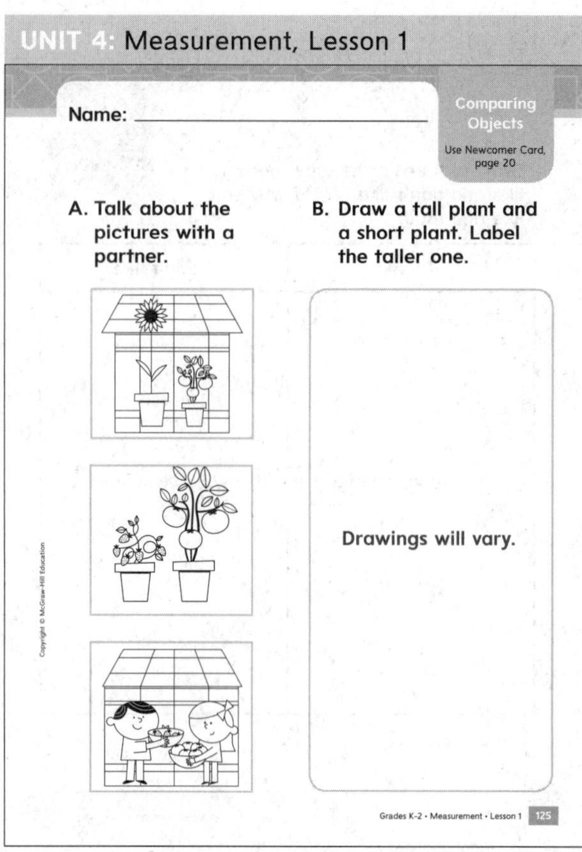

Name:
Comparing Objects
Use Newcomer Card, page 20
A. Talk about the pictures with a partner.
B. Draw a tall plant and a short plant. Label the taller one.
Drawings will vary.
Copyright © McGraw-Hill Education
Grades K-2 • Measurement • Lesson 1
125

UNIT 4: Measurement, Lesson 2

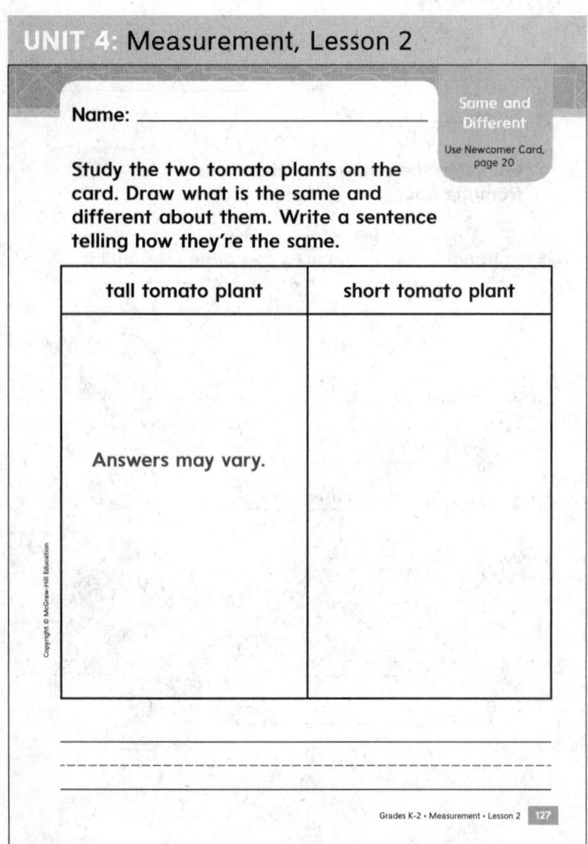

Name:
Same and Different
Use Newcomer Card, page 20
Study the two tomato plants on the card. Draw what is the same and different about them. Write a sentence telling how they're the same.
tall tomato plant
short tomato plant
Answers may vary.
Copyright © McGraw-Hill Education
Grades K-2 • Measurement • Lesson 2
127

UNIT 4: Measurement, Lesson 3

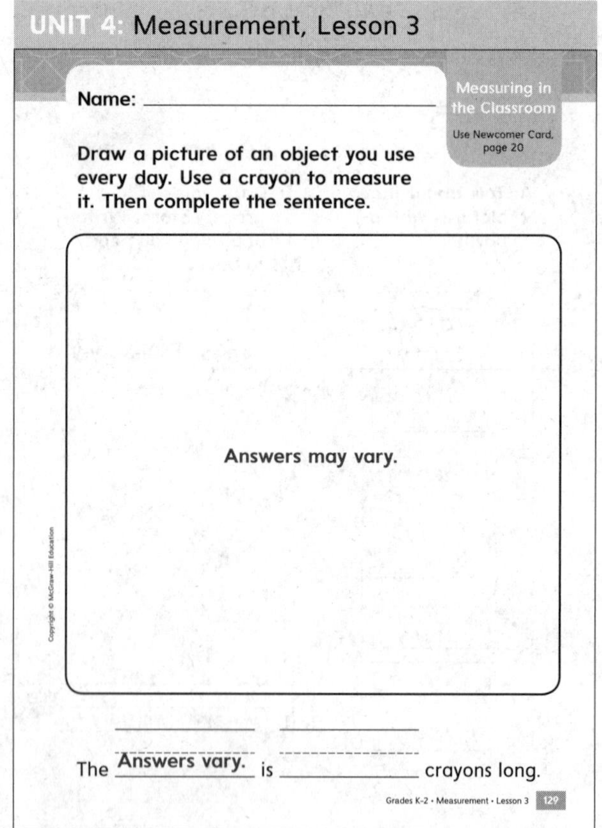

Name:
Measuring in the Classroom
Use Newcomer Card, page 20
Draw a picture of an object you use every day. Use a crayon to measure it. Then complete the sentence.
Answers may vary.
The Answers vary. is crayons long.
Copyright © McGraw-Hill Education
Grades K-2 • Measurement • Lesson 3
129

UNIT 4: Animals, Lesson 1

Wild Animals and Insects

Use Newcomer Card, page 21

Name: ____________________

Write the word from the box to match each picture.

ant bear bee deer raccoon praying mantis

1. deer
2. bee
3. raccoon
4. praying mantis
5. ant
6. bear

UNIT 4: Animals, Lesson 2

Pets

Use Newcomer Card, page 21

Name: ____________________

A. Talk to your partner about the pictures.

B. Draw and label what you can do with a pet.

Answers will vary.

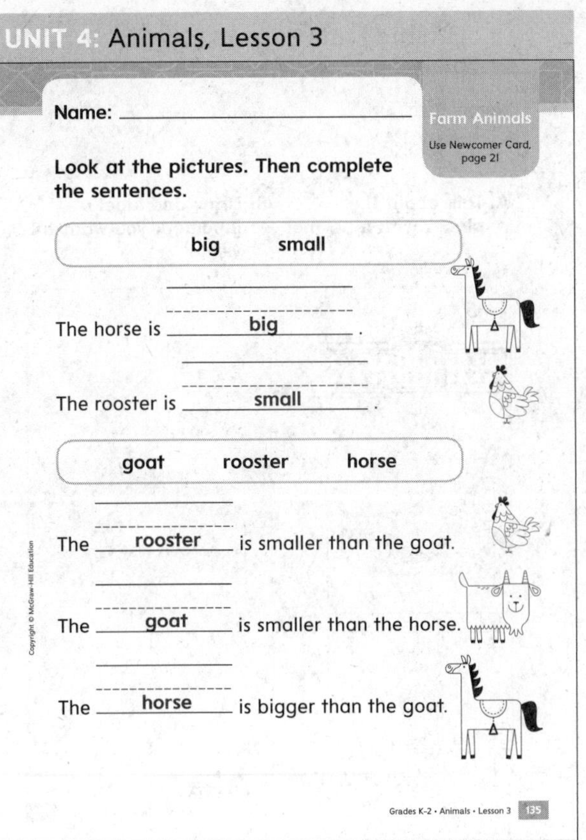

UNIT 4: Animals, Lesson 3

Farm Animals

Use Newcomer Card, page 21

Name: ____________________

Look at the pictures. Then complete the sentences.

big small

The horse is big.

The rooster is small.

goat rooster horse

The rooster is smaller than the goat.

The goat is smaller than the horse.

The horse is bigger than the goat.

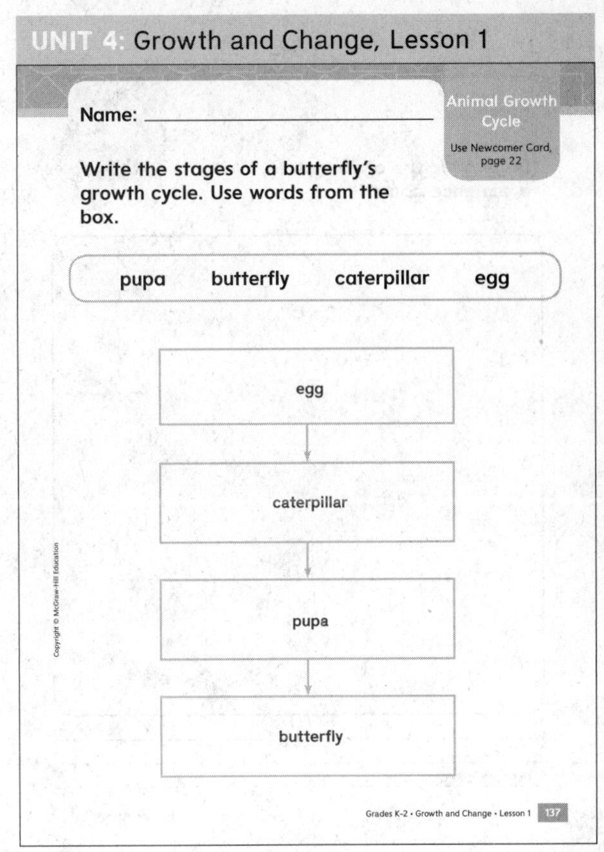

UNIT 4: Growth and Change, Lesson 1

Animal Growth Cycle

Use Newcomer Card, page 22

Name: ____________________

Write the stages of a butterfly's growth cycle. Use words from the box.

pupa butterfly caterpillar egg

egg → caterpillar → pupa → butterfly

ANSWER KEY

UNIT 4: Growth and Change, Lesson 2

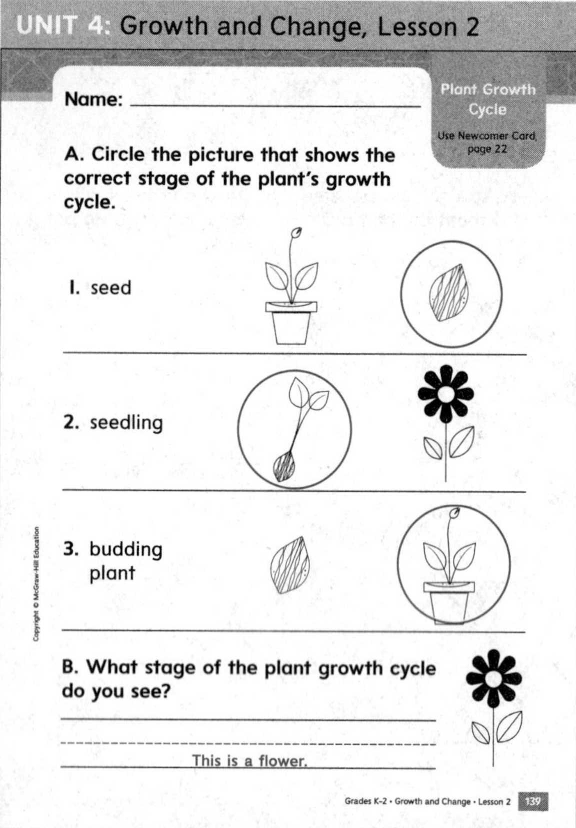

Name: ______________________

Plant Growth Cycle

Use Newcomer Card, page 22

A. Circle the picture that shows the correct stage of the plant's growth cycle.

1. seed
2. seedling
3. budding plant

B. What stage of the plant growth cycle do you see?

This is a flower.

Grades K–2 • Growth and Change • Lesson 2 139

UNIT 4: Growth and Change, Lesson 3

Name: ______________________

Human Growth

Use Newcomer Card, page 22

A. Draw a picture of your family.

Drawings will vary.

B. Use words from the box to compare two people in your drawing.

younger	baby	child
adult	teenager	

Answers may vary.

Grades K–2 • Growth and Change • Lesson 3 141

UNIT 4: United States, Lesson 1

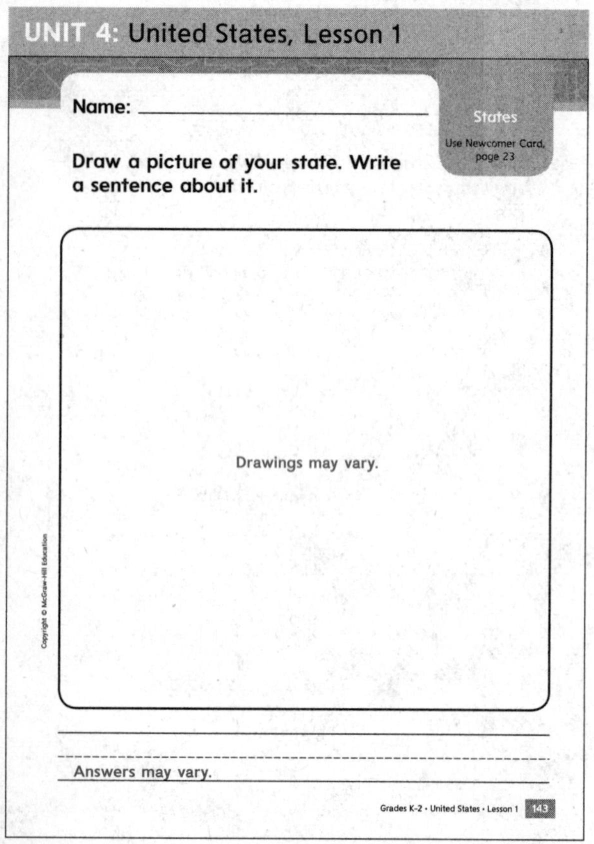

Name: ______________________

States

Use Newcomer Card, page 23

Draw a picture of your state. Write a sentence about it.

Drawings may vary.

Answers may vary.

Grades K–2 • United States • Lesson 1 143

UNIT 4: United States, Lesson 2

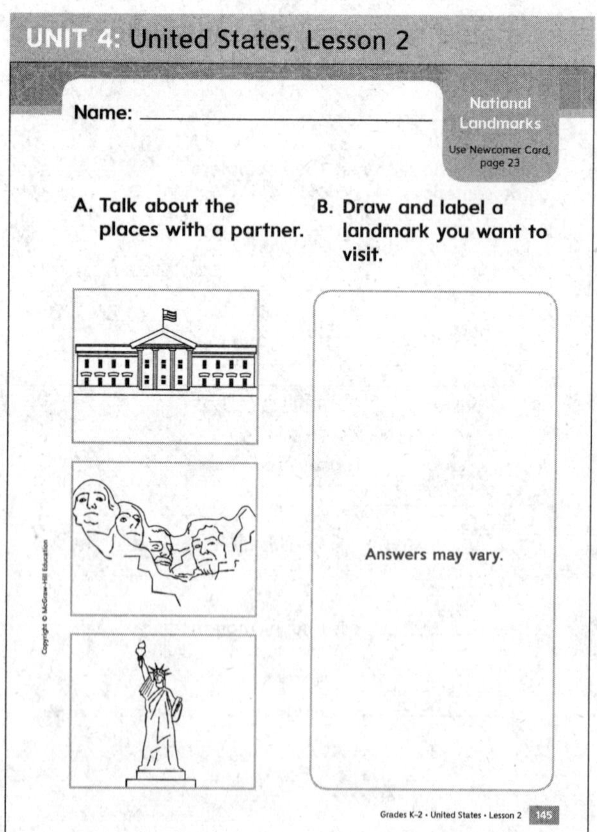

Name: ______________________

National Landmarks

Use Newcomer Card, page 23

A. Talk about the places with a partner.

B. Draw and label a landmark you want to visit.

Answers may vary.

Grades K–2 • United States • Lesson 2 145

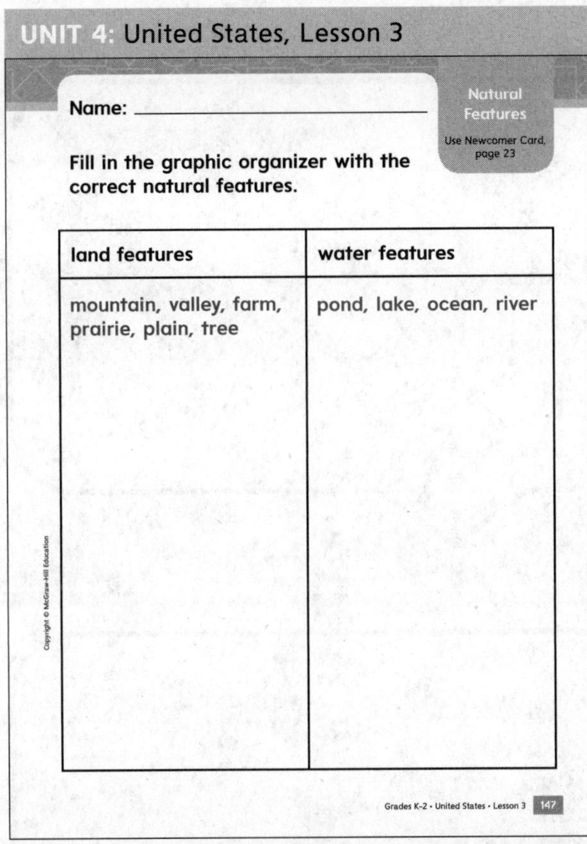

UNIT 4: United States, Lesson 3

Natural Features

Use Newcomer Card, page 23

Name: ____________________

Fill in the graphic organizer with the correct natural features.

land features	water features
mountain, valley, farm, prairie, plain, tree	pond, lake, ocean, river

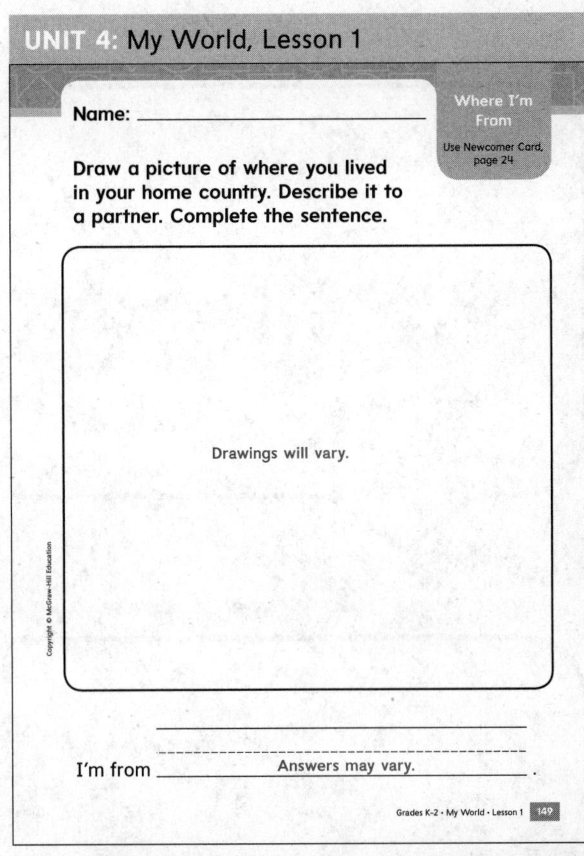

UNIT 4: My World, Lesson 1

Where I'm From

Use Newcomer Card, page 24

Name: ____________________

Draw a picture of where you lived in your home country. Describe it to a partner. Complete the sentence.

Drawings will vary.

I'm from Answers may vary.

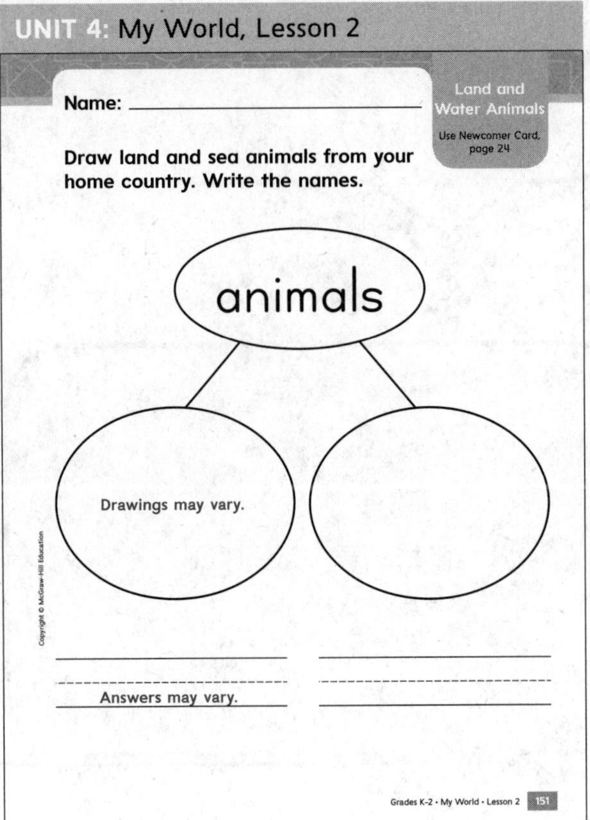

UNIT 4: My World, Lesson 2

Land and Water Animals

Use Newcomer Card, page 24

Name: ____________________

Draw land and sea animals from your home country. Write the names.

animals
Drawings may vary.
Answers may vary.

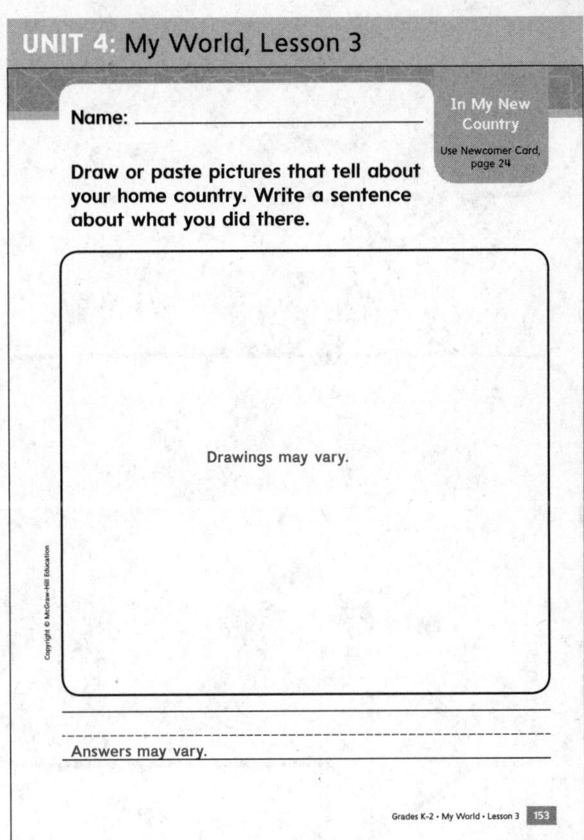

UNIT 4: My World, Lesson 3

In My New Country

Use Newcomer Card, page 24

Name: ____________________

Draw or paste pictures that tell about your home country. Write a sentence about what you did there.

Drawings may vary.

Answers may vary.

Name: ______________________

SPEECH BALLOONS

Name: ____________________

CONVERSATION STARTERS

Hello, my name is ____.

What's your name?

What country are you from?

I'm from ____________.

How old are you?

I'm ________ years old.

I like ________.

I don't like ____________.

What are you doing?	I'm ______________.
Where do you live?	I live in ______________.
What's your phone number?	My number is ______________.
How do you feel?	I'm ________.

CONVERSATION STARTERS

What's this?	It's a _______________.
Where is the _______________?	The ____ is _____ the ___________.
What are you eating?	I'm eating _______________.
What do you need to buy?	I need ________.

GAMES

These collaborative games will help children practice the language learned and can be used to extend the Practice/Apply section of any lesson.

What Are You Doing?

YOU NEED Index cards showing pictures of activities; timer

PURPOSE Children practice using *-ing* words.

INSTRUCTIONS Children play in pairs or small groups. Set a time for acting and guessing. Children take turns taking a card and acting out the pictured activity. The partner or other children in the group guess the activity.

EXAMPLES *eating, reading, calling, running, delivering, cleaning, dusting, recycling*

Save Five!

PURPOSE Children practice *nouns.*

INSTRUCTIONS Children take turns saying "Say Five!" and naming five words they have learned. Children can add words to the command to play more challenging rounds: *"Say five things that are red!"*

EXAMPLES First round: *yellow, fire fighter, house, happy, window*

Second round: (Say five things that are red) *apple, crayon, flower, car, sign*

GAMES

Yes or No?

PURPOSE Children practice *asking* and *answering* questions with the verbs *see, have, like,* and *need.*

INSTRUCTIONS Children play with partners. A child uses the verbs *see, have, like,* or *need* to ask a question about an animal, activity, food, or drink. The partner answers with a *yes* or *no* response and the same verb. Partners switch roles.

EXAMPLES

Do you see/have a cat?
No, I don't see/have a cat.

Do you like/need milk?
Yes, I like/need milk.

Count with Me

YOU NEED Index cards with numbers; small objects such as paper clips

PURPOSE Children practice *counting* and *describing* groups of objects.

INSTRUCTIONS Children play in pairs. One child takes a card and says the number. The partner makes a group of objects that shows the number. Both children count the objects aloud and make a statement about them.

EXAMPLES

First round: 7: *Seven.*
Partner shows 7 items.

Partners count from one to seven.

Second round: 10: *Ten.*
Partner shows 10 items.

Partners count from one to ten and say: *There are ten pens.*

Follow My Command

YOU NEED Index cards with different commands written on them; timer

PURPOSE Children practice *commands.*

INSTRUCTIONS Children play in small groups. Set a time. Each group takes a card. Read the command with the group. Group members discuss the command. One child in the group raises a hand, follows the instruction on the card, and says what he or she is doing. The game continues until all children have raised hands and followed commands. Children can suggest new commands to play more rounds.

Bingo with Letters

YOU NEED Letter cards; graph paper with four to six letters written on it; small objects such as erasers or paper clips

PURPOSE Children practice the *letters of the alphabet.*

INSTRUCTIONS Children play in small groups. A child shuffles the letter cards and then says the letters. Children place items on their grids as they find the letters. The child who completes a grid first says "Bingo!" and wins the game.

Say It with Opposites

YOU NEED Classroom items that can be compared

PURPOSE Children practice *describing* and *comparing* objects.

INSTRUCTIONS Children play several rounds in pairs. Partners get pairs of objects. Children say opposite words or phrases to describe their objects. The pair that says the most words or phrases wins.

EXAMPLES

I like/I don't like blue crayons.

Big/Small: *This backpack is big. This backpack is small.*

Short/Tall: *The red block is short. The blue block is tall.*

GAMES

Alphabet Time

YOU NEED Two sets of letter cards

PURPOSE Children practice *ordering the letters of the alphabet.*

INSTRUCTIONS Children play in small groups. Each group gets a set of cards. Shuffle the cards. Children put the cards in order to complete the alphabet. The group that finishes first wins the game. If the order is not correct, remaining groups play again.

Play to Compare

YOU NEED Timer

PURPOSE Children practice *describing* and *comparing objects.*

INSTRUCTIONS Children play in small groups. Set a time. Group members look for items or pictures in the classroom that can be compared. When the time is up, children take turns saying sentences that compare their items. The group with the highest number of correct sentences wins the game.

EXAMPLES *The blue book is big and the red book is small.*
The eraser is short. The ruler is longer than the eraser.
The yardstick is the longest.
Summer is hot and winter is cold.

Step by Step

YOU NEED Index cards with series of commands; timer

PURPOSE Children practice *saying* and *following commands.*

INSTRUCTIONS Children play in small groups. Each group takes a card. Set a time. Help groups read the card. Then the groups discuss the commands and complete them in order, as stated on the card. The group that completes the commands wins the game.

EXAMPLES

Find four objects. Point to the objects and count them.
Make two groups of two. Talk about your groups.

Spelling Bee

YOU NEED Index cards with letters of the alphabet; timer

PURPOSE Children *spell lesson vocabulary* and familiar names (their own or names of friends and family)

INSTRUCTIONS Children play in pairs. Give each child a word from the lesson or a name to spell. Children look for the cards with the letters they need and put them in order to spell the word or name. The child who finishes first wins the game.

Rock-Paper-Scissors, Word!

PURPOSE Children practice *verbs in the present tense.*

INSTRUCTIONS Children play with partners. Partners play rock-paper-scissors. The winner says a word from the lesson. The other child says a sentence with that word. Children play several rounds.

EXAMPLES

Winner says: *park*
Partner says: *I visit the park.*
Winner says: *bus*
Partner says: *She drives a bus.*

GAMES

True or False

YOU NEED Picture cards

PURPOSE Children practice *describing* objects by using the verbs *to be* and *to have* and the pronoun *it.*

INSTRUCTIONS Children play in pairs. A child takes a card. The partner says statements about the card. The first child answers with *True* or *False* until the partner guesses the word on the card. (Provide support as needed.) Partners switch roles.

EXAMPLES

Nurse

It's an object. False	*It works at a store.* False.
It's a person. True.	*It works at the school.* False.
It works at a hospital. True.	*It's a doctor.* False.
It's a nurse. True!	

Can You?

YOU NEED A ball for each group

PURPOSE Children practice using *affirmative* and *negative* sentences with the modal verb *can.*

INSTRUCTIONS Children play in small groups. A child takes the ball, says something he or she can do and something he or she can't do, then throws the ball to another child. Repeat until all children have said what they can and can't do. Encourage them to make silly sentences.

EXAMPLES

S1: *I can fly a kite. I can't play soccer.*

S2: *I can jump four times. I can't jump ten times.*

S3: *I can play in the afternoon. I can't play at night.*

S4: *I can ride a bicycle. I can't ride a kite.*

Follow the Path

YOU NEED Picture cards

PURPOSE Children practice *vocabulary*.

INSTRUCTIONS Place the cards on the floor creating a path. Children take turns following the path. When they step on a card, they say the corresponding word. If they can't say the word, they return and start again.

I See

YOU NEED Paper strips with the following sentence frames:

I see ________ .
I have ________ .
You have _______ .

PURPOSE Children practice *present tense* verbs *to see* and *to have*, and *adjectives*.

INSTRUCTIONS Children play with partners. A child gets a sentence frame. (Say it aloud.) The child points to an object and uses the frame to begin a description of the object. The child passes the frame to a partner. The partner adds descriptive words or phrases to complete the description, and then points to a different object and starts another round. Partners can play a few rounds and then change partners or use another frame.

EXAMPLES

Child: *I see a shirt.*

Partner: *I see a yellow shirt.*

Child: *I have two crayons.*

Partner: *You have one blue crayon and one red crayon.*

GAMES

What Is It?

YOU NEED Index cards with the words *this, these, that, those*

PURPOSE Children practice using *demonstrative pronouns.*

INSTRUCTIONS Children play in pairs. Each child chooses a card and creates a sentence with the word. The sentence should be about an object or objects nearby, and should include *my, his, her, their,* and *our.* The partner who creates sentences from all four words is the winner.

EXAMPLES

These: *These are my shoes.*

That: *That is our teacher.*

This: *This is our classroom.*

Those: *Those are her pencils.*

Here, There, Everywhere!

PURPOSE Children practice using the verb *to be* and *prepositions.*

INSTRUCTIONS Children play in pairs. Partners take turns. One child asks about the location of an item or person. The partner says where the item or person is.

EXAMPLES

Where is Sam? Sam is here/there/in the classroom/by the door.

Where are the pencils? The pencils are on the table/in the bag/ by the computer.

PROGRESS MONITORING

Oral Language Proficiency Benchmark Assessment

The Oral Language Proficiency Benchmark Assessment can be given at different points throughout the use of these materials to monitor children's oral language proficiency growth. It is suggested that this assessment be administered twice a year.

How to Administer the Assessment

Work with children individually. Show the illustrations, and use the prompts on page T41. Ask one question at a time, recording the children's answers. The guidelines at the bottom of the prompts page will help you to evaluate children's oral proficiency. The first time you administer the assessment, you may wish to model the responses after children give their responses. Model how each question could be answered, using complete sentences, restating, rephrasing, or elaborating on children's responses.

Oral Language Proficiency Benchmark Record Sheet

Use the results of this assessment, as well as quick checks, to monitor children's growth and determine areas in which to focus instruction for each student. Note children's progress on the Oral Language Proficiency Benchmark Record Sheet on page T42 to chart their development over time.

Student Profile

Use the Student Profile on pages T43-T44 to record observations throughout the unit.

Self-Assessment

Have children fill out the Self-Assessment on page T45 to evaluate their own progress during the course of each unit and determine areas in which they may need additional practice and support.

1
flour
sugar
MILK
2
3
4

PROMPTS	STUDENT RESPONSES
Picture 1: Where are the boy and his father?	
Picture 1: Who is cooking breakfast? What does the boy do?	
Picture 2: Where are the boy and his father now?	
Picture 2: What are they doing together? Who is talking now? What does the boy do?	
Picture 3: Where is the boy now? Who does the boy wave to?	
Picture 4: Where is the boy now? Who is the boy with?	
Picture 4: What are they doing together?	
All Pictures: Let's look at all of the pictures together. Tell what happened to the boy using the words *first, then, next,* and *finally.*	

Review children's responses to the prompts. Use the following as a guide to inform instruction:

IF the child is able to use new vocabulary and language structures to respond to questions, **THEN** he or she may be ready for more challenging tasks.

Oral Language Proficiency Benchmark Assessment Record Sheet

STUDENT NAME	AFTER UNIT ______	AFTER UNIT ______

Student Profile

Name ______________________ **Date** ______________

Unit ____________

Use this chart to record student performance data and inform instruction.

INSTRUCTION	OBSERVATION/NOTES
Language Objectives Child can: • name and describe objects • ask and answer questions • recount events	
Language Structures/Grammar Child can: • use language structures to communicate • use language structures to ask and answer questions	
Vocabulary Child can: • use new vocabulary to ask and answer questions • use new vocabulary during collaborative conversations • use new vocabulary to name and describe things	

Student Profile

Name ______________________ Date ____________

Unit __________

Use this chart to record student performance data and inform instruction.

INSTRUCTION	OBSERVATION/NOTES
Writing Child can: • write to label objects • write to fill in sentences • write complete sentences • write his/her name, address, and phone number	
Foundational Skills Child can: • understand the sounds of English letters • understand that some words are made of smaller parts, such as inflectional endings, prefixes, suffixes • recognize and use high-frequency words	
Collaborative Listening Child can: • listen to short, focused conversations	
Collaborative Speaking Child can: • answer yes/no questions during conversations about familiar topics • employ first language and gestures to try to participate more	

Self-Assessment

Read each question. Circle your answer.

Can I name and describe things on the Newcomer Card?	**YES**	**NO**
Can I talk with a partner?	**YES**	**NO**
Can I use new words when I talk?	**YES**	**NO**
Can I write a few words?	**YES**	**NO**

Write new words you have learned.

Mark the boxes.

This week I became better at:	I want to become better at:
☐ speaking ☐ listening ☐ writing	☐ speaking ☐ listening ☐ writing